Yours for the Taking ... Great Wages, Excellent Benefits, and Unbeatable Job Security !!!

No more waiting for test dates. Apply anytime you want!

Your new career is  .... ⇒

Just listen to what others have to say about Mr. Parnell's Postal job & exam guides ...

Accept no imitation. This is the best Postal book. I purchased all the other books but quickly returned the others when I found this one. Thanks to Mr. Parnell, I'm now in the second month of my career as a Postal City Carrier. – W.F., NY

Your guide is amazing. Thanks to you, I got hired within six weeks. I could not have gotten my job without your help. – B.R., Postal Carrier

After trying all the others, T. W. Parnell's books are the only ones we use for curriculum in our Postal employment classes and the only books we recommend. – R.H., Adult Ed Instructor, CA

Your book is fantastic, and the price is very affordable. Another Postal book I bought did not help me at all, and it was more expensive. I would definitely recommend your products! – S.G., NC

Thank you for such an outstanding package. I wish I had known about your book before I wasted my money on three others. – J.V., FL

How to Really Get Postal Jobs

Mr. Parnell welcomes feedback from his customers.

Tell us about your Postal job search. Let us know how this guide worked for you.

Pathfinder Distributing Inc., P.O. Box 1368, Pinehurst, TX 77362-1368.

info@pathfinderdc.com

Published by Pathfinder Distributing Inc., P.O. Box 1368, Pinehurst, TX 77362-1368

ISBN: 978-0-940182-29-5 (How to Really Get Postal Jobs)

Manufactured in the United States of America

This book is dedicated to

Maw Maw & Gaga Parnell

The most wonderful parents and grandparents in the world!

I grew up learning from a hero even greater than John Wayne. That hero is my father. If you look up "self-made man" in a dictionary, you see likely my father's picture. Even though it sounds like a story out of the Wild West, he literally began life in a log cabin with dirt floors and not much else. His background denied him an education, but a quick mind and a strong back more than made up for that slight inconvenience. My father survived the Great Depression, served in World War II, and achieved personal and profession success that few with many years of education can claim.

I would like to list all the life skills my father taught me, but this book is not big enough. He taught me to be a man, a gentleman, a husband, and a Daddy. (Any man can be a father, but it takes a special kind of man to be a "Daddy".) And he taught me more by his living example than by word or deed. Being a red-blooded American boy, I did require occasional disciplinary sessions, but looking back I truly appreciate those lessons. As a matter of fact, I didn't get nearly as much punishment as I deserved, but don't tell him because he may decide to make up for lost time.

Then we come to my mother. If you don't believe in angels, you've never met my mother. She came from a similar meager background and survived the Great Depression, yet she made her way in life with only the support of her own strength and an indomitable husband. If you do a web search for "loving and nurturing parent", you will find a picture of my mother. Her life revolves around her family. To say that she sacrifices all for her family would be the understatement of the year.

If more of us could have my mother's loving, cheerful, fun-loving personality, this world would be a far better place. She invariably finds the good in everybody and everything. She simply chooses to ignore the dark cloud and to see only the silver lining. This is even true of health issues. She has medical problems that might cause a strong man to give up, but not her. Other than accepting needed treatments, she ignores these issues and merrily goes her way having fun and delighting others by being herself. My mother is my hero as well. If I can ever manage to display even a small portion of her bright sunny personality, I will consider myself a complete success.

You cannot imagine how sensational they are as grandparents. Their official titles, bestowed upon them by my oldest before she had fully mastered the art of speech, are Maw Maw and Gaga. My children love and admire their Maw Maw and Gaga beyond measure. And true to form, Maw Maw and Gaga continue to share lessons and life skills with their grandchildren by their living examples of love, faith, and virtue.

I am immensely proud of my children, and I am happy with how my life has progressed. But this pride and happiness would never have come to pass without the innumerable contributions made by my parents. There's no way I could have said this enough in my life, so I will take this opportunity to say it one more time right here … Mom and Dad, I love you!

A message from the author ...

Ladies and gentlemen, this is a first!

This is the first time the Postal Service ever made a revision that was truly an improvement. Under the new application system, you can literally apply anytime you want without having to wait for test dates. As many of you know, simply trying to find out how or when you could apply for an exam or job under the old system was next to impossible. And, historically, every "improvement" only made everything more difficult. That's why this is a first – it's a revision that's really an improvement – at least in terms of convenience. The new process is fully explained in this book.

That's the good news. Now for the bad news ...

Getting to apply is far more convenient now, but the actual application process is a nightmare. The new Postal eCareer application system is one of the most confusing and frustrating processes ever conceived by a bureaucratic mind. Among other problems, due to programming glitches and chronic posting errors, it would be a miracle if the eCareer job search function actually reported full and accurate information for you.

To make matters worse, they are still using the old application system that eCareer was supposed to replace. Some jobs and exams continue to float back and forth between the two systems. The net result is a convoluted pair of application systems seemingly designed to prevent a successful job search. It's enough to drive you nuts.

And while they were at it, they revised virtually all their employment exams. But, even though the tests were changed, they still carry the same high failure rates. The lowest failure rate is 80%, and some exams have failure rates of 95% or more. Yes – you heard me right – at least 80% of all applicants fail on even the easiest tests, and over 95% fail on the more challenging ones.

But don't panic. There is hope.

That's why I'm here. It's my job to get *you* a job. You've come to the right place. If you check the many reviews for my books, you will find that I'm ranked the #1 selling Postal job/exam author for one reason --- my customers succeed --- my tools and my support team assure their success.

Again, the new system is more convenient, but it most certainly is not easy. Effort and diligence are required, but it's nothing you can't handle with guidance. Just follow along as I walk you through the process step-by-step, and you will be enjoying a rewarding new job in no time.

Keep turning pages to explore the career options and to choose your personal path to success.

T. W. Parnell

8

Table of Contents

It amazes me that applying for a job – what should be a simple and straightforward affair – can be made into such a complicated, time consuming, and frustrating process by a federal agency. But it's their ballgame, so we have to play by their rules. To assure that your Postal job quest is successful, I've broken the complex process down into three manageable steps. Trying to skip a step or take a shortcut will only hurt your chances for success.

Before You Apply & Choosing Your Job

Table of Contents continued on the next page ...

Identifying & Preparing for Your Exam

In Step 1 detailed on the previous page, you learned what must be done before you apply, and you chose your target job. Here in Step 2, you will learn about the exam required for your chosen job. If you skipped Step 1, stop and go back right now. There are already enough obstacles in the path of your Postal job quest. Don't add more complications by trying to skip steps!

Table of Contents continued on the next page …

Application, Interview, & Final Details

If you followed my directions, chose your job, identified your exam, and got your study guide before even thinking about the application, you're now ready to tackle the convoluted process with its contradictory duplicate systems by following the step-by-step instructions outlined below.

However ...

If you jumped straight to this page without following my directions, you're not cheating the system; you're cheating yourself out of a job. Turn to page 15 to learn why success is so difficult without guidance. Then keep turning pages until you're really ready to apply, and don't even think about the application until you've completed all the preparations necessary to assure your success.

Table of Contents continued on the next page ...

Application, Interview, & Final Details

New eCareer Application System (continued)

Table of Contents continued on the next page …

Application, Interview, & Final Details

The New World of Postal Jobs & Exams

As I write these words, the Postal Service is wrapping up a series of sweeping revisions. They've rewritten their entire hiring and testing program from the ground up. Nothing is the same. There have been revisions before, but never have they dismantled the whole program and rebuilt it from scratch. *Anything you learned before about Postal jobs and exams is useless. And any Postal job or exam book from before is almost certainly obsolete. It's a whole new ballgame with all new rules.* As a matter of fact, it's so new that the Postal Service had not even updated their own website to reflect these changes as of the publish date of this book. The site may be updated by the time you look, but I wouldn't place any large bets on it.

To assure accurate and complete information, I delayed publication of this book until the end of the transition period. At long last I am now able to offer full info. Most of the revisions have been completed, and the few lingering items are in the last stages of transition. I am particularly happy to finally have this book in print because in recent months there have been no up-to-date guides available for Postal job seekers. My office has provided limited help by e-mail, but now I can provide comprehensive assistance via this book. The below chart is a recap of the major revisions implemented and their current status.

Item	Revision / Status
Application System	The new eCareer application system is being used for many jobs and exams. *The best feature of the new system is that you can now apply anytime you want without having to wait for test dates.* However, the original application system that was supposed to be retired is still in use as well, and some jobs/exams float back and forth between the two.
Exam 460 Exam 470 Exam 473/473C	These tests were retired and replaced by a single new exam … electronic test 473E … used to fill all fulltime processing, distribution, delivery, and retail career positions plus part-time Rural Carrier Associate jobs.
Exam 931 Exam 932 Exam 933	These tests were retired and replaced by a single new exam … electronic test 955 … used to fill all fulltime technical maintenance jobs including Building Equipment Mechanic, Electronic Technician, MPE Mechanic, etc.
Exam 943/944	These were converted to electronic tests but kept the same titles/numbers.
Exam 710 Exam 916	These exams are in final stages of transition. At this point they are hybrids. Their application and administration processes are being handled partially on an electronic basis and partially on paper.

As you progress through this book, you will find updated and detailed information on all jobs and exams. More importantly, you will find detailed instructions for successfully navigating through the convoluted dual application system. Each system has its own unique challenges. Being forced to deal with both of them multiplies the obstacles you must overcome. With all the movement back and forth between the old and new systems, you're basically aiming at a moving target. And as any sharpshooter will tell you, a moving target is the most difficult one to hit. The first step in your path to success is turning to the next page to find step-by-step instructions for using this guide …

Recap: The world of Postal jobs and exams has been turned upside-down. Nothing's the same. Everything's different. Forget everything from before, and start all over again with this book.

How to Get Postal Jobs
Whether the Economy Is Up or Down

It may be easier to get a Post Office job when the economy is booming … but if you know where to look, jobs are plentiful in tough times as well … and even when they may be going through budget cuts. A huge federal agency, they remain one of the largest employers in the country and still have many opportunities even when trying to cut payroll costs. Charged with processing and delivering mail to 150 million addresses daily, Postmasters know how to play the games necessary to fill jobs, and they are always in need of motivated workers. *The key is learning their rules so you can get in on the game. That's where I come in. I'm your coach, and this is your playbook.*

When the Postal Service makes necessary employment adjustments, they always do so by thinning midlevel management ranks. As a matter of fact, this is true with any organization that is forced to cut payroll costs. The Postal Service is required by constitutional mandate to provide daily universal delivery to every commercial and residential address in the U.S. In order to live up to this mandate, they need an army of "workers". Notice that I said "workers", as in people who actually process and deliver mail, maintain facilities and equipment, etc. I did not say that they need an army of "pencil pushers" who sit at desks all day and never even see a piece of mail, much less deliver it. They can live without midlevel managers, but they cannot survive without "workers".

So, how do Postmasters continue to hire workers when faced with budget cuts and even occasional hiring freezes? They play the game we talked about above, and here's how it works. First of all, hiring freezes are for career positions only, not temporary or part-time jobs. So, when prevented from hiring career employees, Postmasters aggressively recruit temporary employees. At any given time, there are hundreds of temporary jobs available, and this number skyrockets in tough times when hiring of career employees is discouraged. Some temporary jobs offer fulltime hours, fulltime wages, and even a partial benefits package that includes vacation leave and access to health insurance. *What's more, some temporary jobs can lead to career appointments, and even those that do not lead to career appointments still offer advantages for jumpstarting a Postal career.*

The Postal Service is a vital component of all commerce and communication in the U.S. So long as the United States exists, this federal agency will remain a cornerstone of our economy. Like any organization, they may be occasionally forced to trim some excess dead weight, but they will always be here, and they will always be recruiting motivated and productive employees. Even if the Postal Service organization was cut by half, they would still offer more opportunities with better wages and benefits than probably any other employer out there.

Whether times are good or bad, just follow my step-by-step instructions to succeed in your Postal job quest. My program will work in any economic environment. But pay closer attention to the temporary/part-time jobs if (1) you don't find postings for the particular career job you want or (2) the Postal Service is in a budget cutting mode when you are searching. *Simply continue turning pages to launch your Postal job search …*

Recap: There are still many Postal jobs available even during bad times and budget cuts; you just need to know the game. This playbook has the winning strategies that lead you to victory.

How to Use this Guide

So, what did you get for the hard earned money you spent on this book? You got a lot. The next several paragraphs will explain why you made such a great purchase and all that this book has to offer you. After you finish the book and successfully complete the Postal hiring process, you will be convinced that you got a real bargain. You will find that the price you paid is an incredibly small investment compared to the returns offered by a career with the U.S. Postal Service.

In these difficult times, many of us are seeking employment opportunities that don't demand specialized education but do come with generous wages, real benefits, and job security. Maybe you've heard that Postal jobs are the way to go. Well, you heard right.

With over 600,000 employees at over 37,000 facilities, the Postal Service offers probably more and better opportunities than any other employer in the U.S. Certainly very few other employers can offer the wages, benefits, and security that come with a federal job. And most Postal jobs have absolutely no education or experience requirements.

There are three major obstacles between you and your Postal job – an application, an exam, and an interview. I know. I can read your mind from thousands of miles away. You're thinking: "What can be so hard about applying for a job and taking a test?" Ask anybody who has ever tried to get a Postal job, and (along with much swearing) you will hear what's so hard about it.

Historically, the application process has seemed to serve two purposes ... to prevent people from applying and to drive them nuts ... and it has generally been quite successful at both. Remember that what we're talking about here is a gigantic federal agency mired in bureaucracy. You will see what the big deal is as we attack the application process shortly.

A little guidance and preparation will go a long way toward your success, and that's the first function of this guide. The hunt for a Postal job is no walk in the park. It's more like a jungle safari. And just like in the movies, the Postal job hunter will likely get lost and eaten by cannibals without a courageous guide to lead the safari. Overlooking the fact that I don't exactly look like a movie star, I am your safari guide. My mission is to lead you to success while fighting off the cannibals.

Thankfully, there's some good news. **Their new eCareer application system makes finding and starting the application process easier, but completing it is a nightmare that can take many hours of frustrating effort without guidance.** And without coaching, it would be very easy to miss job opportunities due to chronic posting errors and to overlook critical steps while attempting to navigate the maze of online forms, attachments, cover letters, addendums, supplements, etc.

Picture the road to a Postal job as a marathon loaded with hazards and potholes where one single misstep can get you tossed out of the competition. However, as long as you follow the personalized route laid out by your safari guide, you should easily be able to avoid the cannibals and pitfalls as you cross the finish line to success. All you have to do is follow along as I help you choose a career path and assure (1) that you find all possible job opportunities including the ones improperly posted and (2) that your application is fully completed in the most convenient, effective, and successful fashion.

A good example of dangerous pitfalls are KSA's. Different jobs call for different KSA's. You are to identify and demonstrate KSA's at particular points within the application. But what in the world is a KSA? How can you demonstrate a KSA if you don't even know what it is? "KSA" is an acronym for Knowledge, Skills, and Abilities. What other employers refer to as a skill-set, the Postal Service calls a KSA. Sometimes – but certainly not always – the job posting will subtly mention  KSA's that are expected of an applicant seeking that particular position. And, without really telling you, they assume that you will supernaturally identify these KSA's and telepathically understand that you are to demonstrate those KSA's at particular points within the application.

If you are a superhero who has supernatural and telepathic powers, then you may not really need this book or my help. But if you are a superhero, why are you looking for a Postal job anyway? If, however, you are a mere mortal like most of us, then some professional guidance and coaching may well make the difference between success and failure.

Your second obstacle is the exam. Most applicants never get past the exam because most of them simply fail. All entry-level fulltime jobs and most part-time/temporary jobs require you to take an exam. All these exams have failure rates of at least 80%, and the failure rate on some is over 95%. For most applicants, success is just not possible without effective test preparation.

That's the second big function of this guide – to give you details on all the exams and to suggest effective test prep tools to assure your success. There are a number of different exams used to fill different jobs. We will cover them all one by one later in the book. For each test, I will give you details on exam content and on the jobs filled from that particular exam. And, I will give you realistic sample test questions where possible. By the time we are through, you will know exactly what to expect, and based upon what you learn about exam content, you will be able to determine what level of test preparation is required for your personal success.

The final step in the employment process is the interview, and the final function of this book is to assure that you ace your interview. Even if you successfully make it through the frustrating application process and blow away the exam, the interview can make you or break you. This is no big deal for you because I've got the actual checklist – the official form – that Postmasters use when conducting interviews. (Don't ask how I got it.)

I will take you step-by-step through the interview checklist explaining exactly what to expect, what they are looking for, and how to highlight specific KSA's that match the different jobs. Oh no! Here we go with KSA's again! That's right, KSA's are just as important in the interview as they are on the application. Just like before, if you have supernatural and telepathic powers, you really don't need my help with the interview. But if you're such a superhero, I still don't understand why you're applying for a Postal job. Is it part of your secret identity like Peter Parker and Spiderman or maybe like Bruce Wayne and Batman? If so, don't worry, your secret is safe with me. Well, not really. Lots of people will be reading this book, and I just published your secret for all of them to see. Sorry about that.

Recap: Even though I'm not a movie star, you will be eaten by cannibals if you do not follow my detailed application, exam, and interview instructions – unless, of course, you are a superhero.

Pathfinder Perks
Online Updates & Support

At this point, most people are itching to start an application. *But that's exactly what you're not going to do yet because you're not nearly ready.* There are several very critically important steps that must be accomplished before you can even think about an application. **The first step is checking Pathfinder Perks online for any updated job or exam information.**

Before doing anything else, you need to assure that the application process, the exams, etc. have not been revised. As of the publish date, everything in this book was absolutely accurate and current. It is possible, however, that revisions may have been implemented since then.

I mentioned earlier that most of the changes in this current series of revisions have been completed and that the few lingering items are in the last stages of transition. However, there is always the possibility that the Postal Service will wake up one lovely morning and suddenly decide out of the clear blue that a completely unanticipated revision should be implemented. **To assure that you have up-to-date information, I use a web tool called Pathfinder Perks to publish updates on any new developments.** These updates are available only to Pathfinder customers who register and create an online account.

If you find revised information at Pathfinder Perks about the particular job or exam you've chosen, you should obviously follow the updated instructions provided there. If you don't find updated information there, simply follow the instructions here in this book.

This is also where you go for support if needed. When visiting Pathfinder Perks, you will be given contact info for reaching my Support Team for help with any questions.

Follow the below instructions to create your online account and access Pathfinder Perks:

1. Go to *www.PostalExam.com* and find the blue box near the top right corner of the page that says "Have a book code?"

2. Enter your book code found on the bottom of page 3 in this book, and click "Go".

3. You will be taken to a new page where you enter your email address, choose a password, etc. to create an account.

4. Login to your account where you will be able to check Pathfinder Perks for updated job and exam information and find contact info for Pathfinder's support team.

Recap: Check Pathfinder Perks online for possible job or exam updates before applying. This is also where you go for support if needed. Do not skip this step. It is very important!

Before You Apply

After checking online for updates, if you truly want to be successful in your Postal job hunt, there are a series of critical steps that absolutely must be completed before you even think about starting an application. Let's review them one-by-one:

✓ **Choose the jobs you want to pursue by reviewing the job descriptions here in this book.** Until recent revisions were implemented, historically you took a test that qualified you for multiple jobs, and then – if your score was high enough – they would call you in for any of those jobs that happened to open up in the local area. However, as you will shortly see, under their new eCareer application system you must apply for individual job postings as openings occur.

Notice that I said "jobs" plural, not "job" singular. **If you limit your opportunities by refusing to consider multiple jobs, you may never get a Postal job at all.** While reviewing the different jobs, you will probably find one that you prefer. Hopefully an opportunity for that job will be available immediately, or at least soon. But then again, it may not. If you hold out for that one job, you may be waiting for a while. It's not uncommon for an applicant to apply for multiple jobs, accept any reasonable offer just to get a career started, and then transfer into a preferred job later. Don't assume, however, that you can get a transfer right away just because you want one. Transfers between crafts do indeed happen all the time, but in order to get one the right circumstances must exist, you must be viewed as a valued employee, and of course management must approve.

Even if you are looking for a fulltime job, do not overlook part-time and/or temporary jobs. As will be explained shortly, part-time and temporary jobs can be stepping stones for fulltime jobs in some situations. If there are not many postings for fulltime jobs when you are looking, and if you can get by with a part-time or temporary job for a while, this may be a good route to follow. If you have a decent job now and are simply looking for a better opportunity, taking a part-time/temporary job may be too big of a sacrifice. But if you are currently unemployed, a part-time/temporary job beats no job at all, and it may jumpstart your fulltime career in some circumstances.

In just a few pages, we will review all the fulltime, part-time, and temporary jobs so you can begin making choices.

✓ **Choose the locations where you are willing to work.** Note the plural "locations" again, not the singular. For more opportunities, applicants often choose a reasonable geographic area rather than one single facility. Putting it all together, you could apply for multiple jobs and locations, and then accept any feasible offer just to get your Postal career started. Like craft transfers, geographic transfers happen all the time under the right circumstances. And again, it is not uncommon for an applicant to accept a job in one location with plans for transferring to a preferred location later.

Under the new eCareer application system, you are able to apply for jobs nationwide. When considering locations, you don't have to limit yourself to your hometown or even your home state. Once you take an exam, you can use your score to apply for jobs anywhere nationwide. If you've ever toyed with the idea of relocating, this may be your big chance.

Recap: You must choose your preferred jobs and locations before applying. You simply cannot apply if you don't know exactly what you're applying for. And try to be flexible when choosing.

✓ **As we review the job choices, I will specify the exam required for each job.** All fulltime jobs and most part-time/temporary jobs require an exam. These exams typically test your performance on job related skills, but some contain vey bizarre sections that don't really relate to anything you would ever do on the job. As a matter of fact, some of the bizarre questions don't seem to relate to anything in world, and you end up wondering about the sanity of the people who create these tests.

After choosing a job and identifying the associated test, go to the exams section of the book for full exam details and information on exam content. Failure rates on Postal exams range from 80% to over 95%. You heard me right. At least 80% of all applicants fail on the easier tests, and over 95% fail on the harder ones. (These are not my numbers; these are actual percentages from the Postal Service.) And the worst part is that, with most exams, these failure rates are avoidable. *With an up-to-date study guide that contains effective test-taking strategies and a quantity of realistic practice tests, it is quite possible to successfully prepare for most exams.*

One of the biggest reasons for these high failure rates is laziness. Most applicants are simply too lazy to really prepare for their exams. If you only learn one point from this book, let it be this: *Do not let laziness cost you the opportunity for a valuable Postal career!!!*

A little research will quickly show you that the #1 bestselling author of Postal job and exam guides is me – T. W. Parnell. I don't say this to brag. I say it so you will listen to me, so you will believe what I say, and so you will heed my advice. I really do know what I'm talking about. Please pay attention while I tell you about the three different types of people who take Postal exams:

1. The vast majority of applicants do not even buy a study guide. They make absolutely no effort to practice or prepare for the exam. So, most of them simply fail. If these tests carry such high failure rates and if I make no attempt whatsoever to prepare, what chance do I have?

2. A small percentage will buy a study guide, but most don't really use it. They are not motivated enough to really do the necessary study and practice work. So, what did I lose if I bought a guide but was too lazy to use it? I lost a lot more than the few dollars I spent for the guide. I lost the opportunity for a career so valuable that it's just not possible to put a price tag on it.

3. A tiny percentage buy a study guide and actually use it. These are the few who are motivated enough to really do the necessary study and practice work. Guess who the successful applicants are? Guess who makes the great scores and gets the jobs? You got it … these guys.

You must choose the group you join. The easy way out is to join the losers in Groups 1 or 2. Joining Group 3 calls for some effort, but the rewards are more than worth it. The good news is that your only real competition is the members of Group 3 who diligently prepare for their exams.

So, what must you do to become a member of Group 3? **Immediately after identifying an exam and <u>before you apply for a job</u>, you must order a study guide.** Once you apply for a job and start the eCareer assessment process, they will give you only about one week to finish. If you wait until after you apply to order a study guide, it will be too late. You probably won't even have enough time to get a guide, much less to use it. By default, you immediately become a Group 1 loser if you don't order a guide before applying for the job. (Note: As mentioned above, you can prepare for and there are study guides for most exams. But there are a few for which this is not true. We will discuss this topic in detail as we look at the exams individually later.)

Recap: Do not lose your chance for a Postal career due to laziness. *Be a Group 3 Winner!* Before you apply for a job, order your study guide and use it. **Study + Practice = Success**

Fulltime Career Jobs

In this section, I will give you details on all entry-level fulltime jobs including employment requirements, required exams, job descriptions, benefits, and beginning wages as of the publish date of this book. We will start with employment requirements and career benefits. Then we will discuss job descriptions for each individual position.

Employment Requirements

One of the great things about Postal jobs is the employment requirements. Almost anyone can meet them. If you're alive, a legal resident of the U.S., and not a serial murderer, you're in. Well, almost anyway. There are a few more requirements besides being alive and not being a murderer, but not many more. All applicants must meet the below requirements regardless of the type of job ... fulltime, part-time, temporary, or whatever:

Age Requirement: Must be at least 18 at time of employment or 16 with high school diploma. There is no maximum age limit. (Notice that they say "at time of employment". There is no minimum age for applying or for taking an exam, but you must be this minimum age before they can hire you.)

Citizenship: Must be a U.S. citizen, a legal permanent resident alien with a green card, or a citizen of American Samoa or any other territory owing permanent allegiance to the U.S. Individuals solely granted asylum status, refugee status or conditional permanent resident status are not eligible for Postal Service employment.

English Competency: Must have basic competency in English. (One purpose of Postal exams is to test for adequate grasp of the English language.)

Selective Service Registration: Male applicants born after December 31, 1959 must be registered with the Selective Service System.

Employment History: Must provide full employment history for the ten year period prior to applying or to the applicant's 16th birthday, whichever is most recent. (Date gaps are not acceptable. Periods of unemployment must be included and identified.)

Military Service: Military service is viewed as prior employment. Military veterans must detail their service history and submit Copy 4 of the DD Form 214, Certificate of Release or Discharge.

Criminal Conviction History: Questions about criminal history are included in the application, and a criminal history check is conducted prior to employment.

Drug Screening: Urinalysis drug screening is conducted prior to employment.

Medical Assessment: A medical assessment is conducted prior to employment to determine ability to perform particular job functions.

Safe Driving Record: A safe driving record is required for employees who may be required to operate Postal or personal vehicles as part of their job functions. An official driving record will be requested prior to employment.

Fulltime Career Benefits

Compensation: Starting wages for the different entry-level jobs will be given as we discuss each of these jobs individually later. However, please be assured that the beginning wages are quite generous and that the potential for growth is almost limitless. Plus, most Postal employees receive regular salary increases, overtime pay, night shift differential, and Sunday premium pay.

Health Insurance: Career employees are offered excellent health insurance coverage with most of the cost paid by the Postal Service.

Retirement: Career employees have access to the federal retirement program which provides a defined benefit annuity at normal retirement age as well as disability coverage.

Thrift Savings Plan: In addition, career employees can choose to make tax deferred contributions to a Thrift Savings Plan (similar to 401k retirement plans). Employees may be eligible for matching contributions from the Postal Service, subject to certain limitations.

Social Security & Medicare: Newly hired employees are covered by Social Security and Medicare.

Life Insurance: Basic life insurance coverage is provided free of charge. Employees have the option to purchase additional coverage.

Flexible Spending Accounts: Career employees are eligible to participate in a Flexible Spending Account (FSA) program after one year of service. Tax-free FSA contributions can be used to cover many out-of-pocket health care and dependent care expenses.

Leave: A generous vacation and sick leave program is available to career employees. Depending upon the employee's length of service, vacation leave can range from 13 to 26 days per year. Fulltime employees earn 13 days of sick leave per year.

Holidays: In addition to vacation and sick leave, employees are granted 10 days of holiday leave per year on holidays observed by the federal government.

Note: If you add up the vacation, sick, and holiday leave, it is possible for a Postal employee to have seven weeks of leave per year. After allowing for normal weekly days off and all this leave, it's possible for a Postal employee to be off work over 40% of the year. Think about it. Where else could you get such great wages, benefits, and job security while only working about half a year? No wonder there's such fierce competition for Postal jobs.

Recap: You've always heard Postal jobs can't be beat. Now you know why. A Postal career is indeed worth a little effort and the small investment you must make for professional coaching.

Explanation of Part-Time Flexible Title

The first thing, and perhaps the most important thing, you need to understand about fulltime jobs is the title "Part-Time Flexible" (PTF). **When you are first hired into most entry-level fulltime jobs, you are required to start out as a PTF.** You need to understand that this is the starting point for your fulltime career.

I've heard horror stories from applicants who, when told they were being hired as a PTF, refused the offer thinking that it was merely a part-time job. In their ignorance, what these unfortunate people really did was turn down the fulltime job they had worked so hard to get.

Postal policy says that PTF's may not work a fixed shift and are not guaranteed 40 hours a week. However, most PTF's do indeed work regular shifts and do indeed get fulltime hours. As a matter of fact, PTF's frequently even have the opportunity to work overtime hours. Perhaps more importantly, PTF's receive career wages and benefits.

Once you're hired, you may be classified as a PTF for anywhere from a few weeks to several years. When "career" vacancies open up, they are given to PTF's on a seniority basis … the PTF's who have been there the longest get converted to career employees first. This conversion, however, is only a bureaucratic formality. If it were me, I wouldn't care what they called me as long as they gave me the hours, wages, and benefits.

Probationary Period

Another important point to understand is that all **new employees serve a 90 day probationary period** so that those who don't perform adequately can be discharged more easily. We have all heard stories about how difficult it is to fire a career federal employee, and this job security is one of the more attractive aspects of working for the Post Office. Since it is so difficult to discharge a career employee, the Postal Service uses this probationary period to weed out undesirables.

What's next?

Beginning on the next page we will discuss each entry-level fulltime job so that you can choose your preferred jobs. In some cases they use a traditional "job description" to describe the position. In others they use official sounding terms like "Functional Purpose", "Qualifications", "Requirements", "Provisions", etc. For accuracy, I will duplicate the methods they use to describe individual jobs.

City Carrier

City Carriers deliver mail in urban areas. Demand for City Carriers continues to grow. A recent Postal publication stated "The number of delivery points increases by 1.7 million each year. This results in 4,800 new Carriers."

Functional Purpose: Delivers and collects mail on foot or by vehicle under varying road and weather conditions in a prescribed area; maintains professional and effective public relations with customers and others, requiring a general familiarity with Postal laws, regulations, products and procedures commonly used, and with the geography of the area. May be required to carry mail weighing up to 35 pounds in shoulder satchels or other equipment and to load or unload mail weighing up to 70 pounds.

Physical Requirements: Must be physically able to efficiently perform duties of the position, which require arduous exertion involving prolonged standing, walking, bending and reaching, and may involve handling heavy containers of mail weighing up to the allowable maximum mailing weight.

Additional Provisions: Must work assigned tour and days. Must follow policies and procedures for personal conduct at work, including adhering to rules and regulations. Required to provide service to the public. Must maintain a neat and professional appearance and demeanor in such interactions, including wearing an approved uniform. Must have a valid state driver's license, and demonstrate and maintain a safe driving record.

Starting Wages: $19.84 per hour

Required Exam: City Carrier applicants must take exam 473E (page 51).

Exam Note: As will be explained later, exam 473E is a new test that recently replaced old exams 460, 470, and 473/473C. As of the publish date of this book, most references to these old exams had been removed from the Postal Service website, but the site had not yet been updated with any info about new exam 473E. If this is still the case when you visit their site, do not be alarmed. If you apply for any of the jobs formerly filled from these old exams and now filled from new exam 473E, you will find that my information is 100% accurate.

Sales, Service, and Distribution Associate

This is the retail clerk at the front counter who sells stamps, money orders, etc.

Functional Purpose: Performs distribution and a variety of sales and customer support services for products. Maintains pleasant and effective public relations with customers and others requiring familiarity with Postal laws, regulations, and procedures commonly used.

Additional Provisions: Must work assigned tour and days of work. Must follow Postal Service policies and procedures for personal conduct at work, including adhering to rules and regulations. Required to provide service to the public. Must maintain a neat and professional appearance in such interactions, including wearing a uniform and name tag when required.

Starting Wages: $19.32 per hour

Required Exam: Sales, Service, and Distribution Associate applicants must take exam 473E (page 51).

Exam Note: As will be explained later, exam 473E is a new test that recently replaced old exams 460, 470, and 473/473C. As of the publish date of this book, most references to these old exams had been removed from the Postal Service website, but the site had not yet been updated with any info about new exam 473E. If this is still the case when you visit their site, do not be alarmed. If you apply for any of the jobs formerly filled from these old exams and now filled from new exam 473E, you will find that my information is 100% accurate.

Mail Processing Clerk

This is an employee who sorts and processes mail inside a Postal facility and who rarely sees the public. Demand for this job is expected to decline over time due to automation.

Functional Purpose: Processes incoming and outgoing mail in both plant and Post Office facilities using automated mail processing equipment or manual methods of sortation and distribution. Must be able to read and sort mail quickly and accurately. Collates, bundles, and transfers processed mail from one area to another. May be required to handle heavy sacks of letter mail or parcels weighing as much as 70 pounds. The work involves continuous standing, stretching, and reaching.

Physical Requirements: Applicants must be physically able to efficiently perform duties of the position.

Starting Wages: $19.29 per hour

Required Exam: Mail Processing Clerk applicants must take exam 473E (page 51).

Exam Note: As will be explained later, exam 473E is a new test that recently replaced old exams 460, 470, and 473/473C. As of the publish date of this book, most references to these old exams had been removed from the Postal Service website, but the site had not yet been updated with any info about new exam 473E. If this is still the case when you visit their site, do not be alarmed. If you apply for any of the jobs formerly filled from these old exams and now filled from new exam 473E, you will find that my information is 100% accurate.

Mail Handler

This is an employee who handles mail inside a Postal facility and who rarely sees the public. Demand for this job is expected to decline over time due to automation.

Functional Purpose: Loads and unloads containers of mail. Transports mail and empty equipment throughout a Postal facility. Opens and empties sacks of mail. Repeatedly lifts and carries parcels and sacks weighing up to 70 pounds and pushes rolling containers weighing up to 1,500 pounds.

Physical Requirements: Applicants must be physically able to efficiently perform duties of the position.

Starting Wages: $19.29 per hour

Required Exam: Mail Handler applicants must take exam 473E (page 51).

Exam Note: As will be explained later, exam 473E is a new test that recently replaced old exams 460, 470, and 473/473C. As of the publish date of this book, most references to these old exams had been removed from the Postal Service website, but the site had not yet been updated with any info about new exam 473E. If this is still the case when you visit their site, do not be alarmed. If you apply for any of the jobs formerly filled from these old exams and now filled from new exam 473E, you will find that my information is 100% accurate.

General Maintenance Group

General Maintenance covers jobs like Building Equipment Mechanic, Maintenance Mechanic, Building Maintenance Custodian, Plumber, Painter, Carpenter, etc. Of all these jobs, the Building Equipment Mechanic and Maintenance Mechanic positions are most common. Maintenance positions require extensive technical skills.

Demand for technical maintenance jobs is significant and is growing rapidly as Postal systems and equipment become more technologically advanced. The maintenance field is expected to be one of the highest growth Postal employment areas within the foreseeable future. Maintenance jobs also offer some of the highest starting wages.

Job Descriptions:
* Building Equipment Mechanics perform involved trouble shooting and complex maintenance work on building and building equipment systems, and preventive maintenance and preventive maintenance inspections of building, building equipment, and systems. Building Equipment Mechanics maintain and operate a large automated air conditioning system and heating system.
* Maintenance Mechanics perform semiskilled preventive, corrective, and predictive maintenance tasks associated with the upkeep and operation of various types of mail processing, buildings, and building equipment, customer service and delivery equipment.

Requirements:
* Applicants must meet the appropriate qualifications and screening requirements associated the specific position(s) of interest.
* Positions require prolonged standing, walking, climbing, bending, reaching and stooping.
* Employees must lift heavy objects on level surfaces, on ladders, and/or on stairways.
* Applicants may be required to qualify on industrial powered lifting equipment.

Starting Wages:
* Building Equipment Mechanic: $23.62 per hour
* Maintenance Mechanic: $20.18 per hour

Required Exam: General Maintenance applicants from the public must take exam 955 (page 199).

Exam Note: As will be explained later, these jobs were formerly filled from exam 931, but new exam 955 recently replaced old exams 931, 932, and 933. As of the publish date of this book, the Postal Service website had not yet been updated to reflect this change. If this is still the case when you visit their site, do not be alarmed. If you apply for any of the jobs formerly filled from old exams 931, 932, and 933, you will find that my information on exam 955 is 100% accurate.

Note for Current Postal Employees: As of the publish date of this book, the Postal Service had not yet updated their internal system for exam 955. For this reason, internal applicants will continue to take old General Maintenance Exam 931 (page 227) for an unknown period of time. Current Postal employees applying for General Maintenance Group jobs should check Pathfinder Perks (page 19) online for any updates on this situation.

Beware improper use of the job title "Maintenance Mechanic". The Postal Service frequently misuses this title. The true Maintenance Mechanic position is described above. However, this title is often incorrectly used when referring to the Mail Processing Equipment Maintenance Mechanic job (page 32). When applying for a job posting under this title, check the description closely to assure exactly which position it really is.

Electronic Technician

Electronic Technicians perform a full range of diagnostic, preventive maintenance, alignment and calibration, and overhaul tasks on both hardware and software on a variety of mail processing, customer service, and building equipment and systems, applying advanced technical knowledge to solve complex problems. Maintenance positions require extensive technical skills.

Demand for technical maintenance jobs is significant and is growing rapidly as Postal systems and equipment become more technologically advanced. This is expected to be one of the highest growth Postal employment fields within the foreseeable future. Maintenance jobs also offer some of the highest starting wages.

Requirements:

- Applicants must meet the appropriate qualifications and screening requirements associated the specific position(s) of interest.

- Positions require prolonged standing, walking, climbing, bending, reaching and stooping.

- Employees must lift heavy objects on level surfaces, on ladders, and/or on stairways.

- Applicants may be required to qualify on industrial powered lifting equipment.

Starting Wages: $25.14 per hour

Required Exam: Electronic Technician applicants from the public must take exam 955 (page 199).

Exam Note: As will be explained later, this job was formerly filled from exam 932, but new exam 955 recently replaced old exams 931, 932, and 933. As of the publish date of this book, the Postal Service website had not yet been updated to reflect this change. If this is still the case when you visit their site, do not be alarmed. If you apply for any of the jobs formerly filled from old exams 931, 932, and 933, you will find that my information on exam 955 is 100% accurate.

Note for Current Postal Employees: As of the publish date of this book, the Postal Service had not yet updated their internal system for exam 955. For this reason, internal applicants will continue to take old Electronic Technician Exam 932 (page 227) for an unknown period of time. Current Postal employees applying for Electronic Technician jobs should check Pathfinder Perks (page 19) online for any updates on this situation.

Mail Processing Equipment Maintenance Mechanic

Mail Processing Equipment Maintenance Mechanic is a really long title for a job. It is usually just called MPE Mechanic, so I will do the same. As indicated in the below job description, MPE Mechanics maintain the automated equipment used to sort and process mail. Maintenance positions require extensive technical skills.

Demand for technical maintenance jobs is significant and is growing rapidly as Postal systems and equipment become more technologically advanced. This is expected to be one of the highest growth Postal employment fields within the foreseeable future. Maintenance jobs also offer some of the highest starting wages.

Job Description:
MPE Mechanics perform involved trouble-shooting and complex maintenance work throughout the system of mail processing equipment and perform preventative maintenance inspections of mail processing equipment, building, and building equipment.

Requirements:

- Applicants must meet the appropriate qualifications and screening requirements associated the specific position(s) of interest.

- Positions require prolonged standing, walking, climbing, bending, reaching and stooping.

- Employees must lift heavy objects on level surfaces, on ladders, and/or on stairways.

- Applicants may be required to qualify on industrial powered lifting equipment.

Starting Wages: $23.62 per hour

Required Exam: MPE Mechanic applicants from the public must take exam 955 (page 199).

Exam Note: As will be explained later, this job was formerly filled from exam 933, but new exam 955 recently replaced old exams 931, 932, and 933. As of the publish date of this book, the Postal Service website had not yet been updated to reflect this change. If this is still the case when you visit their site, do not be alarmed. If you apply for any of the jobs formerly filled from old exams 931, 932, and 933, you will find that my information on exam 955 is 100% accurate.

Note for Current Postal Employees: As of the publish date of this book, the Postal Service had not yet updated their internal system for exam 955. For this reason, internal applicants will continue to take old MPE Mechanic Exam 933 (page 227) for an unknown period of time. Current Postal employees applying for MPE Mechanic jobs should check Pathfinder Perks (page 19) online for any updates on this situation.

Beware improper use of the job title "Maintenance Mechanic". The Postal Service frequently misuses this title. The true Maintenance Mechanic position is a General Maintenance Group job (page 30). However, this title is often incorrectly used when referring to the Mail Processing Equipment Maintenance Mechanic job described on this page. When applying for a job posting under this title, check the description closely to assure exactly which position it really is.

Automotive Mechanic / Technician

The Postal Service has over 200,000 vehicles, the largest civilian fleet of vehicles in the world. And the number grows larger each year to keep pace with population and business growth. Keeping all these vehicles running properly requires a fleet of skilled Automotive Mechanics and Automotive Technicians.

The Postal Service publishes the one below job description for both the Automotive Mechanic and Automotive Technician positions.

Job Description:

- Perform routine and complex repairs and maintenance on all types of motor vehicles.

- Troubleshoot and diagnose more complex vehicle malfunctions using a variety of computerized test equipment.

However, there are indeed differences as follows:

- Exams
  - o Automotive Mechanic applicants take exam 943 which covers basic automotive mechanic skills.
  - o Automotive Technician applicants take exam 943 plus exam 944 which is more challenging.
- Functions
  - o Automotive Mechanics perform basic automotive repairs, maintenance, etc.
  - o Automotive Technicians are expected to handle more complex repairs, maintenance, etc.

Starting Wages:

- Automotive Mechanic - $19.29 per hour
- Automotive Technician - $20.18 per hour

Required Exams:

- Automotive Mechanic applicants must take exam 943 (page 196).
- Automotive Technician applicants must take exam 943 and exam 944 (page 196).

Motor Vehicle Operator / Tractor Trailer Operator

With the largest civilian fleet of vehicles in the world, the Postal Service needs a fleet of professional drivers to operate all these vehicles. As detailed below, there are three different types of driving positions.

Motor Vehicle Operator (MVO)
MVO's operate mail trucks to pick up and transport mail in bulk.

Tractor Trailer Operator (TTO)
TTO's operate heavy-duty tractor trailers either in over-the-road service, city shuttle service, or trailer spotting operations.

Motor Vehicle Operator / Tractor Trailer Operator (MVO/TTO)
MVO/TTO's perform both the above types of driving functions.

Requirements:

• Must have at least two years of driving experience, with at least one year of fulltime experience (or equivalent) driving at least a 7 ton capacity truck or 16 passenger bus. For Tractor Trailer Operators, at least six months of the truck driving experience must be with tractor trailers. The driving must have taken place in the United States or its possessions or territories, or in U.S. military installations worldwide.

• Safe driving record required

• At the time of appointment, you must have a valid Commercial Driver's License from the state in which you live, with air brakes certification, for the type(s) of vehicle(s) used on the job.

Starting Wages:
Motor Vehicle Operator - $20.98 per hour
Tractor Trailer Operator - $21.38 per hour
Motor Vehicle Operator / Tractor Trailer Operator - $21.38 per hour

Required Exams:
Motor Vehicle Operator applicants must take exam 230 (page 49).
Tractor Trailer Operator applicants must take exam 240 (page 49).
Motor Vehicle Operator / Tractor Trailer Operator applicants must take exam 238 (page 49).

Custodial Maintenance

Custodians clean and maintain buildings and grounds. Postal policy states that this job and its exam are restricted to preference eligible military veterans (page 345). If you're a preference eligible military veteran, read on. If not, you might as well skip this section and move on to other possible jobs and/or exams.

Requirements:

- Must have the ability to stand, stoop, bend and stretch for long periods of time, and to manually lift and carry objects weighing 45 pounds or more without assistance.

- Must have the ability to understand and carry out oral instructions expressed in English.

- Must operate power assisted tools and power driven custodial equipment, and must have the ability to work at heights from ladders, walkways, and scaffolds.

Starting Wages: $16.64 per hour

Required Exam: Custodial Maintenance applicants must take exam 916 (page 183).

Professional Corporate Jobs

This job group covers a number of professional positions at Postal headquarters and key locations nationwide. A very limited number of people will be interested in this job group because it represents very few opportunities, and each of these opportunities carries demands for education, training, experience, etc. At any given time, only a handful these Professional Corporate jobs will be posted online compared to hundreds of the more traditional Postal jobs.

Below is a sampling of the professions included under this category:

Accounting / Finance	Information Technology
Architecture	Labor Relations
Economics	Legal
Education	Marketing / Advertising
Emergency Preparedness	Public Affairs / Communication
Employee Development / Training	Real Estate
Engineering	Sales
Government Relations	Statistics
Healthcare	Strategic Planning
Human Resources	Supply Management / Purchasing

There is obviously no single job description, set of requirements, or salary range that can cover all these fields. Whenever they post such an opening, full details including the salary, job description and requirements for that particular job are provided.

There is no exam required of applicants for these type positions. Rather than taking a test to prove suitability for a particular job, as part of the application process the applicant is expected to provide credentials evidencing ability to adequately perform the duties of that position.

All Professional Corporate job openings are posted online via the new eCareer system. Applicants for such jobs apply in the very same fashion as any other applicant and as instructed later in the book. The only difference is that a Professional Corporate job applicant is expected to provide more credentials and is not required to take an employment exam.

Temporary & Part-Time Jobs

There's a wide variety of temporary and part-time jobs. Temporay jobs typically offer fulltime hours, but as indicated by the name, they are not permanent positions. Even part-time jobs can provide fulltime hours in some circumstances.

These jobs can be excellent for people not seeking a permanent career position. But even if a long-term career is your goal, in some cases these jobs can contribute to your success. We will look at each temporary and part-time job individually to discuss what it entails and how it might assist in your quest for a career opportunity.

These jobs become even more important during economic downturns when many other jobs ... perhaps even career Postal jobs ... are hard to find. Even in the worst of times when the Postal Service has temporary hiring freezes in place for fulltime jobs, they are always hiring temporary and part-time employees. You will find hundreds of temporary and part-time jobs posted anytime you search no matter what the economy is like.

As a matter of fact, recruiting temporary/part-time employees is one of the strategies they use to reduce operating costs. The wages for many temporary/part-time jobs are similar to fulltime wages, but temporary/part-time jobs don't come with full benefits ... and not having to provide full benefits saves them a ton of money. (As explained later, some temporary jobs offer partial benefits like vacation leave and access to health insurance.) Regardless of the circumstances, they can never stop hiring altogether. They are always shorthanded and in need of motivated workers. So when faced with budget cuts, they simply recruit more temporary and part-time employees.

If there are not many postings for career jobs when you are looking, and if you can get by with a temporary or part-time job for a while, this may be a good route to follow. If you have a decent job now and are simply looking for a better opportunity, taking a temporary/part-time job may be too big of a sacrifice. But if you are currently unemployed, a temporary/part-time job beats no job at all, and it may jumpstart your fulltime career in some circumstances.

All Postal job applicants must meet the employment requirements listed on page 23. This is true regardless of the type of job ... fulltime, part-time, temporary, or whatever.

Following are all the different types of part-time and temporary Postal jobs. We will discuss them individually in the order given below.

• Transitional City Carrier

• Rural Carrier Associate (RCA)

• Temporary Relief Carrier / Temporary Rural Carrier (TRC)

• Data Conversion Operator (DCO)

• Postmaster Relief / Postmaster Replacement (PMR)

• Casual Jobs

Transitional City Carrier

A transitional job is a long-term temporary position that typically comes with hours and wages similar to its career counterpart, but it is not a permanent position. Transitional employees are hired to supplement the career workforce on an as-needed basis.

A Transitional City Carrier is appointed (hired) for a 360 day term. At the end of this term, and after a five day break, the Transitional City Carrier can be reappointed for additional 360 day terms if supplemental help is still needed. Transitional City Carriers can be reappointed for multiple terms, but there must be a five day employment break between each term. The 360 day term limit exists because a Postal worker who works a full year (365 days) without an employment break must be considered a career employee. Since a Transitional City Carrier is not a career employee, he/she must be given the five day employment break each year.

A Transitional City Carrier performs the same functions and must meet the same requirements described on page 26 for career City Carriers, but it is not necessary to take an exam to get a Transitional City Carrier job. An applicant for this position simply applies as detailed later in the book without having to take a test. However, if you go for one of these positions, be very sure to follow my instructions because the same confusion, complications, and pitfalls await you in both the application and interview processes no matter what type job you seek.

Transitional City Carrier wages vary across the country. Depending upon the location, the pay rate is about $20.00 per hour. One of the best features of this job is that, even though it is not a career position, it comes with some benefits. Transitional City Carriers earn one hour of vacation leave for every 20 hours worked. Depending upon the actual hours worked, this could be up to two weeks of paid vacation per year. And, after completing one term and being reappointed for a second term, a Transitional City Carrier is eligible to enroll in the health insurance program. The Transitional City Carrier is responsible for the full cost of this health insurance, but it typically costs far less than purchasing private health insurance and offers far better benefits than private health insurance.

There is continuing and growing demand for Transitional City Carriers. If there are no postings for your preferred career positions when you are looking, there will likely be a number of postings for Transitional City Carriers. You may want to consider taking one of these transitional jobs and using it as a starting point as described below.

Even though a Transitional City Carrier is a Postal employee, he/she cannot move directly into a career position without first taking an exam just like anybody on the outside. Most Transitional City Carriers want to go career, so most of them are always on the lookout for posted career openings. You will likely do the same if you accept one of these jobs. So, how can a Transitional City Carrier job help you get a career position? Like this …

If, while working as a Transitional City Carrier, you find an opening posted for one of your preferred career positions, apply for it. If you prepared diligently for the exam and therefore scored high enough, you will be called in for an interview. Here's where the Transitional City Carrier job helps out – assuming of course that you have proven to be a productive employee. If you've already proven your value to them, you will breeze through the interview without question. The interview will be a mere formality. If they are comparing a known productive employee against several unknowns, the known productive employee will be chosen every time.

Rural Carrier Associate

The Postal Service is always desperate to recruit people for Rural Carrier Associate (RCA) positions. This means that the job is easy to get because there is little competition. And the job does offer several distinct advantages. For one thing, as explained below, this is one of only two part-time or temporary jobs that can work directly into a career position without having to go through extra steps, exams, or applications. (The other one is the Data Conversion Operator job on page 42.)

The RCA job is a long-term part-time relief position. RCA's cover for fulltime career Rural Carriers when the fulltimer is out due to leave, days off, etc. Since RCA's are not career employees, the job does not come with benefits. RCA wages vary by location, but the average pay rate is $18.00 per hour. An RCA must own a reliable personal vehicle and is expected to use this personal vehicle for delivering mail. However, the RCA is compensated on a generous per-mile basis for using the personal vehicle. An RCA performs functions similar to a City Carrier (page 26) but in a rural environment. RCA applicants must take exam 473/473E (page 51).

(Exam Note: As will be explained later, exam 473E is a new test that recently replaced old exams 460, 470, and 473/473C. As of the publish date of this book, most references to these old exams had been removed from the Postal Service website, but the site had not yet been updated with any info about new exam 473E. If this is still the case when you visit their site, do not be alarmed. If you apply for any of the jobs formerly filled from these old exams and now filled from new exam 473E, you will find that my information is 100% accurate.)

The hours worked by an RCA vary as described below:

• The official statement is that an RCA typically works only one or two days a week on a call-in basis. And the term "call-in" is an apt description. There may be some days when the RCA knows that he/she is expected to work, but he/she is also required to respond immediately when called in unexpectedly because a fulltimer is out sick or whatever. Refusing a call-in is not an option. Like in baseball, a Postmaster typically uses a "three strikes and you're out" rule. After refusing three call-in's, the RCA is usually discharged for failing to fulfill his/her responsibilities.

• However, some RCA's work forty hours or more a week. Some larger suburban (as opposed to inner city) Post Offices employ a number of fulltime Rural Carriers. In such a case, there will be more opportunities to cover for fulltimers because there are simply so many more of them. This means that the RCA will be called upon to work more often and more hours.

• Another way RCA's can get more hours is to cover for fulltimers at other nearby Post Offices. If an RCA can only expect a few days work each week at his/her home facility, it is not uncommon (with his/her home Postmaster's approval) for the RCA to volunteer to work relief at additional facilities within a reasonable distance. As mentioned above, the Postal Service never has enough RCA's and is always trying to recruit more. It is therefore almost a given that other nearby Post Offices will be short-handed and will jump at the chance to get your help.

Turn to the next page for a discussion on how an RCA job can help you get a career position.

How can an RCA job help you get a career position? Two different ways as follows:

- There is only one way to get a career Rural Carrier job. When one of these fulltime jobs becomes available, it is offered to the RCA who has worked at that particular facility the longest. Typically an RCA must work part-time at least a few years before such an opportunity is presented, but it can be shorter. Some RCA's are converted to career employees shortly after or even immediately upon being hired, but having to work part-time for a few years is more typical. By the way, many Postal employees will tell you that a career Rural Carrier position is the best possible Postal job to have. They say that you work with little supervision almost like being self-employed and in a rural environment that is far more comfortable than an inner-city or metro area.

- Most RCA's are always watching eCareer for fulltime jobs. Even though an RCA is a Postal employee, he/she cannot move directly into a career position (other than the career Rural Carrier job discussed above) without first taking an exam just like anybody on the outside. As described for Transitional City Carriers on page 38, proving your value as an RCA will enable you to breeze through the interview process – assuming that you diligently prepared for your exam to assure a high score. Of course, you already took exam 473E to get the RCA job. So if you apply for a job that is filled from exam 473E, you do not have to take it again unless you want to do so in order to improve your score.

Temporary Relief Carrier / Temporary Rural Carrier

In my opinion, this is the strangest Postal job of all. A Temporary Relief Carrier (TRC) performs the exact same job as a Rural Carrier Associate discussed on the previous page. The only difference is that a TRC applicant is not required to take an exam (you simply apply for the job), and a TRC does not make as much money. Yes, you heard me right. A TRC job is the same as an RCA job, but TRC's get paid less. TRC's earn about $13.00 per hour compared to about $18.00 per hour for RCA's.

Why would you accept a TRC job instead of an RCA job and do the same work for less pay? The only reason you should do this is if the only jobs available at the locations where you are willing to work are TRC jobs. And if you do take a TRC job, watch eCareer like a hawk for chances to move up the job ladder. If they post an RCA opening for your area, jump on it because it would give you an immediate $5.00 per hour raise for doing the same job you already have.

Of course, it goes without saying that you should watch eCareer for fulltime postings as well unless you don't have career ambitions. Again, just as described for Transitional City Carriers on page 38, proving your value as a TRC will enable you to breeze through the interview process for a fulltime career job – assuming that you diligently prepared for your exam to assure a score high enough to get you an interview invitation.

However, even though a TRC is a Postal employee, he/she cannot move directly into an RCA job or into a career position without first taking an exam just like anybody on the outside.

Data Conversion Operator

As transitional employees, Data Conversion Operators (DCO's) are hired for a 360 day term. At the end of this term and after a five day break, the DCO can be reappointed for additional 360 day terms. The 360 day term limit exists because a Postal worker who works a full year (365 days) without an employment break must be considered a career employee. Since a DCO is not a career employee, he/she must be given the five day break each year. A DCO can be reappointed for multiple terms, but each time there must be a five day break between terms.

To prepare mail for automated sorting, a DCO (1) reads a typed or handwritten address from the image of a letter on a monitor and then (2) selects essential information from the address and types this information using a keyboard so that (3) the computer can covert the address information to a bar code to be applied to the actual letter. Hence the job title ... Data Conversion Operators operate a computer to convert typed or handwritten data into bar codes that can be scanned and sorted by automated equipment. The DCO job obviously requires typing or data entry skills.

DCO jobs are not career positions and do not come with benefits. However, as explained below, this is one of only two part-time or temporary jobs that can work directly into a career position without having to go through extra steps, exams, or applications. (The other one is the Rural Carrier Associate job on page 39.) DCO applicants must take exam 710 (page 143), and those who pass are required to demonstrate typing or data entry skills on a performance test. The starting pay rate for a DCO is $13.12 per hour.

The bad news is that DCO jobs are only available at a few facilities scattered across the country. These facilities are called Remote Encoding Centers (REC's). But the good news is that there's anywhere from several hundred to over a thousand employees at one of these facilities. The bottom line is that there are many opportunities for DCO jobs, but they are limited to certain sites.

In the 1990's, there were 55 REC's in operation. But as Postal processing systems became more automated, the need for these facilities fell sharply. The REC's were closed one by one until, as of the publish date of this book, all but two either had been closed or were in the process of closing. The two REC's still in operation are located in Salt Lake City, UT and Wichita, KS.

So, how can a DCO job help you get a career position? Two different ways as follows ...

- At any given Remote Encoding Center, there's typically a larger number of transitional employees and a smaller number of career employees. There is only one way to get a career position at one of these facilities. When a career job becomes available, it is offered to the DCO with the highest 710 exam score. So, with this job, your exam score is twice as important as with other jobs. You need a good score just to get hired as a DCO in the first place. And, the score is just as important later if you want progress into a career position.

- Most DCO's are always watching eCareer for fulltime jobs. If one opens up and you apply for it, having proved your value as a DCO will enable you to breeze through the interview process as described for Transitional City Carriers on page 38 ... assuming, of course, that you diligently prepared for the exam and scored high enough to be invited to an interview. Even though a transitional DCO is a Postal employee, he/she cannot move directly into a career position (other than the career DCO job discussed above) without first taking an exam just like anybody on the outside.

Postmaster Relief / Postmaster Replacement

The Postmaster Relief / Replacement (PMR) position is yet another strange job. Before I can describe the job, I must first describe where these jobs are available.

There are small Post Offices in communities across the country (many more than you might expect) that have only one single employee. This employee has the title of Postmaster, but in fact he/she does it all. The functions available in one of these small Post Offiices are usually limited to P.O. Boxes and a retail counter where you can get stamps, buy money orders, drop off packages to be mailed, etc. These small facilities may not even offer mail delivery. Due to lesser business demands, these small Post Offices may not keep normal business hours. They may be open only certain hours of the day and/or certain days of the week.

Even in one of these small Post Offices, the one single employee - the "Postmaster" - gets days off, takes vacations, needs to occasionally take sick leave, etc. When this employee is out, it is the job of a PMR to cover for him/her. The PMR position is a part-time relief job to cover for the Postmaster at one of these small Post Offices when the Postmaster is out for whatever reason. PMR's are not career employees and do not get benefits.

As you might expect, a PMR gets limited hours. The actual Postmaster may not even get fulltime hours, so what can the PMR expect? As with the Rural Carrier Associate job, it may be possible to get more hours by providing the PMR function for a few nearby Post Offices, but a person is simply never going to get rich from this job. The pay rate for PMR's is around $9.50 per hour depending upon the location. At least you don't have to take an exam to get a PMR job. You simply apply online following my directions to be given later.

I view this as a true part-time job for people who really only want a part-time job. I do not see this job as a starting point for people whose goal is a fulltime career. However, as discussed with all the previous part-time and temporary jobs, there is one way that a PMR job can help you get a career position. While working as a PMR, you can keep checking for career job postings. If one comes up, apply for it. If you diligently prepared for the test and scored high enough to be called in for an interview, the interview will be a breeze if you've proven to be a productive employee while working as a PMR. However, note that even though a PMR is a Postal employee, he/she cannot move directly into career position without taking an exam just like anybody on the outside.

43

Casual Jobs

A Casual Job can be anything anywhere anytime. How's that for a job description? And it's really true. The best I can do with this job category is list a bunch of facts.

- Casuals are hired to supplement the career workforce on an as-needed basis.

- Casual applicants do not have to take a exam. They simply apply as directed later in the book without being required to take a test.

- Casuals can be hired for stated terms of 21 days, 90 days, or 360 days. Or they can be hired for just about any length of time in between and/or without a term being specified.

- Casuals cannot work over 360 days without an employment break of at least five days. And like transtional employees, Casuals can be rehired for additional terms if so desired.

- Casuals can be hired to perfom a single job function or any combination of job functions. If you look back over every job discussed in this book, Casuals may be assigned any or all of them.

- Casual wages vary greatly depending upon the location and the job function. The pay rates range from a low of just under $10.00 to a high of almost $20.00 per hour.

- Casuals are not career employees and therefore do not get benefits.

- When a Casual job is posted, details on location, wages, hours, job fuctions, etc. are provided. Until you see a posting, there's no way to guess what the details for a Casual job might be.

As with every other part-time or temporary job, there is one way that a Casual job could help in your quest for a career position. If, while working as a Casual, you find an opening posted for one of your preferred career positions, apply for it. If you prepared for the exam and scored high enough, you will be invited to an interview. If you've proven to be a productive employee while working as a Casual, you will breeze through the interview without question. If they are comparing a known productive employee against several unknowns, the known employee will be chosen every time. However, even though a Casual is a Postal employee, he/she cannot move directly into career position without taking an exam just like anybody on the outside.

Before the Exam

In this section of the book we will discuss all the different Postal employment exams. And if there's one subject I know about, it's Postal exams. I've been writing Postal exam study guides for years. As a matter of fact, I'm ranked the #1 bestselling Postal test prep author in the U.S. I say this not to brag, but to assure you that I do indeed know what I'm talking about. So please pay close attention while we discuss the different exams, and please take the advice I offer to heart.

Why do they use employment exams?

Exams are used for selecting and screening potential employees. Some exams are used to fill one job only, and others are used to fill several different types of jobs. All exams supposedly test an applicant's aptitude for job-related skills, but I don't find this to always be true. By the time we finish looking at the exams, you will agree that some of the skills being tested are not like anything you would ever do on the job – or like anything you would ever do on planet Earth for that matter.

The personality inventory section of an exam builds a psychological profile of the applicant. They supposedly use this for selecting the best potential employees, but I think it's the other way around. Instead of using this psychological test to select the best applicants, I think they use it to screen out the nutcases that might go "Postal". And that's just fine with me. I certainly don't want some lunatic bringing a gun to work at the Post Office when you get a job there or when I go in to buy some stamps. Right now this personality inventory section is only included on two tests, but I'm told that eventually it will probably be added to all the exams.

The final purpose for exams is to assure that the selection process is completely objective so discrimination cannot take place. Personal feelings and opinions cannot influence the decision if hiring is based for the most part upon exam scores, and that leads us right into the next topic ...

How important is your exam score?

As discussed, most jobs require an exam, so the facts I'm about to share apply to most Postal jobs. Here's the first and most important fact: **With Postal jobs, your exam score means everything.**

It is true that you must successfully navigate through the complicated application process in order to get a job. And it is true you must go through the interview process to get a job. And it is true that you won't get a job if you handle either the application or the interview improperly. **But the simple fact is, if your exam score isn't good enough, you don't need to worry about the application or the interview.** If your score isn't good enough, you wasted your time on the application, and you will never be invited to an interview. If your score isn't good enough, you will simply never get a job.

And, as mentioned earlier, Postal exams carry incredibly high failure rates of 80% to 95% or more. Do the math. If a hundred people take one of these exams, only a handful will even pass, much less score high enough to really get a job. Here's the bottom line ... **If you really want a job, you must do everything humanly possible to achieve the highest possible score on your exam.** And that leads us directly into our next topic of how to prepare for Postal exams.

Note: The Postal Service has recently begun to use the term "assessment" frequently rather than "exam" or "test". Don't let this confuse you. A test is a test no matter what they call it.

How to Prepare for Postal Exams

To assure a successful score, you can prepare for most exams by studying and practicing. As we discuss the different exams individually in this section of the book, you will learn about the types of test preparation available for each. But the bottom line is that if you want to succeed, you can – indeed you must – prepare for most Postal exams.

So, what do you need to prepare? **Successful test preparation calls for two critical elements ... motivation and an effective study guide.** For the most popular exams, I can help you with a study guide, but you must provide the motivation yourself. Nobody can give you motivation; it must come from within. Look back for a moment to page 21 where I told you how so many people lose the opportunity for a Postal job simply because they are lazy. They are too lazy to do the test prep work necessary for success. Please do not let this happen to you. I beg of you ... *Do not let laziness cost you the opportunity for a valuable Postal career!!!*

What do I mean by an "effective" study guide? **To successfully help you prepare for an exam, a study guide must offer four features:**

1. **The study guide must be 100% up-to-date.** Period. No exceptions. Like all exams, Postal tests are revised from time to time for various reasons. How can you successfully prepare with a guide that has old information – a guide that is teaching you about exam content that no longer exists? Obsolete study guides have always been a big problem in the Postal test prep field. Sometimes it is simply a matter of old guides still floating around from long ago, but other times it is outright fraud where a study guide known to be obsolete is sold with claims that it is fully up-to-date. You cannot be too careful when choosing a study guide. One big reason for my success as an author is that my materials are always 100% up-to-date. As a matter of fact, the one and only reason my Pathfinder Perks web tool (page 19) exists is to make sure that you are kept fully up-to-date. And when significant revisions take place, I pull my old products off the market and publish new ones. (Sorry for getting so wordy and carried away, but as you can tell, I have very passionate feelings about this subject.)

2. **A study guide must provide full information on exam content.** How can you prepare for a test if you don't even know what's on it? There are different exams used to fill different jobs. For the most part, the different exams are completely different from each other and have nothing in common. An exam consists of several sections, and these sections are completely different from each other. The instructions, timing, and tasks on one section will have absolutely nothing in common with another section on the very same test. You simply cannot prepare for an exam without first learning exactly what's on it.

3. **The study guide must provide simple yet effective test-taking strategies.** This is far more important that you might realize. When taking an exam, you are asked to perform completely foreign skills that you've never dreamed of before and to do so at an incredible rate of speed. To a large degree, Postal exams are speed tests. Most sections are timed, and you are forced to work at a brutal pace. The strategies we're discussing are tricks of the trade that help make the foreign tasks and inhuman speed manageable. For instance, the memorization section of exam 473E is by far the hardest part of the test and one of the biggest reasons for the high failure rates. But when using my memory strategies, people often report that the memorization section goes from the hardest part of the test to the easiest.

4. **Most importantly, the study guide must contain a quantity of realistic practice tests.** The key to successful test preparation is practice. You can learn everything there is to know about an exam, but if you don't practice, you're nowhere. Extensive practice is the only way to master the foreign skills and incredible speed demanded. And the practice means nothing if it is not realistic. The practice tests must be formatted exactly like the actual exam, and you must time yourself precisely like on the actual exam in order to derive any real benefit.

Another reason for my success as an author is my ultra-realistic practice tests. Before publishing a study guide for a particular exam, I research that test thoroughly and actually take it numerous times. By the time I start creating the guide, I know the test inside and out. I refuse to publish a guide until I can guarantee that my practice tests are exactly like the real thing. When it comes to practice tests, there is no gray area. It's either exactly right, or it's completely wrong. One of the features frequently mentioned in reviews for my study guides is that my practice tests are so much more realistic than those in other books.

Believe it or not, with paper tests, one purpose of practice is to enhance eye-hand coordination and improve fine muscle control. This illustration will help demonstrate my point …

Per the above example, imagine that you're taking a test with a full size test booklet to your left and a full size answer sheet booklet to your right (or vice versa if you're left-handed). The test booklet contains hundreds of questions printed on dozens of pages. The answer sheet booklet consists of several pages, but only one page is really important to you, the actual answer sheet page with over 2,000 answer bubbles on it. So, you're taking this speed test racing along at a million miles an hour going back and forth from the test booklet to the answer sheet booklet to darken an answer bubble, and then back to the test booklet for the next question, and then back to the answer sheet booklet to darken an answer bubble, etc. Particularly at the speed demanded, you need exceptional eye-hand coordination and fine muscle control just to successfully manage all this movement and marking.

But there's another challenge. Can you picture how easy it would be to get out of order and to mark an answer in the wrong spot? And once you've marked a single answer out of place, all your remaining answers will be marked in the wrong spots as well. Let's say that you're marking an answer for question 93, but when you start to mark an answer at item 93 on the answer sheet, you suddenly realize that there's already an answer marked there --- the answer for question 92. Somewhere along the way you got out of order by one spot on the answer sheet, and you have been marking answers one spot off since that point. It could be that you got out of order fifty questions back and have therefore marked the last fifty answers incorrectly. If so, you may as well quit and go home right now. There's no recovery at this point, and there's no way to pass if you miss fifty questions. Remember, this is a rigidly timed speed test. You may not even have time to answer all the questions in the time allowed, and you certainly don't have time to go back to correct fifty questions. In fact, you probably would not have time to correct even ten or fifteen questions, much less fifty.

An Important Message about Study Guides

This book is an exhaustive directory of Postal jobs and exams that provides every single bit of information you could ever need to know about how to get a Post Office job. Included in this book are job descriptions and full details on wages, benefits, exams, etc. It gives in-depth directions and tips for successfully navigating the complicated duplicate Postal job and exam application systems. In addition, the book features exclusive insider tips for acing the employment interview.

But this book is not a study guide, and I made very sure that it was never described as such. This book provides extensive information about all Postal exams, and it includes sample test questions where possible, but it does not offer full test preparation by itself. As explained below, combining full test prep materials for several different exams into a single book with this comprehensive Postal job search guide is simply not possible. So, if your preferred job requires an exam, you will need to get a study guide for that test as a separate product.

On the average, one of my printed study guides for a single Postal exam is about 350 pages long. Some are considerably longer. (Yes, it really takes that many pages to teach you what you need to know about one single exam and to give you a reasonable number of realistic practice tests.) As outlined in the table of contents, the Postal Service uses several different employment exams, and all of them are covered in this book. This book is already 352 pages long itself. If I tried to include full test preparation for all these different tests in one publication along with this Postal job guide, it would create a mountain of paper thousands of pages tall. And publishing a book that large is just not possible.

So, all that brings us to this point ...

(1) This book is a tremendously valuable asset for your Postal job quest. It will assure your success every step of the way as you attempt to navigate the confusing and contradictory duplicate Postal application systems. But it is not a study guide, and it cannot prepare you for an exam.

(2) If your chosen job requires an exam, you almost certainly need a study guide, which means that you must purchase the guide as a separate product. But I'm sure that you don't want spend much more money if you don't have to, and I don't want you to either.

(3) Here's the solution --- I've arranged for my study guides to be offered to repeat customers at discounted prices. And if you have this book, regardless of where you got it, you're a repeat customer, so you're entitled to the special discounted prices.

(4) As we look at each individual exam over the following pages, I will provide full details on the content of that exam. If I have a study guide available for that test, I will tell you about the guide and explain how to order it at the special discounted price. Plus, there is a catalog at the end of the book with information on my Postal job and exam guides.

Recap: Most jobs require an exam, and your exam score means everything. If you really want a Postal job, you must do everything humanly possible to achieve your highest possible score.

About Exam 230/238/240

This is one of the most unusual exam discussions we will have. We're going to talk about three different exams that are used to fill three different professional driving jobs. **But these three exams aren't really different at all. They're all identical to each other. And believe or not, they aren't really exams in the first place.** These exams and jobs are recapped below:

Exam 230 – Motor Vehicle Operator (page 34)
Exam 238 – Motor Vehicle Operator / Tractor Trailer Operator (page 34)
Exam 240 – Tractor Trailer Operator (page 34)

If you're not confused yet, let me try a little harder … **Rather than a traditional test, each of these exams is really only a questionnaire about the applicant's driving record and experience.** Even though these "exams" have different numbers and are for different jobs, the questionnaires for all three are identical. The Postal Service somehow converts your questionnaire answers into a numerical score that is used for hiring purposes.

Even though they are identical, each exam is assigned to a particular job. However, **the Postal Service frequently uses these exam titles interchangeably and in random combinations.** For instance, you may see the 230 exam associated with a Tractor Trailer Operator job when it is really assigned to Motor Vehicle Operator jobs. Or you may see the title "230/240" associated with any of the above jobs. This is completely irrelevant since they are all identical, but I want to warn you so that you don't become confused when applying for or taking one of these exams.

These exams are electronic. You do everything associated with these jobs and exams online … apply, complete the questionnaire, etc.

They will not disclose their secret formula for converting your answers into a score, but obviously the better your driving record, the better your score. **Do not even think about exaggerating to assure a high score,** however, because you will be forced to document your answers if you are called in for an interview.

How to Prepare for Exam 230/238/240

The questionnaire topics are listed on the next page. Since these are not true exams, you cannot study or practice for them. There is only one thing you can and should do in advance. **You should use the list of questionnaire topics on the next page as a checklist to gather and organize facts and figures about your driving history.** If you have this information at hand when starting the questionnaire, you should be able to complete it in short order. But if you have to go scurrying around searching for information each time you look at a new question, it will take you forever to finish it, and you may be timed out and kicked out of the Postal application program before finishing the questionnaire. You will be timed out after a period of inactivity that, depending upon which Postal statement you believe, may be as short as 10 minutes or as long as 30 minutes. Just to be safe, assume that 10 minutes is correct and prepare accordingly.

The 230/238/240 questionnaire asks about the following topics:

- Number of drug, alcohol, or other controlled substance driving offense convictions in the past 5 years.

- Number of hit and run convictions in the last 5 years.

- Number of reckless or careless driving convictions in the past 5 years.

- Number of fatal accidents judged to be your fault. (Note: There is not a stated number of years for this topic. They want to know about all such accidents no matter when they happened.)

- Number of driver's license suspensions in the last 3 years.

- Number of driver's license revocations in the last 5 years.

- Number of accidents judged to be your fault in the last 5 years.

- Number of traffic/driving offenses (moving violations) in the past 3 years.

- Number of traffic/driving offenses (moving violations) in the last year.

- Years of driving experience with passenger cars or larger vehicles.

- Months of fulltime experience driving a 7 or more ton truck, a tractor-trailer, or a 16 or more passenger bus. (Note: This item asks for months of experience, not years.)

- Months of fulltime experience driving a 7 or more ton truck, a tractor-trailer, or a 16 or more passenger bus within the past 7 years. (Note: This item is identical to the one above except that it asks for months of experience within the past 7 years.)

- Months of fulltime experience driving a tractor-trailer. (Note: This item asks for months of experience, not years.)

- Months of fulltime experience driving a tractor-trailer within the past 7 years. (Note: This item is identical to the one above except that it asks for months of experience within the past 7 years.)

About Exam 473/473E

This is the biggie ... the most popular Postal exam ... the one used to fill all over 90% of all fulltime jobs, all entry-level career positions in the Processing, Distribution, Delivery, and Retail category. And, this exam is used to fill the high demand part-time Rural Carrier Associate job as well. This test is also called the General Entrance Test Battery, the Battery Exam, and the Mega Test. Listed below are the actual jobs filled from this exam:

City Carrier – page 26
Mail Handler – page 29
Mail Processing Clerk – page 28
Rural Carrier Associate – page 39
Sales, Service, and Distribution Associate (Retail / Front Counter Clerk) – page 27

A brief history lesson is needed as we begin discussing this exam. **The actual title for this test is 473E, but you will also hear it called the 473, and you may even see the title 473C.** You see, exam 473/473C was first introduced as a pencil & paper test in late 2004 to replace old exam 470. This new exam was the very same whether it was called 473 or 473C. The difference was in the type of jobs being filled. When given as the 473, it was used to fill all entry-level career Processing, Distribution, Delivery, and Retail positions as mentioned above. When given as the 473C, they were using it to fill only City Carrier jobs. The "C" stood for "Carrier".

Pencil & paper exam 473/473C was recently converted to online electronic test 473E. The "E" stands for "Electronic". In truth, exams 473 and 473C no longer exist, but you may still hear those titles used when this test is being discussed. And at the same time this conversion took place, old exam 460 was retired, and the Rural Carrier Associate job formerly filled from old exam 460 was assigned to new exam 473E.

Note: As of the publish date of this book, most references to old exams 460, 470, and 473/473C had been removed from the Postal Service website, but the site had not yet been updated with any info about new exam 473E. If this is still the case when you visit their site, do not be alarmed. If you apply for any of the jobs formerly filled from these old exams and now filled from new exam 473E, you will find that my information is 100% accurate.

That's enough of a history lesson. The next question is "What's on the exam?" Per the following discussion, **exam 473E is taken in two separate sessions** (or assessments, as they call it).

Session 1 is a self-administered Personal Characteristics & Experience Inventory test. You take this session on your own without supervision. Most people take this online test at home using their own computer, but you can take it anywhere using whatever computer is convenient for you (at a library, borrow a friend's computer, etc.). This is a psychological test that is used to identify the best potential employees. Basically, this part of the exam builds a profile of your personality.

Session 2 is an online electronic test as well, but it is taken at a testing site in a strictly supervised environment. This testing site is a facility with a quantity of computers where a number of people can take computerized tests simultaneously. **Session 2 consists of three parts as follows:**

Part A – Address Checking has 60 questions. Each question is a pair of items consisting of an address (street/P.O. Box, city, and state) and a ZIP code. You are given 11 minutes to compare the items and answer "A" if they are exactly alike, "B" if they are different and the difference is in the address, "C" if they are different and the difference is in the ZIP code, or "D" if they are different and the difference is in both the address and the ZIP code. Considering the detailed comparisons to be made, the speed demanded on this section is quite challenging for most applicants.

In **Part B – Forms Completion**, you are shown various forms used by the Postal Service and asked questions about how they should be completed. You are given 15 minutes to answer 30 multiple-choice questions. The answer choices are A, B, C, or D. If you were an experienced Postal employee, this task would probably be easier. But, since you've never seen any of these forms and never even heard of many of the topics involved, it becomes a most challenging ordeal. And one of the complaints I regularly hear is that choosing an answer is made even more difficult by the ambiguous and confusing content of the forms. (Did you really think that a federal agency's bureaucratic forms would be logical or easy to understand?)

Part C – Coding and Memory consists of two sections as described below. As the title suggests, one section is the Coding Section, and the other is the Memory Section. For both sections, you are shown a chart of delivery routes and various address ranges that fit within the delivery routes.

In the Coding Section, you are given 6 minutes to answer 36 questions. Each question is an address, and the answer should be the delivery route (A, B, C, or D) where the chart indicates that the address belongs. In the Coding Section, you are allowed to look at the chart as you answer the questions. This section is like an open-book test you took in school. The answers are right there on a chart waiting for you to look them up. The real problem, the reason most people fail, is the next section.

In the Memory Section, you have 7 minutes to answer 36 similar address questions. Again, the answer is the delivery route (A, B, C, or D) where the chart indicates that the address belongs. But in the Memory Section, you are not allowed to look at the chart as you answer the questions. Instead, you are given a few minutes to memorize the addresses and delivery routes, and then you must answer the questions from memory.

This Memory Section is the Bad Boy! This section is one of the big reasons that so many people fail. The memorization is inhuman. Success calls for unique memorization strategies developed explicitly for this test … which is one of the key benefits of my 473E study guide (page 348). Those who post reviews for my guide often say that the memory section went from being the hardest part of the test to the easiest once they used my memory strategies.

How to Prepare for Exam 473/473E

Postal contacts nationwide state that exam 473/473E carries an 80-90% failure rate. It's hard to imagine such a high failure rate. But the simple fact is that, if 100 people took this test, 80-90 of them would fail, and only 10-20 would pass. There's really no need for me to say anything more about why test preparation for this exam is so important. These figures tell the story better than I could ever hope to.

So, how do you prepare for exam 473/473E to assure a good enough score to get a job? As discussed earlier, successful test preparation requires motivation and an effective study guide. And again, I can help with the study guide, but you must provide the motivation. This test, however, calls for a whole different kind of study guide.

As an electronic test, this exam calls for a different type of study guide. **To provide the realistic practice tests demanded, the test prep materials for this exam must be electronic just like the exam.** A printed book just won't work. As emphasized over and over again, successful test preparation calls for extensive and realistic practice. In the case of electronic tests, you must practice with interactive online sample exams formatted precisely and exactly like the real thing. Taking an electronic exam is completely and totally different from taking a paper & pencil test. *Succeeding on an electronic exam demands an altogether different set of skills that can only be mastered by practicing with electronic sample tests.* The last few sentences you just read are much more important than might be realized at first glance. Allow me to elaborate on a few key terms …

- **Different set of skills:** When first explaining the need for realistic practice some pages back, I detailed the skills needed to succeed on a paper & pencil exam. Well, the Postal Service has already converted some tests from paper to electronic. Eventually all exams will be converted to electronic. Eye-hand coordination and fine muscle control are still required on electronic tests, but the particular challenges faced and skills demanded are different. I could talk about this at great length, but the differences are difficult to grasp without actually experiencing them.

- **Online practice tests:** Electronic practice tests can be presented two ways – online or on a CD. But the only right way is online. An important function of test preparation is for you to become intimately familiar with the exam so that you can approach the real thing with complete confidence and familiarity. This enables you to rapidly and accurately breeze through the exam without the distraction of trying to figure out what in the world you're supposed to be doing. The actual exam is online. You must login and access the online materials multiple times. So, when practicing, you should realistically do the very same thing to gain the necessary level of familiarity.

- **Formatted exactly the real thing:** Referring again some pages back to our discussion on the need for realistic practice, I went to great length to explain how important it is for the practice tests to be formatted and timed 100% exactly like the real thing. And, as mentioned above, it is imperative that you are able to approach the real exam with complete confidence and familiarity. Imagine what would happen if you practiced your heart out to prepare for the test, but when taking the real exam, you found it was way different from your practice tests. This would surely destroy your confidence, your composure, your performance, and in turn your score. When it comes to practice tests, it's either 100% right or it's 100% wrong. There's nothing in between.

- **Interactive practice tests:** The actual electronic exam is interactive. When taking the exam, you are able to navigate and maneuver in various fashions. You can control (within reasonable limits) when the exam clock starts. You can navigate back and forth within one section of the test from question to question and from page to page (screen to screen). After completing one section, if you have time left over, you can selectively check your answers in that section for accuracy. (And, with sufficient realistic practice, you should indeed build up your speed to the point that you will have time to check answers.) After completing one section, you control (within reasonable limits) when to start the next section. And, at all times there should be a count-down timer at the top of the screen showing you exactly how much time remains on the section of the exam you are taking at that point. Again for realistic practice, electronic practice tests should provide this same exact level of interactivity. And, really, they should provide even more interactivity for test prep value. For instance, to track your progress and focus your energies, the practice tests should automatically and immediately be scored upon completion. And, the scores should be recorded so that you can chart your performance over time. Static practice tests that cannot provide this level of interactivity are simply unacceptable.

For these reasons, immediately after exam 473 was converted to an online test, I began building an electronic study guide for new exam 473E. **My comprehensive new electronic 473E guide was completed a few months after the conversion, and I'm proud to say that it offers everything described over the last few pages plus even more.** The experience taught me that, even though creating an electronic study guide is far more challenging and expensive than publishing a book, the test prep benefits greatly surpass those offered by a simple book. Among other benefits, there's no excuse for an out-of-date online guide because it can be updated instantly and continuously.

Building ultra realistic electronic practice tests was no small task. **It turns out that creating tests exactly like the actual exam required some very deep programming.** I had to contract a team of computer gurus from different companies and in different locations to complete the project. Both I and they took the new 473E electronic test a number of times to learn firsthand how it works and how my electronic practice tests needed to work. The finished product exceeded my greatest expectations. It is truly the finest test prep product I've ever published. It cost a ton of money to build, but it was worth it. (Between you and me, building this online 473E guide cost more than most people make in a whole year.)

To order my Complete Postal Exam 473/473E Interactive eGuide at the special repeat customer price, see page 348.

Exam 473/473E – Complete Sample Test

The only way to fully appreciate the 473E and its challenges is to personally experience it. Following over the next 87 pages is a complete sample test presented as realistically as possible. Since the 473E is an electronic test, it is not possible for a paper sample test to meet my usual ultra realistic standards. Two obvious differences are that the questions are presented on paper rather than on a computer monitor, and you use a pencil to mark answers rather than clicking a mouse. Your experience with this paper sample test cannot exactly match the real thing, but it is presented as realistically as possible.

To receive any benefit from this sample test, you must follow the instructions and timing restrictions precisely. The instructions are worded almost exactly the same as on the real exam. Most importantly, if you do not time yourself specifically as directed, you will gain nothing at all from this experience. And to take this test realistically, *you must not write or make any marks whatsoever except for marking your answers!* Even though notes would help in some exam sections, since the real test is electronic, writing or making notes of any kind will not be possible when taking it.

I would like to take this opportunity to confuse you about Postal exam scoring formulas. The Postal Service refuses to release the scoring formulas used to calculate the final overall scores for any of its tests. They publish the scoring formulas used to score most (but not all) of the individual sections of their exams, but they will not tell us how those individual section scores are combined together to create the final overall exam score. The only thing we know for sure about the final scores is that on all exams the passing score is 70 and the highest possible score without veterans preference points (page 345) is 100.

We do know what the overall scoring formula is _not_. It is not simply a combination of the individual section scores because, if you add up the individual section scores, the total can easily exceed 100. And the overall score is not a simple percentage. For instance, it does not mean that your score is an 85 just because you answered 85% of the questions correctly. We know lots of things that the formula is _not_, but unfortunately we do not know what it _is_.

To measure your performance on my sample tests, I will give you the scoring formula for each section separately (where the scoring formula is known). Gauging your results on each section should give you a reasonable indication of how you might have fared on the overall exam.

As detailed in the below index, exam 473E is a monster. This sample exam is 87 pages long even after I radically condensed the number of pages in the Personal Characteristics & Experience Inventory section to make the size of the test as manageable as possible.

Turn to the next page when you are ready to begin the 473E sample test.

DIRECTIONS

Personal Characteristics & Experience Inventory (PCEI) is the first session that you take on your own without supervision. The PCEI is both simple and confusing at the same time. It is simple in that you read a question/statement and then respond by simply stating how it applies to you. It is confusing in that both the questions and the answers can seem ambiguous. And you will notice that they ask about the same topic multiple times. They ask in different ways each time, but the topic (frustration, stress, temper, organization, tolerance, motivation, safety, etc.) is the same.

In this session, you have 90 minutes to answer 150 questions. Unlike all other exams/sections, the time allowed for the PCEI is generous. This is a rare Postal exam situation where speed is not an issue. Most people finish before the 90 minutes run out. However, do set some type of a timer for 90 minutes to make sure that you don't exceed the specified allotment of time.

All PCEI questions are multiple choice. The number and type of answer choices vary as follows:

- For the first portion, approximately one third of the questions, the answer choices are "Strongly Agree", "Agree", "Disagree", and "Strongly Disagree".

- For the second portion, the choices are "Very Often", "Often", "Sometimes", and "Rarely or Never".

- On the final portion, the questions can have from four to nine answer choices, and the answer choices are worded differently for each question.

Regardless of how many answer choices are presented or how the answer choices are worded, you are only supposed to mark one answer choice per question. Even if two or more choices seem appropriate, you must choose only one.

The format of this paper sample test varies from the real electronic exam in only two significant ways. On the real test, there is only one PCEI question per page/screen. If I followed that format here, this one section of the test alone would be 150 pages long. To prevent this book from being a zillion pages long, I included as many PCEI sample questions as possible on each page.

The second difference has to do with answer choices. The answer choices appear under each question just like on the actual exam. But since this is a paper test, you must choose answers by darkening them with a pencil rather than clicking them with a mouse. On every section of the real electronic exam except this one, you choose an answer by clicking a typical small round radio button. On the PCEI section only, there are large square buttons rather than small round ones. However, to save space/pages on this paper sample test as described in the above paragraph, I used small round radio buttons instead of the large square ones.

SCORING

There are no right or wrong answers on this section. Whatever answer choice best describes you is the right answer for you. They somehow convert your answers into a numerical score, but they will not share any details about how this is accomplished. Since there are no official right or wrong answers and since there is no formula we can give you for scoring the PCEI, we have not included an answer key for this section. Since you cannot score yourself in this case, it will not be possible for you to interpret how your performance on this section of the sample test might contribute to your final exam score. I have given you this PCEI sample test simply for you experience it.

Turn the page and begin when you are prepared to time yourself for exactly 90 minutes.

1)   After finishing one task, you automatically move on to other duties without having to be told to do so.
- A)   Strongly Agree
- B)   Agree
- C)   Disagree
- D)   Strongly Disagree

2)   You are valued as an employee for not having to be continually managed.
- A)   Strongly Agree
- B)   Agree
- C)   Disagree
- D)   Strongly Disagree

3)   You are offended if a customer is not satisfied with the service you provide.
- A)   Strongly Agree
- B)   Agree
- C)   Disagree
- D)   Strongly Disagree

4)   You can easily and comfortably associate with almost everyone.
- A)   Strongly Agree
- B)   Agree
- C)   Disagree
- D)   Strongly Disagree

5)   You like to learn new concepts that can be helpful personally or professionally.
- A)   Strongly Agree
- B)   Agree
- C)   Disagree
- D)   Strongly Disagree

6)   Even if you don't enjoy a particular duty, you complete it without having to be prompted.
- A)   Strongly Agree
- B)   Agree
- C)   Disagree
- D)   Strongly Disagree

7)   Multitasking is one of your strongest skills.
- A)   Strongly Agree
- B)   Agree
- C)   Disagree
- D)   Strongly Disagree

8)   You strongly believe in the adage "A job worth doing is a job worth doing well".
- A)   Strongly Agree
- B)   Agree
- C)   Disagree
- D)   Strongly Disagree

 Continued on next page …

9) You believe that occasionally being a little late for work is okay.
   - ○ A) Strongly Agree
   - ○ B) Agree
   - ○ C) Disagree
   - ○ D) Strongly Disagree

10) You prefer a job that offers challenges more than a job that is routine.
   - ○ A) Strongly Agree
   - ○ B) Agree
   - ○ C) Disagree
   - ○ D) Strongly Disagree

11) You are willing to bypass safety procedures sometimes to get a job finished faster.
   - ○ A) Strongly Agree
   - ○ B) Agree
   - ○ C) Disagree
   - ○ D) Strongly Disagree

12) You are more productive and efficient that most of the people you work with.
   - ○ A) Strongly Agree
   - ○ B) Agree
   - ○ C) Disagree
   - ○ D) Strongly Disagree

13) You are willing to learn exactly what you need to know to do your job but no more.
   - ○ A) Strongly Agree
   - ○ B) Agree
   - ○ C) Disagree
   - ○ D) Strongly Disagree

14) It is difficult for you to focus on one thing for an extended amount of time.
   - ○ A) Strongly Agree
   - ○ B) Agree
   - ○ C) Disagree
   - ○ D) Strongly Disagree

15) You're always willing to start a new task but sometimes have trouble completing it.
   - ○ A) Strongly Agree
   - ○ B) Agree
   - ○ C) Disagree
   - ○ D) Strongly Disagree

16) People enjoy being with you.
   - ○ A) Strongly Agree
   - ○ B) Agree
   - ○ C) Disagree
   - ○ D) Strongly Disagree

Continued on next page …

17) When you are frustrated it affects your relationships and your performance on the job.
- A) Strongly Agree
- B) Agree
- C) Disagree
- D) Strongly Disagree

18) You can deal with frustration on the job better than most of your co-workers.
- A) Strongly Agree
- B) Agree
- C) Disagree
- D) Strongly Disagree

19) You do not need to own up to mistakes if nobody else catches them and they do not affect anyone.
- A) Strongly Agree
- B) Agree
- C) Disagree
- D) Strongly Disagree

20) Safety is a priority in everything you do.
- A) Strongly Agree
- B) Agree
- C) Disagree
- D) Strongly Disagree

21) If a co-worker is very busy, pointing out a safety concern to him or her may be counterproductive.
- A) Strongly Agree
- B) Agree
- C) Disagree
- D) Strongly Disagree

22) If a customer treats you unfairly, you should not be expected to treat the customer any better.
- A) Strongly Agree
- B) Agree
- C) Disagree
- D) Strongly Disagree

23) You arrive at work early more often than late.
- A) Strongly Agree
- B) Agree
- C) Disagree
- D) Strongly Disagree

24) Organization is essential for success.
- A) Strongly Agree
- B) Agree
- C) Disagree
- D) Strongly Disagree

Continued on next page …

Personal Characteristics & Experience Inventory

continued

25) You always keep a promise.
- ○ A) Strongly Agree
- ○ B) Agree
- ○ C) Disagree
- ○ D) Strongly Disagree

26) It is not necessary to point out a problem at work if nobody else is aware of it.
- ○ A) Strongly Agree
- ○ B) Agree
- ○ C) Disagree
- ○ D) Strongly Disagree

27) Deadlines are usually flexible.
- ○ A) Strongly Agree
- ○ B) Agree
- ○ C) Disagree
- ○ D) Strongly Disagree

28) You have a variety of friends from different ethnic backgrounds.
- ○ A) Strongly Agree
- ○ B) Agree
- ○ C) Disagree
- ○ D) Strongly Disagree

29) You like working with customers on a daily basis.
- ○ A) Strongly Agree
- ○ B) Agree
- ○ C) Disagree
- ○ D) Strongly Disagree

30) When assigned a job, you begin promptly and continue until it is complete.
- ○ A) Strongly Agree
- ○ B) Agree
- ○ C) Disagree
- ○ D) Strongly Disagree

31) Some people are difficult for anyone to get along with.
- ○ A) Strongly Agree
- ○ B) Agree
- ○ C) Disagree
- ○ D) Strongly Disagree

32) You find that assisting people on the job is personally rewarding.
- ○ A) Strongly Agree
- ○ B) Agree
- ○ C) Disagree
- ○ D) Strongly Disagree

Continued on next page ...

33) You enjoy expanding your horizons.
- ○ A) Strongly Agree
- ○ B) Agree
- ○ C) Disagree
- ○ D) Strongly Disagree

34) You are known for accomplishing more in less time than your fellow employees.
- ○ A) Strongly Agree
- ○ B) Agree
- ○ C) Disagree
- ○ D) Strongly Disagree

35) Friends know that they can depend on you when they need help.
- ○ A) Strongly Agree
- ○ B) Agree
- ○ C) Disagree
- ○ D) Strongly Disagree

36) Making notes is a waste of time if you are too busy.
- ○ A) Strongly Agree
- ○ B) Agree
- ○ C) Disagree
- ○ D) Strongly Disagree

37) Juggling several assignments simultaneously is easy for you.
- ○ A) Strongly Agree
- ○ B) Agree
- ○ C) Disagree
- ○ D) Strongly Disagree

38) Your supervisor knows to come to you if a project must be completed quickly.
- ○ A) Strongly Agree
- ○ B) Agree
- ○ C) Disagree
- ○ D) Strongly Disagree

39) You enjoy helping co-workers.
- ○ A) Strongly Agree
- ○ B) Agree
- ○ C) Disagree
- ○ D) Strongly Disagree

40) You use as many safety precautions at home as you do at work.
- ○ A) Strongly Agree
- ○ B) Agree
- ○ C) Disagree
- ○ D) Strongly Disagree

41) You enjoy trying new practices you've learned.
- ○ A) Strongly Agree
- ○ B) Agree
- ○ C) Disagree
- ○ D) Strongly Disagree

42) You look forward to training classes that help you perform your job better.
- ○ A) Strongly Agree
- ○ B) Agree
- ○ C) Disagree
- ○ D) Strongly Disagree

43) If you are overwhelmed at work your performance is hindered.
- ○ A) Strongly Agree
- ○ B) Agree
- ○ C) Disagree
- ○ D) Strongly Disagree

44) You are recognized for your patience.
- ○ A) Strongly Agree
- ○ B) Agree
- ○ C) Disagree
- ○ D) Strongly Disagree

45) You enjoy helping people find solutions for their problems.
- ○ A) Strongly Agree
- ○ B) Agree
- ○ C) Disagree
- ○ D) Strongly Disagree

46) You are recognized for your organization.
- ○ A) Strongly Agree
- ○ B) Agree
- ○ C) Disagree
- ○ D) Strongly Disagree

47) You handle stress well.
- ○ A) Strongly Agree
- ○ B) Agree
- ○ C) Disagree
- ○ D) Strongly Disagree

48) You are always looking for ways to improve your job performance.
- ○ A) Strongly Agree
- ○ B) Agree
- ○ C) Disagree
- ○ D) Strongly Disagree

Continued on next page …

49) Problems at home influence your performance on the job.
- ○ A) Strongly Agree
- ○ B) Agree
- ○ C) Disagree
- ○ D) Strongly Disagree

50) You can remain focused on a single issue for extended periods.
- ○ A) Strongly Agree
- ○ B) Agree
- ○ C) Disagree
- ○ D) Strongly Disagree

51) You have the natural ability of defuse volatile situations.
- ○ A) Strongly Agree
- ○ B) Agree
- ○ C) Disagree
- ○ D) Strongly Disagree

52) You do exactly what is expected of you and no more.
- ○ A) Strongly Agree
- ○ B) Agree
- ○ C) Disagree
- ○ D) Strongly Disagree

53) You make friends easily.
- ○ A) Strongly Agree
- ○ B) Agree
- ○ C) Disagree
- ○ D) Strongly Disagree

54) Accomplishing your team's goals is as important as accomplishing your personal goals.
- ○ A) Strongly Agree
- ○ B) Agree
- ○ C) Disagree
- ○ D) Strongly Disagree

55) Safety is more of a priority for you than for most your co-workers.
- ○ A) Strongly Agree
- ○ B) Agree
- ○ C) Disagree
- ○ D) Strongly Disagree

56) You welcome suggestions that may help you personally or professionally.
- ○ A) Very Often
- ○ B) Often
- ○ C) Sometimes
- ○ D) Rarely or Never

Continued on next page ...

57) You complete all assignments even if some do not seem very important to you.
- ○ A)   Very Often
- ○ B)   Often
- ○ C)   Sometimes
- ○ D)   Rarely or Never

58) Stress can distract your focus.
- ○ A)   Very Often
- ○ B)   Often
- ○ C)   Sometimes
- ○ D)   Rarely or Never

59) You adhere to the safety practice of lifting with your legs, not your back.
- ○ A)   Very Often
- ○ B)   Often
- ○ C)   Sometimes
- ○ D)   Rarely or Never

60) Even in a tense situation when everyone else is irritated, you control your temper.
- ○ A)   Very Often
- ○ B)   Often
- ○ C)   Sometimes
- ○ D)   Rarely or Never

61) Completing tasks seems to take you more time than it should.
- ○ A)   Very Often
- ○ B)   Often
- ○ C)   Sometimes
- ○ D)   Rarely or Never

62) You make a great first impression.
- ○ A)   Very Often
- ○ B)   Often
- ○ C)   Sometimes
- ○ D)   Rarely or Never

63) You are willing to listen to someone's opinion even if you don't agree.
- ○ A)   Very Often
- ○ B)   Often
- ○ C)   Sometimes
- ○ D)   Rarely or Never

64) You immediately offer to help when you see a fellow employee in need of assistance.
- ○ A)   Very Often
- ○ B)   Often
- ○ C)   Sometimes
- ○ D)   Rarely or Never

                                     Continued on next page …

65) You first create a prioritized plan when beginning an assignment.
- ○ A) Very Often
- ○ B) Often
- ○ C) Sometimes
- ○ D) Rarely or Never

66) You share new information with fellow employees if it will improve their job performance.
- ○ A) Very Often
- ○ B) Often
- ○ C) Sometimes
- ○ D) Rarely or Never

67) People look to you for resolving tense situations.
- ○ A) Very Often
- ○ B) Often
- ○ C) Sometimes
- ○ D) Rarely or Never

68) You employ safety precautions when doing odd jobs at home.
- ○ A) Very Often
- ○ B) Often
- ○ C) Sometimes
- ○ D) Rarely or Never

69) You get aggravated by people reminding you of safety precautions.
- ○ A) Very Often
- ○ B) Often
- ○ C) Sometimes
- ○ D) Rarely or Never

70) You maintain thorough records on the job.
- ○ A) Very Often
- ○ B) Often
- ○ C) Sometimes
- ○ D) Rarely or Never

71) You respond respectfully regardless of how another person treats you.
- ○ A) Very Often
- ○ B) Often
- ○ C) Sometimes
- ○ D) Rarely or Never

72) Fellow employees say that you are calm even in stressful situations.
- ○ A) Very Often
- ○ B) Often
- ○ C) Sometimes
- ○ D) Rarely or Never

Continued on next page …

73) When you discover a better system or practice on the job, you tell fellow employees about it.
- ○ A) Very Often
- ○ B) Often
- ○ C) Sometimes
- ○ D) Rarely or Never

74) You react quickly without always considering the results of your actions.
- ○ A) Very Often
- ○ B) Often
- ○ C) Sometimes
- ○ D) Rarely or Never

75) You practice the adage: "Do unto others as you would have them do unto you".
- ○ A) Very Often
- ○ B) Often
- ○ C) Sometimes
- ○ D) Rarely or Never

76) You do not readily accept suggestions for improvement without proof the suggestions are valid.
- ○ A) Very Often
- ○ B) Often
- ○ C) Sometimes
- ○ D) Rarely or Never

77) Your fellow employees can tell very easily when you are in a bad mood.
- ○ A) Very Often
- ○ B) Often
- ○ C) Sometimes
- ○ D) Rarely or Never

78) You must be reminded of appointments and schedules.
- ○ A) Very Often
- ○ B) Often
- ○ C) Sometimes
- ○ D) Rarely or Never

79) You treat people respectfully even when they treat you disrespectfully.
- ○ A) Very Often
- ○ B) Often
- ○ C) Sometimes
- ○ D) Rarely or Never

80) People get angry at you because you refuse to consider their suggestions.
- ○ A) Very Often
- ○ B) Often
- ○ C) Sometimes
- ○ D) Rarely or Never

Continued on next page …

continued

81) You maintain an optimistic outlook in discouraging circumstances.
- ○ A) Very Often
- ○ B) Often
- ○ C) Sometimes
- ○ D) Rarely or Never

82) You are more careful when driving in inclement weather than most other people.
- ○ A) Very Often
- ○ B) Often
- ○ C) Sometimes
- ○ D) Rarely or Never

83) You overcome any obstructions to assure that an assignment is completed.
- ○ A) Very Often
- ○ B) Often
- ○ C) Sometimes
- ○ D) Rarely or Never

84) You offer to assist fellow employees after completing your own tasks.
- ○ A) Very Often
- ○ B) Often
- ○ C) Sometimes
- ○ D) Rarely or Never

85) You do what is expected of you plus a little more.
- ○ A) Very Often
- ○ B) Often
- ○ C) Sometimes
- ○ D) Rarely or Never

86) You complete assignments on schedule.
- ○ A) Very Often
- ○ B) Often
- ○ C) Sometimes
- ○ D) Rarely or Never

87) You do not take a risk without completely understanding the possible results.
- ○ A) Very Often
- ○ B) Often
- ○ C) Sometimes
- ○ D) Rarely or Never

88) When working with a team, you encourage input from all teammates.
- ○ A) Very Often
- ○ B) Often
- ○ C) Sometimes
- ○ D) Rarely or Never

Continued on next page …

89) You give people your respect even if they have not earned it.
- ○ A) Very Often
- ○ B) Often
- ○ C) Sometimes
- ○ D) Rarely or Never

90) You get more done on the job than others.
- ○ A) Very Often
- ○ B) Often
- ○ C) Sometimes
- ○ D) Rarely or Never

91) Fellow employees are astonished at how you can manage stress on the job.
- ○ A) Very Often
- ○ B) Often
- ○ C) Sometimes
- ○ D) Rarely or Never

92) You are only courteous to people who are courteous to you.
- ○ A) Very Often
- ○ B) Often
- ○ C) Sometimes
- ○ D) Rarely or Never

93) Fellow employees frequently comment on how reliable you are.
- ○ A) Very Often
- ○ B) Often
- ○ C) Sometimes
- ○ D) Rarely or Never

94) You find it difficult to meet schedules when assigned multiple tasks.
- ○ A) Very Often
- ○ B) Often
- ○ C) Sometimes
- ○ D) Rarely or Never

95) When someone is disrespectful to you, it is difficult to be respectful to that person.
- ○ A) Very Often
- ○ B) Often
- ○ C) Sometimes
- ○ D) Rarely or Never

96) You plan your assignments by prioritizing tasks.
- ○ A) Very Often
- ○ B) Often
- ○ C) Sometimes
- ○ D) Rarely or Never

Continued on next page …

97) You do not take advantage of all training opportunities that would improve your job performance.
- ○ A)   Very Often
- ○ B)   Often
- ○ C)   Sometimes
- ○ D)   Rarely or Never

98) When you observe a need at work, you act on it right away without having to be told to do so.
- ○ A)   Very Often
- ○ B)   Often
- ○ C)   Sometimes
- ○ D)   Rarely or Never

99) You see a project through to completion even when faced with interruptions and conflicts.
- ○ A)   Very Often
- ○ B)   Often
- ○ C)   Sometimes
- ○ D)   Rarely or Never

100) You are quick to offer assistance if a fellow employee has a problem.
- ○ A)   Very Often
- ○ B)   Often
- ○ C)   Sometimes
- ○ D)   Rarely or Never

101) When there is a problem on the job, who or what is usually at fault?
- ○ A)   Management
- ○ B)   Equipment
- ○ C)   Other employees
- ○ D)   Insufficient scheduling
- ○ E)   Something you did or did not do
- ○ F)   Something else
- ○ G)   I don't know.

102) How do you handle stressful circumstances on the job?
- ○ A)   My performance is better under stressful circumstances.
- ○ B)   Stressful circumstances don't affect me one way or the other.
- ○ C)   I don't enjoy stressful circumstances, but I can endure it.
- ○ D)   I do not handle stressful circumstances very well.
- ○ E)   I don't know.

103) What motivates you the most at this point in your life?
- ○ A)   Status and prestige
- ○ B)   Wages, benefits, and job security
- ○ C)   Generating new concepts and ideas
- ○ D)   Personal freedom
- ○ E)   Helping those in need
- ○ F)   Something else
- ○ G)   I don't know.

      Continued on next page …

104) How frequently have you voluntarily stayed late after work or school to finish a special project?
- ○ A) Never
- ○ B) Less than five times
- ○ C) Five to ten times
- ○ D) More than ten times
- ○ E) I don't know.

105) How frequently do you establish personal goals or objectives that are virtually unachievable?
- ○ A) All the time
- ○ B) Frequently
- ○ C) Occasionally
- ○ D) Not very often
- ○ E) Not at all
- ○ F) I don't know.

106) What rating were you given in your latest performance review?
- ○ A) Excellent
- ○ B) Superior
- ○ C) Satisfactory
- ○ D) Unsatisfactory
- ○ E) I've never had a performance review.
- ○ F) I don't know.

107) How would you feel about having to work several nights every week?
- ○ A) I prefer working at night.
- ○ B) I would do it but would not like it.
- ○ C) I would refuse to work at night.
- ○ D) I don't know.

108) If you were in an assembly of 100 diverse people, how would others rank your talent for getting along?
- ○ A) #1
- ○ B) In the top 10
- ○ C) In the top 25
- ○ D) In the top 50
- ○ E) I'm not interested in getting along with other types of people.
- ○ F) I don't know.

109) Of the below factors, which would make your job the most unpleasant or unacceptable?
- ○ A) Not being given a specific job description
- ○ B) Not having the freedom to call my own shots
- ○ C) Having to perform repetitive tasks over and over
- ○ D) Having to frequently explain why I did something
- ○ E) All of these factors would make my job difficult.
- ○ F) None of the factors would bother me.
- ○ G) I don't know.

Continued on next page …

110) Which of these have you been responsible for?
- A) Locking and securing a facility at the end of the day
- B) Balancing the books, accounts, etc.
- C) Managing cash, receipts, etc.
- D) Two of the above
- E) All of the above
- F) None of the above
- G) I don't know.

111) Have you met with more or less success than other people with similar education?
- A) Much less success
- B) Less success
- C) About the same success
- D) More success
- E) Much more success
- F) I don't know.

112) Which of the below management circumstances bothers you the most?
- A) Not having the freedom to do the work my way
- B) Being told what to do all the time
- C) Having a manager who is not willing to consider my suggestions
- D) None of the above circumstances bother me.
- E) I don't know.

113) How are you at learning new procedures?
- A) Much better and quicker than my co-workers
- B) A little better and quicker than my co-workers
- C) About the same as everybody else
- D) A little slower than my co-workers
- E) I don't know.

114) How would you handle it if a fellow employee's personal habits really bothered you?
- A) Try to ignore it and hope that it stops
- B) Drop hints about the problem
- C) Confront him or her and demand that it stop
- D) Submit a complaint to management
- E) Try something else
- F) I don't know.

115) How do you prefer to schedule tasks at work?
- A) Concentrate on one thing at a time
- B) At the most, handle two or three things at the same time
- C) Multitask several assignments simultaneously
- D) I don't know.

116) If you resigned from your most recent job, how much notice did you give?
- A) None
- B) One week or less
- C) More than one week
- D) Does not apply

Continued on next page ...

117) If you have changed jobs in the past, what was your greatest motivation for the change?
- ○ A) More challenging work
- ○ B) Better co-workers
- ○ C) Better wages
- ○ D) Better use of your skills, education, etc.
- ○ E) None of the above
- ○ F) I've never had a job or never changed jobs.

118) How did you get along with your teachers in high school?
- ○ A) Much better than my classmates
- ○ B) A little better than my classmates
- ○ C) About the same as my classmates
- ○ D) Not as good as my classmates
- ○ E) I did not get along with my teachers at all.
- ○ F) Does not apply

119) At this point in your life, which of the below factors is most important when seeking a new job?
- ○ A) Better wages
- ○ B) Greater status
- ○ C) Relocation
- ○ D) Less stress
- ○ E) Better hours
- ○ F) More challenging work
- ○ G) None of the above

120) Which of the below items best describes your management experience?
- ○ A) I have been self-managed.
- ○ B) I have managed one other employee.
- ○ C) I have managed two or more other employees.
- ○ D) None of the above

121) How much experience do you have working in a manufacturing environment?
- ○ A) More than ten years
- ○ B) Five to ten years
- ○ C) One to five years
- ○ D) Less than one year
- ○ E) I have no manufacturing experience.

122) Which of the below items would be easiest for you?
- ○ A) Trying to assist someone who has a limited grasp of your native language
- ○ B) Prompting a fellow employee to be more productive
- ○ C) Pacifying an irritated customer
- ○ D) A public speaking engagement for a large group
- ○ E) Convincing a manager to consider your suggestions
- ○ F) All of these items would be easy for me.
- ○ G) None of these items would be easy for me.
- ○ H) I don't know.

Continued on next page ...

123) Which of the below situations bothers you most at work?
- ○ A)   Your suggestion is misunderstood
- ○ B)   Your suggestion is ignored
- ○ C)   A fellow employee criticizes your work
- ○ D)   A manager tells you to complete a job left unfinished by another employee
- ○ E)   All of these situations bother me.
- ○ F)   None of these situations bother me.
- ○ G)   I don't know.

124) Have you ever wanted to quit a job because of a management problem?
- ○ A)   No
- ○ B)   Yes, one time
- ○ C)   Yes, several times
- ○ D)   Yes, quite a number of times
- ○ E)   I don't remember.

125) Does it bother you to work under many strict rules and regulations?
- ○ A)   Yes, quite a lot
- ○ B)   Yes, somewhat
- ○ C)   No, not much
- ○ D)   No, not at all

126) How would your latest manager rate your dependability?
- ○ A)   Better than anyone else
- ○ B)   Better than most
- ○ C)   The same as most
- ○ D)   Less than most
- ○ E)   Not dependable at all
- ○ F)   I don't know.

127) Compared to others, how frequently are you asked to take on a special project?
- ○ A)   Much more frequently than others
- ○ B)   More frequently than others
- ○ C)   The same as others
- ○ D)   Less frequently than others
- ○ E)   Never
- ○ F)   I don't know.

128) How long does it take to calm your temper enough to work normally when you become angry?
- ○ A)   I never lose my temper.
- ○ B)   A few minutes
- ○ C)   A few hours
- ○ D)   One day
- ○ E)   More than one day
- ○ F)   I don't know.

Continued on next page ...

129) How do you handle fellow employees that are having family or personal problems?
- ○ A)   Tell them to leave their problems at home and leave you alone
- ○ B)   Offer your help if they would like it
- ○ C)   Be compassionate and encouraging
- ○ D)   Suggest how they could take care of their problems
- ○ E)   Force them to discuss it with you
- ○ F)   Ignore them
- ○ G)   None of the above

130) In which of the below school functions did you excel?
- ○ A)   Class participation
- ○ B)   Team projects
- ○ C)   Papers or reports
- ○ D)   Test taking
- ○ E)   None of the above

131) How would you describe your ability to function as a member of a team?
- ○ A)   Not as good as most
- ○ B)   About the same as most
- ○ C)   Better than most
- ○ D)   I don't know.

132) As a team leader, how are you at convincing others to follow your instructions?
- ○ A)   Not as good as most
- ○ B)   About the same as most
- ○ C)   Better than most
- ○ D)   I've never been a team leader.
- ○ E)   I don't know.

133) In what area do you really stand out?
- ○ A)   Helping people
- ○ B)   Keeping records
- ○ C)   Prioritizing
- ○ D)   Setting goals
- ○ E)   None of the above

134) How much of a risk taker are you?
- ○ A)   I take risks frequently.
- ○ B)   I occasionally take small risks.
- ○ C)   I never take risks.
- ○ D)   None of the above
- ○ E)   I don't know.

135) How much experience do you have working at a facility that runs 24 hours a day?
- ○ A)   None
- ○ B)   Less than 1 month
- ○ C)   1 to 12 months
- ○ D)   1 to 5 years
- ○ E)   Over 5 years

                                    Continued on next page …

continued

136) Which type duty do you enjoy more?
- ○ A)   Manual labor
- ○ B)   Customer service
- ○ C)   Record keeping
- ○ D)   None of the above

137) How quickly do you finish assignments?
- ○ A)   Slower than most
- ○ B)   About the same as most
- ○ C)   Faster than most
- ○ D)   I don't know.

138) Which of these job situations bothers you the most?
- ○ A)   Being asked to begin additional assignments before current ones are completed
- ○ B)   Having to revise a project repeatedly before it is approved
- ○ C)   Helping disrespectful or rude people
- ○ D)   Being overwhelmed with more assignments than one person should be expected to handle
- ○ E)   None of the above
- ○ F)   I don't know.

139) How frequently would your high school teachers say you participated in class discussions?
- ○ A)   More than most
- ○ B)   About the same as most
- ○ C)   Less than most
- ○ D)   Never
- ○ E)   I don't know.

140) While in high school, how frequently were you in fights or physical confrontations?
- ○ A)   Daily
- ○ B)   Weekly
- ○ C)   Monthly
- ○ D)   Once or twice
- ○ E)   Never

141) What is your opinion of working nights?
- ○ A)   I enjoy working nights.
- ○ B)   I will work nights if required.
- ○ C)   I avoid working nights.
- ○ D)   I refuse to work nights.
- ○ E)   I don't know.

142) Which word best describes you?
- ○ A)   Motivated
- ○ B)   Tolerant
- ○ C)   Reliable
- ○ D)   Intelligent
- ○ E)   Pleasant
- ○ F)   None of the above
- ○ G)   I don't know.

Continued on next page …

143) As an employee, what level of management do you require?
- ○ A) More than most
- ○ B) About the same as most
- ○ C) Less than most
- ○ D) Almost none

144) How do you feel when being introduced to a stranger?
- ○ A) Relaxed
- ○ B) Okay
- ○ C) Nervous
- ○ D) I don't know.

145) How much input should employees have in supervisory decisions?
- ○ A) None
- ○ B) Employee suggestions should be considered.
- ○ C) Employees should play a key role in the decision making process.
- ○ D) I don't know.

146) What type goals are easier for you to achieve?
- ○ A) Organizational goals
- ○ B) Team goals
- ○ C) Personal goals
- ○ D) None of the above

147) Which duty as a team member is easier for you?
- ○ A) Prioritizing
- ○ B) Record keeping
- ○ C) Mediating
- ○ D) Communicating
- ○ E) None of the above

148) Which of these employment factors means the most to you?
- ○ A) Wages
- ○ B) Job security
- ○ C) Status
- ○ D) Advancement

149) Which employment factor(s) would be the worst for you personally?
- ○ A) Low wages
- ○ B) Lack of communication
- ○ C) Inferior working conditions
- ○ D) Disrespectful supervisor
- ○ E) Vague job description
- ○ F) All the above

150) What type management do you prefer?
- ○ A) General and occasional
- ○ B) Consistent and sensible
- ○ C) Constant and detailed
- ○ D) None of the above

DIRECTIONS

The Address Checking section consists of 60 questions to be completed in 11 minutes. You are given a **Correct List** of addresses and ZIP codes. A **List to be Checked,** also with addresses and ZIP codes, appears next to the Correct List. The List to be Checked should be exactly like the Correct List, but it may contain errors.

Your task is to compare each row of information in the Correct List and the List to be Checked to find if there are **A) No Errors**, an error in the **B) Address Only**, an error in the **C) ZIP Code Only**, or an error in **D) Both** the address and the ZIP code. Mark your answer (A, B, C, or D) accordingly.

Even though this is a paper sample test, the Address Checking section is formatted as much like the real exam as possible. It is laid out very similarly to the Address Checking section on the actual electronic exam. For instance, there are 10 questions per page (screen) just like on the real test. And the answer choices are radio buttons that appear to the right of each question just like on the real test. But since this is a paper test, you must choose answers by darkening the radio buttons with a pencil rather than clicking them with a mouse.

SCORING

Formula: To score the Address Checking section, first use the answer key at the end of the test to identify your correct and incorrect answers. Then count your correct answers and your incorrect answers. Subtract 1/3 of the number of incorrect answers from the number of correct answers. The result is your score. (Yes, I know this is a goofy formula. But it's theirs, not mine. All I can do is explain it the best way I can.)

Example: Let's say that, out of the 60 questions, I answered 50 in the time allowed. And, of the 50 that I answered, 41 were correct, and 9 were wrong. To score myself, I subtract 3 (1/3 of the 9 of wrong answers) from 41 (the number of correct answers). My score is a 38.

HOW TO INTERPRET YOUR SCORE

Process: If I answered all the questions correctly within the time allowed, the best possible score on this section is a 60. (Yes, I know this sounds confusing. You're accustomed to thinking of 100 as a top score. But with the Postal Service you need to learn how to think unnaturally.) Since nobody knows the top-secret formula for calculating the final exam score, the only way you can measure your performance on this section is to compare your score to the best possible score of 60.

Example: Looking back to the above sample, we figured my score to be a 38. When comparing my score to the best possible score of 60, it's obvious that my score is only about half as good as it could have been. More specifically, there's a maximum of 60 points available on this section, and I was only able to capture 63% of them.

Interpretation: So, does 38 sound like a good score? Absolutely not. It sounds terrible. If I want to excel on this section, I obviously need a lot of practice to master the skills and speed demanded. If your performance on this sample test indicates that you need some help, my 473E study guide (page 348) can provide the strategies and realistic practice tests required. (Bear in mind that, since we don't have the final scoring formula, we are basically making an educated guess when interpreting your performance on this section.)

Turn the page and begin when you are prepared to time yourself for exactly 11 minutes.

A) No Errors   **B) Address Only**   **C) ZIP Code Only**   **D) Both**

	Correct List		List to be Checked		
	Address	**ZIP Code**	**Address**	**ZIP Code**	
1)	1404 Wilson Ave Bowie, TX	77362	1404 Wilson Ave Bowie, TX	77632	○A) ○B) ○C) ○D)
2)	2309 S. Bridge Greenville, MS	36127-4410	2309 S. Bridge Greenville, MN	36127-4410	○A) ○B) ○C) ○D)
3)	1313 S Main Union City, MI	52149-5548	1313 S Main Union City, WI	52419-5548	○A) ○B) ○C) ○D)
4)	4801 NW Cooper James Island, S.C.	27103-9412	4801 NW Cooper James Island, S.D.	27103-9412	○A) ○B) ○C) ○D)
5)	2254A ASHLEIGH JACKSON, TN	70069-5123	2254A ASHLEIGH JACKSON, TN	70069-5123	○A) ○B) ○C) ○D)
6)	P.O. Box 823 Rapid City, SD	48959	P.O. Box 832 Rapid City, SD	48059	○A) ○B) ○C) ○D)
7)	970 E Liberty Ave. San Francisco, C.A.	61259-7812	970 E Liberty Ave. San Francisco, C.A.	61259-7812	○A) ○B) ○C) ○D)
8)	7600 Greenville Hwy Colorado Springs, CO	84010-6492	7600 Greenville Hwy Colorado Springs, CO	84100-6492	○A) ○B) ○C) ○D)
9)	853 Broad Blvd Apt. 2C Tulsa, OK	21793-5412	853 Broad Blvd Apt. 2C Tulsa, OK	21793-4512	○A) ○B) ○C) ○D)
10)	2019 E 81st St Hanover, P.A.	70012-3164	2019 E 81st St Handover, P.A.	70112-3164	○A) ○B) ○C) ○D)

continued on next page

continued

A) No Errors **B) Address Only** **C) ZIP Code Only** **D) Both**

	Correct List		List to be Checked		
	Address	**ZIP Code**	**Address**	**ZIP Code**	
11)	50739 Valley Plaza Warwick, R.I.	23975-5791	50739 Valley Plaza Warwick, R.I.	23975-5791	○A) ○B) ○C) ○D)
12)	1189 Thomas Dr. Bismarck, ND	79781-1462	1189 Thomas Dr. Bismarck, NY	79781-1462	○A) ○B) ○C) ○D)
13)	990 Rebecca Ln. Wilton, NY	84561-3971	990 Rebecca Ln. Wilton, NY	84561-3971	○A) ○B) ○C) ○D)
14)	26 Hampton House #4 Toms River, N.J.	79462	26 Hampton House #4 Toms River, N.J.	79462	○A) ○B) ○C) ○D)
15)	1000 Roberts Rd. Las Cruces, NM	69731-4987	100 Roberts Rd. Las Cruces, NM	69731-4987	○A) ○B) ○C) ○D)
16)	2525 King Ave. Helena, MO	52169-7621	2525 King Ave. Helen, MO	52769-7621	○A) ○B) ○C) ○D)
17)	701 Snekter Ave NE Cecil, PA	91203-7522	701 Sneaker Ave NE Cecil, PA	91203-7522	○A) ○B) ○C) ○D)
18)	179 Edgewood Dr. Lake City, SC	37941	179 Edgewood Dr. Lake City, SC	37941	○A) ○B) ○C) ○D)
19)	2035 Whiskey Rd. S Alcoa, T.N.	79134-6548	3025 Whiskey Rd. S Alcoa, T.N.	79134-6548	○A) ○B) ○C) ○D)
20)	1243 Jonathan Ln Vinita, OK	63178-1002	1243 Jonathan Ln Vinita, OK	63178-1002	○A) ○B) ○C) ○D)

continued on next page

continued

A) No Errors   B) Address Only   C) ZIP Code Only   D) Both

	Correct List		List to be Checked		
	Address	ZIP Code	Address	ZIP Code	
21)	37853 Chardon Rd. Waverly, OH	49872-6547	37853 Chardon Rd. Waverly, OK	49072-6547	A) B) C) D)
22)	PO Box 5646379 Gibsonia, P.A.	20897-6379	PO Box 5646379 Gibsonia, P.A.	20891-6379	A) B) C) D)
23)	4141 Jeremy St. Foley, AL	30013-7319	4144 Jeremy St. Foley, AL	30013-7319	A) B) C) D)
24)	1050 RICHARDSON GLENDALE, AZ	50130	1050 RICHARDSON GLENDALE, AZ	50130	A) B) C) D)
25)	1100 S Beltline Hwy. Kodiak, AK	90640-3197	1100 S Beltline Hwy. Kodiak, AK	90640-3199	A) B) C) D)
26)	655 Fieldstone Dr. Red Bluff, C.A.	97800-7391	655 Fieldstone Dr. Red Stone, C.A.	97800-7391	A) B) C) D)
27)	900 S Bowline St. Florida City, FL	60014-7865	900 S Bowline St. Florida City, FL	60014-7865	A) B) C) D)
28)	444 W Vine Ave Dover, DE	20614-6521	4444 W Vine Ave Dover, DE	26614-6521	A) B) C) D)
29)	538 N Church Apt. 34 Petal, MS	36804-6731	538 N Church Apt. 3B Petal, MS	36804-6731	A) B) C) D)
30)	705 Dixon Blvd. Utica, N.Y.	09541-5440	705 Dixon Blvd. Utica, N.Y.	09541-5400	A) B) C) D)

continued on next page

continued

A) No Errors   B) Address Only   C) ZIP Code Only   D) Both

	Correct List		List to be Checked		
	Address	**ZIP Code**	**Address**	**ZIP Code**	
31)	1538 E Floyd Baker Pierre, SD	72159-9421	1538 E Floyd Baker Pierre, SD	72159-9421	○A) ○B) ○C) ○D)
32)	3950 Grandview St. Big Spring, TX	32157	3950 Grandview St. Big Spring, TN	32157	○A) ○B) ○C) ○D)
33)	913 Seaboard St. Lenoir City, T.N.	40201-6547	913 Seaboard AV. Lenoir City, T.N.	40200-6547	○A) ○B) ○C) ○D)
34)	2377 Dave Lyle Blvd. Rutland, VT	21036-4897	2377 Dave Lilly Blvd. Rutland, VT	21036-4897	○A) ○B) ○C) ○D)
35)	3201 E Waco Apt. 3C Sandy, Utah	40691-3321	3201 E Waco Apt. 3B Sandy, Utah	40691-3321	○A) ○B) ○C) ○D)
36)	PO BOX 17002 GILLETTE, WY	80128-7002	PO BOX 17002 GILLETTE, WY	80128-7002	○A) ○B) ○C) ○D)
37)	234 Springs Way N Logan, WV	70021	234 Springs Hwy N Logan, WV	70012	○A) ○B) ○C) ○D)
38)	100 McGinnis Ave. Natchez. MS	39125-7458	100 McGinnis Ave. Natchez. MS	39125-7458	○A) ○B) ○C) ○D)
39)	235 Frontage Rd. Lees Summit, MO	41791-5469	235 Frontage Rd. Lees Summit, MO	41791-5469	○A) ○B) ○C) ○D)
40)	935 THARP RD VISTA, C.A.	90107-6197	935 THARP RD VISTA, C.A.	90107-6107	○A) ○B) ○C) ○D)

continued on next page

continued

A) No Errors	B) Address Only	C) ZIP Code Only	D) Both

	Correct List		List to be Checked		
	Address	ZIP Code	Address	ZIP Code	
41)	21945 9th Ave. Russellville, AL	29130-7391	21495 9th Ave. Russellville, AL	29130-7391	○A) ○B) ○C) ○D)
42)	333 Boyd Blvd. Kokomo, IN	49731-9874	333 Boyd Blvd. Kokomo, IN	49731-9784	○A) ○B) ○C) ○D)
43)	3240 Southwester Ave. Mt. Pleasant, IA	59871	3240 Southwester Ave. Mt. Pleasanton, IA	59871	○A) ○B) ○C) ○D)
44)	4040 Newton St. Wellington, K.S.	65419-3278	4040 Newton St. Wellington, K.S.	65419-2278	○A) ○B) ○C) ○D)
45)	735 GOSPEL DR. ABBEVILLE, LA	30069	735 GOSPEL DR. ABBEVILLE, LA	30060	○A) ○B) ○C) ○D)
46)	1310 N Eisenhower Dr. Appleton, WI	73215-6127	1310 N Eisenhower Dr. Appletown, WI	73215-6127	○A) ○B) ○C) ○D)
47)	4 Charles Town Plaza Laurel, MS	34897-5412	4 Charles Town Plaza Laurel, MS	34897-5412	○A) ○B) ○C) ○D)
48)	19034 Shows St. Spearfish, SD	90453	19034 Shows St. Spearfish, ND	90543	○A) ○B) ○C) ○D)
49)	2401 Augusta Rd. Rock Hill, TN	64500-6471	2401 Augusta Rd. Rock Hill, TN	64509-6471	○A) ○B) ○C) ○D)
50)	2795 North Rd Princeton, NJ	13197-3042	2975 North Rd Princeton, NJ	13197-3042	○A) ○B) ○C) ○D)

continued on next page

continued

A) No Errors   B) Address Only   C) ZIP Code Only   D) Both

	Correct List		List to be Checked		
	Address	ZIP Code	Address	ZIP Code	
51)	1236 Route 6 Carlsbad, N. M.	59430-2001	1236 Route 6 Carlsbad, N. M.	59430-2001	○A) ○B) ○C) ○D)
52)	400 Eubank Blvd. Dexter, MI	49601	400 Eubank Blvd. Nester, MI	49601	○A) ○B) ○C) ○D)
53)	89234 THELMA LN ALMA, NEBRASKA	77912-6014	89234 THELMA LN ALMA, NEBRASKA	77912-6014	○A) ○B) ○C) ○D)
54)	2401 Foothill Blvd. Sheridan W.Y.	89761-3312	2407 Foothill Blvd. Sheridan W.Y.	89761-3112	○A) ○B) ○C) ○D)
55)	2863 Heritage Dr. Dodgeville, W.I.	10365-9812	2868 Heritage Dr. Dodgeville, W.I.	10365-9815	○A) ○B) ○C) ○D)
56)	1255 E. Chestnut Arcola, IL	88245	1255 E. Chestnut Arcola, IL	88215	○A) ○B) ○C) ○D)
57)	8976 Tompkins Blvd. Crossett, AR	60081-4937	8976 Tompkins Blvd. Crossett, AR	60081-4937	○A) ○B) ○C) ○D)
58)	75 Centennial Pky N Humacao, PR	51198-2004	75 Centennial Pky N Sombrero, PR	51198-2004	○A) ○B) ○C) ○D)
59)	800 Niagara St. Williston, V.T.	40647-3789	800 Niagara St. Williestown, V.T.	40647-3789	○A) ○B) ○C) ○D)
60)	1084 Success Road Pinehurst, TX	77362	1084 Success Road Pinehurst, TX	77362	○A) ○B) ○C) ○D)

End of Address Checking

DIRECTIONS

The Forms Completion section tests your ability to identify information needed to complete various Postal Service forms. This part of the exam consists of 30 questions to be completed in 15 minutes. You will be shown 5 different forms and be asked to answer 6 questions about each form. In every case, the form will be displayed on the left-hand page facing you, and the questions about that form will be on the right-hand page facing you. As you progress through the test, the same format (forms to the left and questions to the right) will continue.

Even though this is a paper sample test, the Forms Completion section is formatted as much like the real exam as possible. It is laid out very similarly to the Forms Completion section on the actual electronic exam. For instance, there are 6 questions per page (screen) just like on the real test. In addition, the radio buttons and answer choices appear below each question just like on the real test. But since this is a paper test, you must choose answers by darkening the radio buttons with a pencil rather than clicking them with a mouse.

SCORING

Formula: To score the Forms Completion section, first use the answer key at the end of the test to identify your correct and incorrect answers. Then count your correct answers, and that is your score. The score for this section is simply your number of correct answers. Wrong answers do not figure into the formula for this section.

Example: Let's say that, out of the 30 questions, I answered 25 in the time allowed. And, of the 25 that I answered, 21 were correct, and 4 were wrong. My score is simply a 21 ... the number of correct answers.

HOW TO INTERPRET YOUR SCORE

Process: If I answered all the questions correctly within the time allowed, the best possible score on this section is a 30. (Again, I know that this sounds confusing and that you're accustomed to thinking of 100 as a top score. But again, with the Postal Service you need to learn how to think unnaturally.) Since nobody knows the top-secret formula for calculating the final exam score, the only way you can measure your performance on this section is to compare your score to the best possible score of 30.

Example: Looking back to the above sample, we figured my score to be a 21. When comparing my score to the best possible score of 30, it's obvious that my score is not nearly as good as it could have been. More specifically, there's a maximum of 30 points available on this section, and I was only able to capture 70% of them.

Interpretation: So, does 21 sound like a good score? No. It sounds like I need to do much better. If I want to excel on this section, I need to practice to master the skills and speed demanded. Where can you find the test-taking strategies and realistic practice tests needed to master these skills and speed? My 473E study guide (page 348) can provide the help needed to manage this section on bureaucratic forms. (Bear in mind that, since we don't have the final scoring formula, we are basically making an educated guess when interpreting your performance on this section.)

Turn the page and begin when you are prepared to time yourself for exactly 15 minutes.

Authorization to Hold Mail

Postmaster - Please hold mail for:

1. Name(s)

2. Address

3a. Begin Holding Mail (Date)	**3b.** Resume Delivery (Date)

4. ☐ **Option A**
I will pick up all accumulated mail when I return and understand that mail delivery will not resume until I do. (This is suggested if your return date may change or if no one will be at home to receive mail.)

5. ☐ **Option B**
Please deliver all accumulated mail and resume normal delivery on the ending date shown above.

6. Customer Signature

For Post Office Use Only

7. Date Received

8a. Clerk	**8b.** Bin Number
9a. Carrier	**9b.** Route Number

Customer Option A Only

Carrier: Accumulated mail has been picked up.

10a. Resume delivery on (date) _____

10b. By: _____

continued on next page

continued

1) The customer's name is Helen Crump, the clerk's name is Alicia Peterson, and the carrier's name is Carlos Rodriguez. Where would Alicia Peterson's name be entered on this form?
- A) Box 1
- B) Box 8a
- C) Box 9a
- D) None of the above

2) The customer's name is Helen Crump, the clerk's name is Alicia Peterson, and the carrier's name is Carlos Rodriguez. Where would Helen Crump's name be entered on this form?
- A) Box 1
- B) Box 8a
- C) Box 9a
- D) None of the above

3) The customer's name is Helen Crump, the clerk's name is Alicia Peterson, and the carrier's name is Carlos Rodriguez. Where would Carlos Rodriguez's name be entered on this form?
- A) Box 1
- B) Box 8a
- C) Box 9a
- D) None of the above

4) How would you indicate that you want your accumulated mail delivered on 3/13/09 and that you want your normal delivery to resume on that date?
- A) Enter 3/13/09 in Box 3b.
- B) Check "Option B" in Box 5.
- C) Enter 3/13/09 on Line 10a.
- D) Enter 3/13/09 in Box 3b and check "Option B" in Box 5.

5) If Option A in Box 4 is checked, which of these is correct?
- A) The accumulated mail should be delivered on the date specified.
- B) The accumulated mail should be delivered and delivery should resume on the date specified.
- C) Mail should no longer be held as of the date specified.
- D) None of the above is correct.

6) A date would be an acceptable entry for each of these EXCEPT
- A) Box 3b
- B) Box 6
- C) Box 7
- D) Line 10a

continued on next page

continued

EXPRESS MAIL   Mailing Label

ORIGIN (POSTAL USE ONLY)			DELIVERY (POSTAL USE ONLY)		
PO ZIP Code **1a.**	Day of Delivery **1b.** ☐ Next ☐ Second	Flat Rate Envelope **1c.** ☐	Delivery Attempt **1d.** Mo. Day	Time **1e.** ☐ AM ☐ PM	Employee Signature **1f.**
Date In **2a.**	**2b.** ☐ Noon ☐ 3 PM	Postage **2c.** $	Delivery Attempt **2d.** Mo. Day	Time **2e.** ☐ AM ☐ PM	Employee Signature **2f.**
Time In **3a.** ☐ AM ☐ PM	Military **3b.** 2nd Day 3rd Day	Return Receipt Fee **3c.**	Delivery Attempt **3d.** Mo. Day	Time **3e.** ☐ AM ☐ PM	Employee Signature **3f.**
Weight **4a.** lbs. ozs.	Int'l Alpha Country Code **4b.**	COD Fee **4c.**	Insurance Fee **4d.**		

No Delivery **5a.** ☐ Wknd ☐ Holiday	Acceptance Clerk Initials **5b.**	Total Postage & Fees **5c.** $	**6.** ☐ WAIVER OF SIGNATURE NO DELVERY ☐ Weekend ☐ Holiday

CUSTOMER USE ONLY

Customer Signature _____

Method of Payment **7a.** Express Mail corporate Acct. No.	Federal Agency Acct. No. or **7b.** Postal Service Acct. No.
8a. FROM: (PLEASE PRINT) PHONE: _____	**8b.** TO: (PLEASE PRINT) PHONE: _____ ZIP + 4: _____

continued on next page

continued

7) An Express Mail package is scheduled for delivery by noon the next day. How should this be noted?
- ○ A) Write "Next" in Box 1d.
- ○ B) Write "Next" in Box 2a.
- ○ C) Check "Next" in Box 1b and "Noon" in Box 2b.
- ○ D) Check box 5a

8) An Express Mail package was dropped off at the Post Office on 9/19/09 at 4:00 in the afternoon. How should the drop off time and date be noted?
- ○ A) Write "9/19/09" in Box 2a, write "4:00" in Box 3a, and check "PM" in Box 3a.
- ○ B) Write "9/19/09" in Box 2a and check "AM" in Box 3a.
- ○ C) Write "9/19/09" in Box 1d and check "PM" in Box 1e.
- ○ D) None of the above

9) Which of these could be an acceptable entry for Box 4d?
- ○ A) 10/20/09
- ○ B) 89705
- ○ C) A check mark
- ○ D) $17.65

10) Which of these could be an acceptable entry for Box 1c?
- ○ A) 10/20/09
- ○ B) 89705
- ○ C) A check mark
- ○ D) $17.65

11) Where would you enter the sender's address?
- ○ A) Box 8a
- ○ B) Box 8b
- ○ C) Box 6
- ○ D) The sender's address is not entered on this form.

12) Where does the clerk who accepts the package identify him/herself?
- ○ A) Box 1a
- ○ B) Box 1f
- ○ C) Box 4b
- ○ D) Box 5b

continued on next page

continued

RETURN RECEIPT FOR MERCHANDISE			
Postage	1.	5.	Postmark Here
Return Receipt for Merchandise Fee	2.		
Special Handling Fee	3.		
Total Postage & Fees	4.		
6.	Waiver of Signature ☐ YES ☐ NO		
7.	Recipient's Name *(Please print clearly)*		
8.	Street, Apt. No.; or P.O. Box		
9.	City, State, ZIP + 4		

continued on next page

continued

13) Janet Cone does not want a waiver of signature. How should she indicate this?
- ○ A) Check "YES" in Box 6
- ○ B) Check "NO" in Box 6
- ○ C) Make a note on the back of the form
- ○ D) None of the above

14) Which of these would be an acceptable entry for Box 8?
- ○ A) $13.57
- ○ B) 07/18/09
- ○ C) Ellen Montgomery
- ○ D) P.O. Box 34778

15) Which of these would be an acceptable entry for Box 7?
- ○ A) $13.57
- ○ B) 07/18/09
- ○ C) Ellen Montgomery
- ○ D) P.O. Box 34778

16) Which of these would be an acceptable entry for Box 1?
- ○ A) 19 47th St., Gulfport, AK
- ○ B) 5:00 p.m.
- ○ C) $29.50
- ○ D) 70042-7899

17) Which of these would be an acceptable entry for Box 6?
- ○ A) Janet Cone
- ○ B) A check mark
- ○ C) 12 lbs. 4 ozs.
- ○ D) $29.78

18) Which of these would be an acceptable entry for Box 9?
- ○ A) $35.67
- ○ B) A check mark
- ○ C) P.O. Box 1699
- ○ D) Atlanta, GA 89320-6754

continued on next page

continued

Certificate of Bulk Mailing

Fee for Certificate	Use Current Rate Chart	**1.** Meter stamp or postage (uncancelled) stamps in payment of fee to be affixed here and cancelled by postmarking, including date.
Up to 1,000 pieces		
For each additional 1,000 pieces, or fraction		
Duplicate Copy		

2a. Number of identical pieces	**2b.** Class of mail	**2c.** Postage on each	**2d.** Number of pieces per lb.	**2e.** Total number of pounds	**2f.** Total postage paid	**2g.** Fee paid

3a. Mailed for	**3b.** Mailed by

Postmaster's Certificate

It is hereby certified that the above-described mailing has been received and number of pieces and postage verified.

4. _____
　　　　　　　(Postmaster or Designee)

continued on next page

continued

19) Where does the Postmaster sign this form?
- A) Box 1
- B) Box 3a
- C) Box 3b
- D) Line 4

20) Which of these would be an acceptable entry for Box 2d?
- A) A check mark
- B) 90843-6700
- C) 620 Fawn Run Road
- D) 35

21) How would you indicate that there are 5,000 identical pieces?
- A) Enter 5,000 in Line 2a
- B) Enter 5,000 in Line 2b
- C) Enter 5,000 in Line 2e
- D) Enter 5,000 in Line 2g

22) This mailing is to be sent by first class mail. Where would this be indicated?
- A) Box 1
- B) Box 2a
- C) Box 2b
- D) Box 2c

23) Where should total postage paid be entered?
- A) Box 2a
- B) Box 2c
- C) Box 2f
- D) Box 2g

24) Which of these would be an acceptable entry for Box 2c?
- A) 55378-1123
- B) $0.22
- C) Sarah Rich
- D) 11/24/09

continued on next page

continued

Application to Mail at Nonprofit Standard Mail Rates

Part 1 *(For completion by applicant)*

No application fee is required. All information must be complete and typewritten or printed legibly.

1. Complete name of organization *(If voting registration official, include title.)*

2. Street address of organization *(Include apartment or suite number.)*

3. City, state, ZIP+4 code

4a. Telephone *(Include area code.)*

4b. Name of applicant *(Must represent applying organization.)*

5. Type of organization *(Check only one.)*

  ☐ Religious   ☐ Scientific   ☐ Agricultural   ☐ Veterans'   ☐ Qualified political committee

  ☐ Educational   ☐ Philanthropic   ☐ Labor   ☐ Fraternal   ☐ Voting registration official

6. Is this a for-profit organization or does any of the net income inure to the benefit of any private stockholder or individual?   ☐ Yes   ☐ No

7a. Is this organization exempt from federal income tax? *(If 'Yes', attach a copy of the exemption issued by the Internal Revenue Service that shows the section of the IRS code under which the organization is exempt.)*   ☐ Yes   ☐ No

7b. Is an application for exempt status pending with the IRS? *(If 'Yes', attach a copy of the application to this form.)*   ☐ Yes   ☐ No

8. Has this organization previously mailed at the Nonprofit Standard Mail rates? *(If yes, list the Post Offices where mailings were most recently deposited at these rates?*   ☐ Yes   ☐ No

7c. Has the IRS denied or revoked the organization's federal tax exempt status? *(If 'Yes', attach a copy of the IRS ruling to this form.)*   ☐ Yes   ☐ No

9. Has your organization had Nonprofit Standard Mail rate mailing privileges denied or revoked? *(If 'Yes', list the Post Office [city and state] where the application was denied or authorization revoked.)*   ☐ Yes   ☐ No

10. Post Office (not a station or branch) where authorization requested and bulk mailings will be made *(City, state, ZIP code)*

11. Signature of applicant

12. Title

13. Date

Part 2 *(For completion by Postmaster at originating office where application filed)*

14. Signature of Postmaster *(Or designated representative)*

15. Date application filed with Post Office *(Round stamp)*

continued on next page

continued

25) How should the type of organization applying be identified if it is devoted to the purpose of religious education?

    A) Check both the "Religious" and the "Educational" choices in Box 5.

    B) Check the "Educational" choice in Box 5 and also write a note about the religious aspect in Box 5.

    C) Check the "Religious" choice in Box 5 and write a note about the educational aspect also in Box 5.

    D) Check either the "Religious" or the "Educational" choice in Box 5, whichever seems more appropriate, but do not check both.

26) Which of these could be an appropriate entry for Box 1?

    A) William Haywood

    B) Calvary Methodist Church

    C) Carl Lee, Voting Registrar, Harris County, TX

    D) Both items B and C above

27) Where on this form is the amount of the application fee noted?

    A) Box 13

    B) Box 8

    C) There is no application fee.

    D) The amount of the fee is dependent upon the location of the Post Office and should therefore be written in Box 10 by the Postmaster.

28) Into which boxes should a city, state, and ZIP code be written?

    A) Boxes 3 and 10

    B) Boxes 2, 3, and 10

    C) Boxes 2, 3, 10 and 13

    D) None of the above

29) A telephone number could be entered into which box or boxes?

    A) Box 1

    B) Box 10

    C) Box 12

    D) None of the above

30) Where does the applicant sign this form?

    A) Box 1

    B) Box 11

    C) Box 13

    D) The applicant does not sign this form.

End of Forms Completion

DIRECTIONS

This part of the exam consists of two sections as detailed below that test your ability to use codes quickly and accurately both from a Coding Guide and from memory. The Coding Guide is a chart that contains four delivery routes (identified by the codes A, B, C, and D) and various address ranges on several streets that are served by those delivery routes. Each question is an address. To answer each question, you must identify the delivery route that serves the address, and mark as your answer the code (A, B, C, or D) for that delivery route.

The Coding Section has 36 questions to be answered in 6 minutes. During the Coding section, you will look at a Coding Guide to find answers. The Coding Section is broken down into 3 segments.

The Memory Section has 36 questions to be answered in 7 minutes. During the Memory Section, you are expected to memorize the Coding Guide and answer questions from memory. You cannot look at the Coding Guide to find answers. The Memory Section is broken down into 4 segments.

I realize that this sounds quite confusing, but that's because this part of the test *is* quite confusing. To minimize the confusion, I will give you instructions separately for each individual segment as we progress through the various Coding & Memory steps.

Even though this is a paper sample test, it is formatted as much like the real electronic exam as possible. For instance, the Coding Guide is to the left, and the questions are to the right in every case. And, there are the same numbers of questions per page (screen) as on the real test. In addition, the radio buttons and answer choices appear to the right of each question just like on the real test. But since this is a paper test, you must choose answers by darkening the radio buttons with a pencil rather than clicking them with a mouse.

Do not write or make marks of any kind except for marking your answers!

This applies to the entire test but is especially important during the Coding section, the Memory section, and all of the various Coding & Memory segments. Notes can make the memorization more manageable. And referring back to notes, if possible, could definitely make answering the Memory questions much easier. The key to this sample test, however, is to take it realistically. And the real exam is an electronic test presented via computer. During this electronic test, you have access to absolutely no pencils, pens, or paper whatsoever. So, writing or making notes of any kind is simply impossible when taking the actual exam. Therefore, in order to make this a realistic experience, *do not write or make marks of any kind except for marking your answers*.

Turn the page when you are ready to begin the first section, the Coding Section.

DIRECTIONS

The Coding Section consists of 3 segments as detailed below.

Coding Section - Segment 1: The first segment is a 2 minute introductory exercise designed to give you a preview of what you are expected to do on the actual test. This segment is not scored.

Coding Section - Segment 2: The second segment is a 90 second (1½ minutes) practice exercise designed to help prepare you for the actual test. This segment is not scored.

Coding Section - Segment 3: The third segment is the actual Coding Section test. You have 6 minutes to answer 36 questions. This segment is scored.

Do not write or make marks of any kind except for marking your answers!

This applies to the entire test but is especially important during the Coding section, the Memory section, and all of the various Coding & Memory segments. Notes can make the memorization more manageable. And referring back to notes, if possible, could definitely make answering the Memory questions much easier. The key to this sample test, however, is to take it realistically. And the real exam is an electronic test presented via computer. During this electronic test, you have access to absolutely no pencils, pens, or paper whatsoever. So, writing or making notes of any kind is simply impossible when taking the actual exam. Therefore, in order to make this a realistic experience, *do not write or make marks of any kind except for marking your answers*.

Turn the page when you are ready to begin Coding Segment 1.

DIRECTIONS

Segment 1 of the Coding Section is an introductory exercise to acquaint you with how the questions are to be answered. In this segment, you have 2 minutes to answer 4 questions.

Each question is an address. Looking at the Coding Guide, you are to find the address range that the address in the question belongs in and then mark as your answer the code (A, B, C, or D) for that that range. Included is an explanation for each question to assure that you fully understand the tasks you are to perform in this part of the test.

Do not write or make marks of any kind except for marking your answers!

This applies to the entire test but is especially important during the Coding section, the Memory section, and all of the various Coding & Memory segments. Notes can make the memorization more manageable. And referring back to notes, if possible, could definitely make answering the Memory questions much easier. The key to this sample test, however, is to take it realistically. And the real exam is an electronic test presented via computer. During this electronic test, you have access to absolutely no pencils, pens, or paper whatsoever. So, writing or making notes of any kind is simply impossible when taking the actual exam. Therefore, in order to make this a realistic experience, *do not write or make marks of any kind except for marking your answers.*

Turn the page and begin when you are prepared to time yourself for exactly 2 minutes.

CODING GUIDE

Address Range	Delivery Route
801 – 1240 Monmouth Dr. 1 – 149 Ellington LN	A
3300 – 3699 Ince Blvd. 1241 – 1300 Monmouth Dr. 150 – 299 Ellington LN	B
22 – 82 Tolling Wood Terrace 14500 – 16500 Sam Houston Toll RD 3700 – 3999 Ince Blvd.	C
All mail that doesn't fall in one of the address ranges listed above	D

QUESTIONS

	Address	Delivery Route			
1)	14545 Sam Houston Toll RD	○ A)	○ B)	○ C)	○ D)
2)	302 Ellington LN	○ A)	○ B)	○ C)	○ D)
3)	3421 Ince Blvd.	○ A)	○ B)	○ C)	○ D)
4)	1601 Hwy 90 East	○ A)	○ B)	○ C)	○ D)

ANSWERS & EXPLANATIONS

1) 14545 Sam Houston Toll RD

Looking at the Coding Guide on the left, we see that Sam Houston Toll RD appears in only one box / delivery route, which is Delivery Route C. More specifically, we see that for Sam Houston Toll RD, only the number addresses 14500 through 16500 are included under Delivery Route C. So, does the address 14545 Sam Houston Toll RD fall between 14500 and 16500? Yes, it does. This means that the address 14545 Sam Houston Toll RD belongs in Delivery Route C, so we mark the answer choice C for this question.

2) 302 Ellington LN

Ellington LN appears twice in the Coding Guide. For Ellington LN, the addresses 1 - 149 belong in Delivery Route A, and the addresses 150 - 299 belong in Route B. Does the address 302 Ellington LN fall within either of these ranges? No, the number 302 is too large to fit in either range. So, this address belongs under Delivery Route D for "All mail that doesn't fall in one of the address ranges listed above". Therefore, we mark answer choice D for this question.

3) 3421 Ince Blvd.

Ince Blvd. also appears twice in the Coding Guide. For Ince Blvd., the addresses 3300 - 3699 belong in Delivery Route B, and the addresses 3700 - 3999 belong in Delivery Route C. Does the address 3421 Ince Blvd. fit into either of these ranges? Yes, it falls between the addresses 3300 and 3699 in Delivery Route B. So, we mark answer choice B for this question.

4) 1601 Hwy 90 East

Does Hwy 90 East appear anywhere in the Coding Guide? No. The address of 1601 in this question doesn't matter at all. Regardless of what the address number is, Hwy 90 East simply does not appear anywhere in our Coding Guide. This address therefore necessarily belongs under Delivery Route D for "All mail that doesn't fall in one of the address ranges listed above". We accordingly mark answer choice D for this question.

End of Coding Segment 1

DIRECTIONS

Segment 2 is a practice exercise designed to expose you to the realistic timing demanded. In this segment, you have 90 seconds to answer 8 questions. You answer questions exactly the same way that we did in the previous segment, and again the Coding Guide is displayed for your use in finding the answers.

This segment is not scored. It does not count toward you final score when you take the real exam. Accordingly, we will not score it on this sample test or use it as a measure of your performance.

Do not write or make marks of any kind except for marking your answers!

This applies to the entire test but is especially important during the Coding section, the Memory section, and all of the various Coding & Memory segments. Notes can make the memorization more manageable. And referring back to notes, if possible, could definitely make answering the Memory questions much easier. The key to this sample test, however, is to take it realistically. And the real exam is an electronic test presented via computer. During this electronic test, you have access to absolutely no pencils, pens, or paper whatsoever. So, writing or making notes of any kind is simply impossible when taking the actual exam. Therefore, in order to make this a realistic experience, *do not write or make marks of any kind except for marking your answers*.

Turn the page and begin when you are prepared to time yourself for exactly 90 seconds.

CODING GUIDE

Address Range	Delivery Route
801 – 1240 Monmouth Dr. 1 – 149 Ellington LN	A
3300 – 3699 Ince Blvd. 1241 – 1300 Monmouth Dr. 150 – 299 Ellington LN	B
22 – 82 Tolling Wood Terrace 14500 – 16500 Sam Houston Toll RD 3700 – 3999 Ince Blvd.	C
All mail that doesn't fall in one of the address ranges listed above	D

QUESTIONS

	Address	Delivery Route			
1)	3762 Ince Blvd.	○ A)	○ B)	○ C)	○ D)
2)	1258 Monmouth Dr.	○ A)	○ B)	○ C)	○ D)
3)	29 Tolling Wood Terrace	○ A)	○ B)	○ C)	○ D)
4)	967 Monmouth Dr.	○ A)	○ B)	○ C)	○ D)
5)	153 Wellington LN	○ A)	○ B)	○ C)	○ D)
6)	3456 Ince Blvd.	○ A)	○ B)	○ C)	○ D)
7)	20 Tolling Wood Terrace	○ A)	○ B)	○ C)	○ D)
8)	178 Ellington LN	○ A)	○ B)	○ C)	○ D)

The correct answers are 1-C, 2-B, 3-C, 4-A, 5-D, 6-B, 7-D, and 8-B.

End of Coding Segment 2

DIRECTIONS

Segment 3 is the actual Coding test. You have 6 minutes to answer 36 questions in the very same way we did on Segments 1 and 2. The Coding Guide is displayed for your use in answering the questions. This segment is scored, and the score from this section does affect your final score on the actual exam. So, we will likewise score Segment 3 on this sample test and use the score to measure your performance.

SCORING

Formula: To score your Coding test, first use the answer key at the end of this sample exam to identify your correct and incorrect answers. Then count your correct answers and your incorrect answers. Subtract 1/3 of the number of incorrect answers from the number of correct answers. The result is your score. (Yes, this is the same goofy formula we used for the Address Checking section. They use the same formula for the Coding test, and as you will see shortly, they use the same formula for the Memory test as well.)

Example: Let's say that I answered all 36 questions in the time allowed. And of the 36 I answered, 33 were correct, and 3 were wrong. To score myself, I subtract 1 (1/3 of the 3 of wrong answers) from 33 (the number of correct answers). My score is a 32.

HOW TO INTERPRET YOUR SCORE

Process: If I answered all the questions correctly within the time allowed, the best possible score on this section is a 36. (Yes, I know this sounds confusing. You're accustomed to thinking of 100 as a top score. But with the Postal Service you need to learn how to think unnaturally.) Since nobody knows the top-secret formula for calculating the final exam score, the only way you can measure your performance on this section is to compare your score to the best possible score of 36.

Example: Looking back to the above sample, my score was a 32. The maximum number of points available is 36, and the best possible score is 36. How does my score compare? I captured 88% of the maximum number of points available.

Interpretation: So, does 32 sound like a good score? Well, it's not bad. You might even say it's pretty good. But if I really want to get a Postal job, my goal is to achieve the highest possible score. So, even with a pretty good score, I better get with the program and do some practicing to improve my score as much as possible. And my 473E study guide (page 348) contains the realistic sample tests needed for this practice work. (Bear in mind that, since we don't have the final scoring formula, we are basically making an educated guess when interpreting your performance on this section.)

Note: In addition to the above interpretation comments, we need to remember that this is basically an open book test. Frankly, there's no good reason why I should answer any questions incorrectly on an open book test. The correct answers are right in front of me. So, if I answered any questions incorrectly, another reason for practicing should be to assure (1) that I know where and how to find the correct answers and (2) that I do indeed find and choose the correct answers.

Turn the page and begin when you are prepared to time yourself for exactly 6 minutes.

CODING GUIDE

Address Range	Delivery Route
801 – 1240 Monmouth Dr. 1 – 149 Ellington LN	A
3300 – 3699 Ince Blvd. 1241 – 1300 Monmouth Dr. 150 – 299 Ellington LN	B
22 – 82 Tolling Wood Terrace 14500 – 16500 Sam Houston Toll RD 3700 – 3999 Ince Blvd.	C
All mail that doesn't fall in one of the address ranges listed above	D

	Address	Delivery Route			
1)	701 Monmouth Dr.	○ A)	○ B)	○ C)	○ D)
2)	3607 Ince Blvd.	○ A)	○ B)	○ C)	○ D)
3)	199 Ellington LN	○ A)	○ B)	○ C)	○ D)
4)	80 Tolling Wood Terrace	○ A)	○ B)	○ C)	○ D)
5)	822 Monmouth Dr.	○ A)	○ B)	○ C)	○ D)
6)	17500 Sam Houston Toll RD	○ A)	○ B)	○ C)	○ D)
7)	3906 Ince Blvd.	○ A)	○ B)	○ C)	○ D)
8)	92 Ellington LN	○ A)	○ B)	○ C)	○ D)
9)	16218 Sam Houston Toll RD	○ A)	○ B)	○ C)	○ D)

continued on next page

CODING GUIDE

Address Range	Delivery Route
801 – 1240 Monmouth Dr. 1 – 149 Ellington LN	A
3300 – 3699 Ince Blvd. 1241 – 1300 Monmouth Dr. 150 – 299 Ellington LN	B
22 – 82 Tolling Wood Terrace 14500 – 16500 Sam Houston Toll RD 3700 – 3999 Ince Blvd.	C
All mail that doesn't fall in one of the address ranges listed above	D

continued on next page

	Address	Delivery Route			
10)	1262 Monmouth Dr.	O A)	O B)	O C)	O D)
11)	25 Tolling Wild Terrace	O A)	O B)	O C)	O D)
12)	111 Ellington LN	O A)	O B)	O C)	O D)
13)	76 Tolling Wood Terrace	O A)	O B)	O C)	O D)
14)	3489 Ince Blvd.	O A)	O B)	O C)	O D)
15)	1294 Monmouth Dr.	O A)	O B)	O C)	O D)
16)	3820 Ince Blvd.	O A)	O B)	O C)	O D)
17)	1100 Monmouth Dr.	O A)	O B)	O C)	O D)
18)	253 Ellington LN	O A)	O B)	O C)	O D)

continued on next page

CODING GUIDE	
Address Range	**Delivery Route**
801 – 1240 Monmouth Dr. 1 – 149 Ellington LN	A
3300 – 3699 Ince Blvd. 1241 – 1300 Monmouth Dr. 150 – 299 Ellington LN	B
22 – 82 Tolling Wood Terrace 14500 – 16500 Sam Houston Toll RD 3700 – 3999 Ince Blvd.	C
All mail that doesn't fall in one of the address ranges listed above	D

continued on next page

continued

	Address	Delivery Route			
19)	934 Monmouth Dr.	○ A)	○ B)	○ C)	○ D)
20)	41 Tolling Wood Terrace	○ A)	○ B)	○ C)	○ D)
21)	290 Ellington LN	○ A)	○ B)	○ C)	○ D)
22)	1650 Sam Houston Toll RD	○ A)	○ B)	○ C)	○ D)
23)	3890 Ince Blvd.	○ A)	○ B)	○ C)	○ D)
24)	1225 Monmouth Dr.	○ A)	○ B)	○ C)	○ D)
25)	227 Ellington LN	○ A)	○ B)	○ C)	○ D)
26)	3584 Ince Blvd.	○ A)	○ B)	○ C)	○ D)
27)	3741 Ince Blvd.	○ A)	○ B)	○ C)	○ D)

continued on next page

CODING GUIDE

Address Range	Delivery Route
801 – 1240 Monmouth Dr. 1 – 149 Ellington LN	A
3300 – 3699 Ince Blvd. 1241 – 1300 Monmouth Dr. 150 – 299 Ellington LN	B
22 – 82 Tolling Wood Terrace 14500 – 16500 Sam Houston Toll RD 3700 – 3999 Ince Blvd.	C
All mail that doesn't fall in one of the address ranges listed above	D

continued on next page

continued

	Address	Delivery Route			
28)	1253 Mammoth Dr.	○ A)	○ B)	○ C)	○ D)
29)	16400 Sam Houston Toll RD	○ A)	○ B)	○ C)	○ D)
30)	27 Ellington LN	○ A)	○ B)	○ C)	○ D)
31)	54 Tolling Wood Terrace	○ A)	○ B)	○ C)	○ D)
32)	119 Ellington LN	○ A)	○ B)	○ C)	○ D)
33)	4220 Ince Blvd.	○ A)	○ B)	○ C)	○ D)
34)	3315 Ince Blvd.	○ A)	○ B)	○ C)	○ D)
35)	1279 Monmouth Dr.	○ A)	○ B)	○ C)	○ D)
36)	15289 Sam Houston Toll RD	○ A)	○ B)	○ C)	○ D)

End of Coding Segment 3

DIRECTIONS

The Memory Section consists of 4 segments as detailed below.

Memory Section - Segment 1: The first segment is a 3 minute study period during which you try to memorize the Coding Guide. There are no questions to answer.

Memory Section - Segment 2: The second segment is a 90 second (1½ minutes) practice exercise containing 8 questions. This segment is not scored.

Memory Section - Segment 3: The third segment is a 5 minute study period during which you try to memorize the Coding Guide. There are no questions to answer.

Memory Section - Segment 4: This fourth segment is the actual Memory Section test. You have 7 minutes to answer 36 questions. This segment is scored.

Do not write or make marks of any kind except for marking your answers!

This applies to the entire test but is especially important during the Coding section, the Memory section, and all of the various Coding & Memory segments. Notes can make the memorization more manageable. And referring back to notes, if possible, could definitely make answering the Memory questions much easier. The key to this sample test, however, is to take it realistically. And the real exam is an electronic test presented via computer. During this electronic test, you have access to absolutely no pencils, pens, or paper whatsoever. So, writing or making notes of any kind is simply impossible when taking the actual exam. Therefore, in order to make this a realistic experience, *do not write or make marks of any kind except for marking your answers.*

Turn the page when you are ready to begin Memory Segment 1.

DIRECTIONS

Memory Segment 1 is a 3 minute study period during which you try to memorize the information in the Coding Guide. There are no answers to mark during this study period.

Turn the page and begin studying when you are prepared to time yourself for exactly 3 minutes.

Do not write or make marks of any kind except for marking your answers!

This applies to the entire test but is especially important during the Coding section, the Memory section, and all of the various Coding & Memory segments. Notes can make the memorization more manageable. And referring back to notes, if possible, could definitely make answering the Memory questions much easier. The key to this sample test, however, is to take it realistically. And the real exam is an electronic test presented via computer. During this electronic test, you have access to absolutely no pencils, pens, or paper whatsoever. So, writing or making notes of any kind is simply impossible when taking the actual exam. Therefore, in order to make this a realistic experience, *do not write or make marks of any kind except for marking your answers.*

Turn the page and begin when you are prepared to time yourself for exactly 3 minutes.

CODING GUIDE	
Address Range	**Delivery Route**
801 – 1240 Monmouth Dr. 1 – 149 Ellington LN	A
3300 – 3699 Ince Blvd. 1241 – 1300 Monmouth Dr. 150 – 299 Ellington LN	B
22 – 82 Tolling Wood Terrace 14500 – 16500 Sam Houston Toll RD 3700 – 3999 Ince Blvd.	C
All mail that doesn't fall in one of the address ranges listed above	D

End of Memory Segment 1

DIRECTIONS

Memory Segment 2 is a practice exercise where you are to answer 8 questions in 90 seconds. You are to answer the questions just as in the Coding Section, but now you must answer from memory. The Coding Guide is not shown for use in finding the answers.

This segment is not scored. It does not count toward you final score when you take the real exam. Accordingly, we will not score it on this sample test or use it as a measure of your performance.

Do not write or make marks of any kind except for marking your answers!

This applies to the entire test but is especially important during the Coding section, the Memory section, and all of the various Coding & Memory segments. Notes can make the memorization more manageable. And referring back to notes, if possible, could definitely make answering the Memory questions much easier. The key to this sample test, however, is to take it realistically. And the real exam is an electronic test presented via computer. During this electronic test, you have access to absolutely no pencils, pens, or paper whatsoever. So, writing or making notes of any kind is simply impossible when taking the actual exam. Therefore, in order to make this a realistic experience, *do not write or make marks of any kind except for marking your answers.*

Turn the page and begin when you are prepared to time yourself for exactly 90 seconds.

QUESTIONS

Address	Delivery Route			
1) 3940 Ince Blvd.	○ A)	○ B)	○ C)	○ D)
2) 136 Ellington LN	○ A)	○ B)	○ C)	○ D)
3) 31 Tolling Wood Terrace	○ A)	○ B)	○ C)	○ D)
4) 1220 Mammoth Dr.	○ A)	○ B)	○ C)	○ D)
5) 184 Ellington LN	○ A)	○ B)	○ C)	○ D)
6) 3352 Ince Blvd.	○ A)	○ B)	○ C)	○ D)
7) 1350 Sam Houston Toll RD	○ A)	○ B)	○ C)	○ D)
8) 1266 Monmouth Dr.	○ A)	○ B)	○ C)	○ D)

The correct answers are 1-C, 2-A, 3-C, 4-D, 5-B, 6-B, 7-D, and 8-B.

End of Memory Segment 2

DIRECTIONS

Memory Segment 3 is a 5 minute study period during which you try to memorize the information in the Coding Guide. There are no answers to mark during this study period.

Turn the page and begin studying when you are prepared to time yourself for exactly 5 minutes.

Do not write or make marks of any kind except for marking your answers!

This applies to the entire test but is especially important during the Coding section, the Memory section, and all of the various Coding & Memory segments. Notes can make the memorization more manageable. And referring back to notes, if possible, could definitely make answering the Memory questions much easier. The key to this sample test, however, is to take it realistically. And the real exam is an electronic test presented via computer. During this electronic test, you have access to absolutely no pencils, pens, or paper whatsoever. So, writing or making notes of any kind is simply impossible when taking the actual exam. Therefore, in order to make this a realistic experience, *do not write or make marks of any kind except for marking your answers*.

Turn the page and begin when you are prepared to time yourself for exactly 5 minutes.

CODING GUIDE	
Address Range	**Delivery Route**
801 – 1240 Monmouth Dr. 1 – 149 Ellington LN	A
3300 – 3699 Ince Blvd. 1241 – 1300 Monmouth Dr. 150 – 299 Ellington LN	B
22 – 82 Tolling Wood Terrace 14500 – 16500 Sam Houston Toll RD 3700 – 3999 Ince Blvd.	C
All mail that doesn't fall in one of the address ranges listed above	D

End of Memory Segment 3

DIRECTIONS

Memory Segment 4 is the actual Memory test. You have 7 minutes to answer 36 questions. You must answer from memory. The Coding Guide is not shown. This segment is scored, and the score from this section does affect your overall exam 473E score. So, we will likewise score Segment 4 on this sample test and use the score to measure your performance.

SCORING

Formula: To score yourself, first use the answer key at the end of this sample exam to identify your correct and incorrect answers. Then count your correct answers and your incorrect answers. Subtract 1/3 of the number of incorrect answers from the number of correct answers. The result is your score. (Yes, this is the same goofy formula we used for Address Checking and for Coding.)

Example: Let's say that, out of the 36 questions, I answered 28 in the time allowed. And of the 28 I answered, 19 were correct, and 9 were wrong. To score myself, I subtract 3 (1/3 of the 9 of wrong answers) from 19 (the number of correct answers). My score is a 16.

HOW TO INTERPRET YOUR SCORE

Process: If I answered all the questions correctly within the time allowed, the best possible score on this section is a 36. (Yes, I know this sounds confusing. You're accustomed to thinking of 100 as a top score. But with the Postal Service you need to learn how to think unnaturally.) Since nobody knows the top-secret formula for calculating the final exam score, the only way you can measure your performance on this section is to compare your score to the best possible score of 36.

Example: Looking back to the above sample, my score was a 16. The maximum number of points available is 36, and the best possible score of 36. How does my score compare? I captured 44% of the maximum number of points available.

Interpretation: So, does 16 sound like a good score? No, it is a horrible score. The unfortunate truth, however, is that nobody does well on the Memory test their first time. Virtually everyone fails it miserably. Per previous discussions, this part of the test is one of the biggest reasons for the incredibly high failure rate. Without particular memorization strategies specifically designed for this test … and without realistic practice to master the skills and speed demanded … success is all but impossible. Most people first experience the Memory test when taking the actual exam, and as just mentioned, virtually everyone fails miserably the first time around. What chance do they have without advance preparation? The facts prove that, unless you are some kind of a genius with a photographic memory, you need to think long and hard about diligently preparing for this test. And the Memory section is where my 473E study guide (page 348) really shines. Reviewers praise my memory strategies and ultra realistic practice tests more often than any other features. Your performance on this sample test will surely indicate that you need to prepare for this exam, and I sincerely believe that my guide will provide the help needed to achieve your highest possible score. (Bear in mind that, since we don't have the final scoring formula, we are basically making an educated guess when interpreting your performance on this section.)

Turn the page and begin when you are prepared to time yourself for exactly 7 minutes.

Address	Delivery Route			
1) 52 Tolling Wood Terrace	○ A)	○ B)	○ C)	○ D)
2) 129 Ellington LN	○ A)	○ B)	○ C)	○ D)
3) 16234 Sam Houston Toll RD	○ A)	○ B)	○ C)	○ D)
4) 196 Ellington LN	○ A)	○ B)	○ C)	○ D)
5) 3367 Inch St.	○ A)	○ B)	○ C)	○ D)
6) 812 Monmouth Dr.	○ A)	○ B)	○ C)	○ D)
7) 16550 Sam Houston Toll RD	○ A)	○ B)	○ C)	○ D)
8) 51 Ellington LN	○ A)	○ B)	○ C)	○ D)
9) 1271 Monmouth Dr.	○ A)	○ B)	○ C)	○ D)

continued on next page

continued

Address	Delivery Route			
10) 3390 Ince Blvd.	○ A)	○ B)	○ C)	○ D)
11) 72 Tolling Wood Terrace	○ A)	○ B)	○ C)	○ D)
12) 1204 Monmouth Dr.	○ A)	○ B)	○ C)	○ D)
13) 279 Ellington LN	○ A)	○ B)	○ C)	○ D)
14) 16000 Sam Houston Toll RD	○ A)	○ B)	○ C)	○ D)
15) 3480 Ince Blvd.	○ A)	○ B)	○ C)	○ D)
16) 35 Tolling Wood Place	○ A)	○ B)	○ C)	○ D)
17) 1290 Monmouth Dr.	○ A)	○ B)	○ C)	○ D)
18) 3900 Ince Blvd.	○ A)	○ B)	○ C)	○ D)

continued on next page

continued

	Address	Delivery Route			
19)	282 Ellington LN	○ A)	○ B)	○ C)	○ D)
20)	987 Monmouth Dr.	○ A)	○ B)	○ C)	○ D)
21)	15500 Sam Houston Toll RD	○ A)	○ B)	○ C)	○ D)
22)	66 Tolling Wood Terrace	○ A)	○ B)	○ C)	○ D)
23)	3849 Ince Blvd.	○ A)	○ B)	○ C)	○ D)
24)	130 Ellington LN	○ A)	○ B)	○ C)	○ D)
25)	3512 Ince Blvd.	○ A)	○ B)	○ C)	○ D)
26)	35 Tolling Wood Terrace	○ A)	○ B)	○ C)	○ D)
27)	3841 Inch Blvd.	○ A)	○ B)	○ C)	○ D)

continued on next page

continued

	Address	Delivery Route			
28)	144 Ellington LN	○ A)	○ B)	○ C)	○ D)
29)	3670 Ince Blvd.	○ A)	○ B)	○ C)	○ D)
30)	244 Ellington LN	○ A)	○ B)	○ C)	○ D)
31)	14800 Sam Houston Toll RD	○ A)	○ B)	○ C)	○ D)
32)	81 Rolling Wood Terrace	○ A)	○ B)	○ C)	○ D)
33)	1140 Monmouth Dr.	○ A)	○ B)	○ C)	○ D)
34)	3730 Ince Blvd.	○ A)	○ B)	○ C)	○ D)
35)	2849 Main St.	○ A)	○ B)	○ C)	○ D)
36)	1280 Monmouth Dr.	○ A)	○ B)	○ C)	○ D)

End of Memory Segment 4

Address Checking

1)	C	11)	A	21)	D	31)	A	41)	B	51)	A
2)	B	12)	B	22)	C	32)	B	42)	C	52)	B
3)	D	13)	A	23)	B	33)	D	43)	B	53)	A
4)	B	14)	A	24)	A	34)	B	44)	C	54)	D
5)	A	15)	B	25)	C	35)	B	45)	C	55)	D
6)	D	16)	D	26)	B	36)	A	46)	B	56)	C
7)	A	17)	B	27)	A	37)	D	47)	A	57)	A
8)	C	18)	A	28)	D	38)	A	48)	D	58)	B
9)	C	19)	B	29)	B	39)	A	49)	C	59)	B
10)	D	20)	A	30)	C	40)	C	50)	B	60)	A

Forms Completion

1)	B	7)	C	13)	B	19)	D	25)	D
2)	A	8)	A	14)	D	20)	D	26)	D
3)	C	9)	D	15)	C	21)	A	27)	C
4)	D	10)	C	16)	C	22)	C	28)	A
5)	D	11)	A	17)	B	23)	C	29)	D
6)	B	12)	D	18)	D	24)	B	30)	B

Coding

1)	D	10)	B	19)	A	28)	D
2)	B	11)	D	20)	C	29)	C
3)	B	12)	A	21)	B	30)	A
4)	C	13)	C	22)	D	31)	C
5)	A	14)	B	23)	C	32)	A
6)	D	15)	B	24)	A	33)	D
7)	C	16)	C	25)	B	34)	B
8)	A	17)	A	26)	B	35)	B
9)	C	18)	B	27)	C	36)	C

Memory

1)	C	10)	B	19)	B	28)	A
2)	A	11)	C	20)	A	29)	B
3)	C	12)	A	21)	C	30)	B
4)	B	13)	B	22)	C	31)	C
5)	D	14)	C	23)	C	32)	D
6)	A	15)	B	24)	A	33)	A
7)	D	16)	D	25)	B	34)	C
8)	A	17)	B	26)	C	35)	D
9)	B	18)	C	27)	D	36)	B

End of Exam 473E Sample Test

About Exam 710

Exam 710 is primarily used to fill Data Conversion Operators jobs (page 42), temporary data entry positions that can lead to fulltime jobs. Occasionally, but very rarely, this exam is used to fill other clerical or administrative type jobs. It is also used as an internal test that Postal employees must take to qualify for certain promotions, transfers, etc. This test is known by several different names – Clerical Abilities Exam, Data Conversion Operator Exam, and DCO Exam.

No revisions to exam 710 are expected in the foreseeable future. However, there is a long term plan to convert all Postal exams from paper to electronic over a period of years. So, even though the 710 is now a paper exam, it will eventually become a computerized test. Just to be safe, make sure to check Pathfinder Perks (page 19) for any updates if you plan to take exam 710.

Exam 710 consists of two major parts ... Clerical Abilities and Verbal Abilities ... which are in turn broken down into smaller sections as detailed below:

The first half of the exam, Clerical Abilities, consists of the following four timed sections:

- **Sequencing**
Each question in this section is a list of four names or codes in alphabetic and/or numeric order. Some codes are numbers only, and others have letters and numbers mixed together. You are given a fifth name or code, and told to find where this fifth name or code should alphabetically and/or numerically fit into the list. This may not sound too very difficult until you discover that they give you only 3 minutes to answer 20 questions. This means that you have only 9 seconds per question to find the answer and then mark it on your answer sheet. The speed required is incredible. Most people are lucky to finish half the questions the first time they try. Success on this section calls for extensive and realistic practice to master the skills and speed required.

- **Comparison**
Each question in this section is a list of three items (names, addresses, codes, etc.) that are either exactly alike or at least very, very similar. You are to compare the three items to see if they are exactly alike or if they are different in any way. Then you are to mark your answers (A, B, C, D, or E) based upon the below instructions:

  A) If all three items are exactly alike.
  B) If only the first and second items are exactly alike.
  C) If only the first and third items are exactly alike.
  D) If only the second and third items are exactly alike.
  E) If all three items are different.

You've never truly experienced utter confusion until trying to answer the 30 questions in this section within the 5 minutes allowed. This means that you have only 10 seconds per question. The really confusing and time consuming part is having to refer back to the instructions again and again after looking at each question so you can figure out which answer choice to mark. As before, most people are lucky to finish about half the questions the first time they try. And again, success calls for extensive practice with up-to-date and authentic practice tests to master the skills and speed required.

- **Spelling**

  In this section you are given 3 minutes to answer 20 questions - which is 9 seconds per question. For each question, answer choices A, B, and C are possible ways to spell a particular word. You are to select the answer choice (A, B, or C) with the correct spelling, or to choose answer choice D if you believe that none of the above possible spellings (A, B, or C) is correct. Of course, the words they give you are the most difficult ones you can imagine. To succeed on this section, you need to review basic spelling principles and to study a lengthy list of commonly misspelled words and a list of words that do not follow normal spelling principles.

- **Mathematics**

  In this section you have 8 minutes to answer 15 mathematical questions ... and before it's all said and done, you will wish that you had more than twice that much time. This is pure math. Each question is an addition, subtraction, multiplication, or division problem. You will be asked to work with whole numbers, decimals, fractions, and percentages. You must solve the problems the old fashioned way with pencil and paper. No calculators are allowed! Success on this section calls for a refresher course on math principles and extensive practice with up-to-date and authentic sample questions to master the required speed and skills.

The second half of the exam, Verbal Abilities, has a total of 55 questions that are broken down into the following three sections. You are given a single 50 minute period to answer the 55 questions. For most people, speed is not a big issue in this section. As a matter of fact, you are usually told that you may leave if you finish before the 50 minutes is up, and most people do indeed leave before time is called.

- **Following Written Instructions**

  The Postal Service claims that this section tests your ability to understand instructions similar to those you might receive on the job. However, we cannot believe that any sane human being would ever give you instructions as strange, convoluted, and confusing as the wording of these 20 questions. Plus, in order to answer a question correctly, you must accomplish three steps as outlined below:

  1. First you must create a preliminary answer based upon the wording of the question. The preliminary answer will be a letter and a number put together like this: T 5
  2. Then, you must look up the preliminary answer on a table provided on the exam to find its correlating answer choice (A, B, C, D, or E).
  3. Finally, you darken the proper answer choice (A, B, C, D, or E) on your answer sheet.

  Many applicants fail this section completely because they never really understand how to find and mark the correct answer. Even though I explained it as simply as possible, you still probably don't understand either, and you won't really be able to understand until you see it on the sample test shortly. Success on this section calls for extensive and realistic practice. Plus, you need detailed instructions to assure that you fully understand how to find and mark the answers.

- **Grammar, Usage & Punctuation**

  In this section, there are 20 questions that deal with the proper use of grammar, words, and punctuation. In each question you are given four similar sentences, and you are to choose the one that is most appropriately structured and/or worded. Success on this section calls for a refresher course on basic grammar, usage, and punctuation principles and extensive practice with up-to-date and authentic sample questions.

- **Vocabulary & Reading Comprehension**

  The final section is really two smaller sections merged into one. It consists of two types of questions, Vocabulary and Reading Comprehension, as detailed below.

  > **Vocabulary Questions**

    There are only 5 Vocabulary questions. For each question you are given a sentence with a particular word highlighted. Then, you are given a list of four words, and you are to choose which of the four listed words most nearly means the same as the highlighted word in the sentence. Success on this section calls for a refresher course on basic vocabulary principles.

  > **Reading Comprehension Questions**

    In each of the 10 Reading Comprehension questions, you are given a paragraph to read. Then you are given four sentences that are related to the subject of the paragraph. You are to choose the sentence that best supports and summarizes the paragraph. Success on this section calls for extensive practice to train yourself to quickly scan paragraphs to determine their meaning and purpose.

One important point to bear in mind about the 710 exam, especially as you take the sample test, is that **you _can_ write, make notes, do calculations, etc. during the exam**. This is not true of all exams. As a matter of fact, on the 710, you will be instructed to do so during some sections. However, you can only make notes, do calculations, etc. in the question/test booklet. You are not allowed to make any marks on the answer sheet except the answer choices you darken.

How to Prepare for Exam 710

Since the 710 has so many different sections, I mentioned the elements needed for success as we discussed the sections individually over the last few pages. But the bottom line is the same sermon that I've preached all along: Successful test preparation requires motivation and an effective study guide - in this case a study guide that provides the needed reviews and refresher courses in addition to test-taking strategies and realistic practice tests.

And here's an interesting bit of trivia … To my knowledge, the only study guide available anywhere for exam 710 is mine. To the best of my knowledge, no other author or publisher offers any type of test prep materials at all for exam 710. You see, there is not tremendous demand for 710 study guides because this test is only offered at a few sites across the country (see page 42). Frankly, there is simply not sufficient demand to justify the huge investment required to print and maintain an inventory of books just for this test.

However, I enjoy great relationships with the various Postal labor unions. Based upon the success that their members had experienced with my other guides, several years ago the largest of these unions asked me to create a study guide for exam 710. I could hardly decline such a request, and in short order I published the first version of my Postal Exam 710 Quick Course. Union members and applicants from the public have used this guide with great success ever since.

I explained earlier that exam 710 is a hybrid test – partially electronic and partially paper. My 710 guide is a hybrid product as well. Since there is not sufficient demand to justify a hard copy book, it is provided as an online PDF file. But you must print it to use it. Since the actual test is taken with pencil and paper, in order to practice realistically you must do so with pencil and paper. Thus the need to print the PDF so that you can practice realistically.

To order my Postal Exam 710 Quick Course at the special repeat customer price, see page 349.

Exam 710 – Complete Sample Test

A complete 710 sample test is presented on the following pages. **This sample test is formatted and broken into various sections exactly like the real exam.** The instructions given for each portion of the practice test are similar to the instructions you will hear on the real exam.

It is imperative that you take this sample test realistically – that you time yourself precisely on each section as directed in the instructions. **Until you experience the speed demanded, you have not really experienced the test at all.**

An answer sheet is provided at the end of this sample test. Either carefully tear it out or make a copy so that you will have a loose answer sheet for marking answers. The answer sheet, by the way, is formatted exactly like the real thing, and the answer bubbles are the exact same size and shape as those on the actual exam. You must fully darken the bubble when marking an answer.

To measure your performance on this sample test, I will give you the scoring formula for each section separately. Use the answer key at the end of this sample test to score yourself as you complete each section. Scoring each section will give you a reasonable indication of how you might have fared on the overall exam. As explained on page 55, they will not release the final overall scoring formulas for any exams, so it is not possible to score this sample test as a whole.

The numbering of the questions on this test may confuse you. As mentioned earlier, this exam consists of two major parts. Please note the below facts about question numbering:

- The first part, Clerical Abilities, has a total of 85 questions broken down into four sections. As you progress from one section to another, the numbering of the questions does not start all over again at number 1. The numbering is simply continued from the previous section. For instance, the Sequencing section questions are numbered 1 through 20. The next section, Comparison, has 30 questions. Ordinarily, you would expect the Comparison questions to be numbered 1 through 30. But, instead, the numbering of the Comparison questions picks up where the Sequencing section stopped. Since the Sequencing questions stopped at 20, the Comparison questions start at 21 and go through 50. And this continues through all the sections as follows:

Section	Questions
Sequencing	1 - 20
Comparison	21 - 50
Spelling	51 - 70
Mathematics	71 - 85

- The second part of this exam, Verbal Abilities, has a total of 55 questions broken down into three sections. The numbering starts again at 1 in the second half of the test. But as with the first half and as detailed below, the numbering continues from one section to another:

Section	Questions
Following Instructions	1 - 20
Grammar, Usage & Punctuation	21 - 40
Vocabulary & Reading Comprehension	41 - 55

- Naturally, the numbering on the answer sheet follows this same pattern.

Turn the page when you are ready to begin the 710 sample test.

The first part of the exam - Clerical Abilities - is divided into 4 sections, each of which is timed differently. I will give you directions, timing, etc. for each section as we progress through the test. Below is the information needed for the first section - Sequencing.

DIRECTIONS

In the Sequencing section, you are given 3 minutes to answer 20 questions. Each question is a name/code in a box followed by a list of four other names/codes in alpha/numeric order. You are to find where, in alpha/numeric order, the name/code in the box would fit into the list below it. The spots where the name/code in the box could fit into the list are labeled with the letters A, B, C, D, and E. To mark answers on the answer sheet, darken the letter for the spot where you think the name/code in the box should go.

SCORING

Formula: To score all sections of exam 710, use the answer key at the end of the test to identify your correct and incorrect answers. Then count your correct answers, and that is your score. Your score for this section is simply your number of correct answers. Wrong answers do not figure into the formula for this section.

Example: Let's say that, out of the 20 questions, I answered 18 in the time allowed. And, of the 18 answered, 15 were correct, and 3 were wrong. My score is a 15 … the number of correct answers.

HOW TO INTERPRET YOUR SCORE

Process: If I answered all the questions correctly within the time allowed, the best possible score on this section is a 20. (I know that this sounds confusing and that you're accustomed to thinking of 100 as a top score. But with the Postal Service, you need to learn how to think unnaturally.) Since nobody knows the secret formula for the final exam score, the only way you can measure your performance on this section is to compare your score to the best possible score of 20.

Example: Looking back to the above sample, we figured my score to be a 15. When comparing my score to the best possible score of 20, it's obvious that my score is not nearly as good as it could have been. More specifically, there's a maximum of 20 points available on this section, and I was only able to capture 75% of them.

Interpretation: So, does 15 sound like a good score? No. It sounds like I need to do much better. If I want to excel on this section, I need to practice to master the skills and speed demanded. Where can you find the help needed to master these skills and speed? My 710 study guide (page 349) offers the tips and realistic practice tests needed for success. (Bear in mind that, since we don't have the final scoring formula, we are basically making an educated guess when interpreting your performance on this section.)

Turn the page and begin when you are prepared to time yourself for exactly 3 minutes.

1. Claus, Larry
   A) ⟶
   Claude, Lowell
   B) ⟶
   Clausel, Jeff
   C) ⟶
   Clausen, Duane
   D) ⟶
   Claussen, Thomas
   E) ⟶

2. Denton, Barbara
   A) ⟶
   Denson, Helen
   B) ⟶
   Dent, James
   C) ⟶
   Dente, Susan
   D) ⟶
   Denty, Maxwell
   E) ⟶

3. 09582-6994
   A) ⟶
   09582-7654
   B) ⟶
   09582-7992
   C) ⟶
   09582-8321
   D) ⟶
   09582-9889
   E) ⟶

4. RKL-77384
   A) ⟶
   RKL-77284
   B) ⟶
   RKL-77296
   C) ⟶
   RKL-77349
   D) ⟶
   RKL-77392
   E) ⟶

5. Greenman, David
   A) ⟶
   Greenlee, Glen
   B) ⟶
   Greenup, William
   C) ⟶
   Greenwald, Joshua
   D) ⟶
   Greenwalt, Karen
   E) ⟶

6. 454990.73P
   A) ⟶
   454990.83P
   B) ⟶
   454994.12P
   C) ⟶
   454994.36P
   D) ⟶
   454996.29P
   E) ⟶

7. Zelayaco
   A) ⟶
   Zeeboco
   B) ⟶
   Zeeco
   C) ⟶
   Zelco
   D) ⟶
   Zenco
   E) ⟶

8. Horton, Winston
   A) ⟶
   Horton, Arthur
   B) ⟶
   Horton, Clyde
   C) ⟶
   Horton, Herbert
   D) ⟶
   Horton, Timothy
   E) ⟶

Continued on next page

Continued

9. 77489
A) ⟶
   77345
B) ⟶
   77530
C) ⟶
   77596
D) ⟶
   77600
E) ⟶

13. 43319 Elmhusrt
A) ⟶
   43246 Elmhurst
B) ⟶
   43309 Elmhurst
C) ⟶
   43446 Elmhurst
D) ⟶
   43468 Elmhurst
E) ⟶

10. Kirby, Bobbie
A) ⟶
   Kinslow, Janice
B) ⟶
   Kinter, John
C) ⟶
   Kinzel, John
D) ⟶
   Kiper, Dale
E) ⟶

14. 4026543298
A) ⟶
   4026543248
B) ⟶
   4026543286
C) ⟶
   4026543302
D) ⟶
   4026543326
E) ⟶

11. 16L-1922B
A) ⟶
   16L-1922M
B) ⟶
   16L-1922P
C) ⟶
   16L-1922S
D) ⟶
   16L-1922Y
E) ⟶

15. McEuen, Alice
A) ⟶
   McElyea, Dale
B) ⟶
   McEwen, Dorothy
C) ⟶
   McFadden, Brett
D) ⟶
   McFadin, Harold
E) ⟶

12. Technico
A) ⟶
   Techaid
B) ⟶
   Techalloy
C) ⟶
   Techclean
D) ⟶
   Techline
E) ⟶

16. Amsler, Guy
A) ⟶
   Amundson, Barbara
B) ⟶
   Amyett, Gene
C) ⟶
   Anders, Henry
D) ⟶
   Andersen, Earl
E) ⟶

Continued on next page

Continued

17. 77542-2301
   A) ⟶
      77552-1890
   B) ⟶
      77552-2201
   C) ⟶
      77552-3345
   D) ⟶
      77552-4950
   E) ⟶

18. SDE1435-X
   A) ⟶
      SDE1452-X
   B) ⟶
      SDE1464-X
   C) ⟶
      SDE1478-X
   D) ⟶
      SDE1489-X
   E) ⟶

19. Constantine, Max
   A) ⟶
      Cornwallis, Charles
   B) ⟶
      Conquistador, Alfred
   C) ⟶
      Constance, Lillian
   D) ⟶
      Constantinople, Zabukos
   E) ⟶

20. Nguyen, Thuan
   A) ⟶
      Nguyen, Tam
   B) ⟶
      Nguyen, Thanh
   C) ⟶
      Nguyen, Thieu
   D) ⟶
      Nguyen, Thuy
   E) ⟶

End of Sequencing Section

DIRECTIONS

In this section you have 5 minutes to answer 30 questions. Each question is a list of 3 names, addresses, or codes. You are to determine if the 3 listed items are exactly alike or if they are different in any way. Then you are to mark your answer choice (A, B, C, D, or E) on the answer sheet based upon the below instructions:

A – If **ALL THREE** names, addresses, or codes are exactly **ALIKE.**
B – If only the **FIRST AND SECOND** names, addresses, or codes are exactly **ALIKE.**
C – If only the **FIRST AND THIRD** names, addresses, or codes are exactly **ALIKE.**
D – If only the **SECOND AND THIRD** names, addresses, or codes are exactly **ALIKE.**
E – If **ALL THREE** names, addresses, or codes are **DIFFERENT.**

SCORING

Formula: To score all sections of exam 710, use the answer key at the end of the test to identify your correct and incorrect answers. Then count your correct answers, and that is your score. Your score for this section is simply your number of correct answers. Wrong answers do not figure into the formula for this section.

Example: Let's say that, out of the 30 questions, I answered 28 in the time allowed. And, of the 28 answered, 24 were correct, and 4 were wrong. My score is a 24 ... the number of correct answers.

HOW TO INTERPRET YOUR SCORE

Process: If I answered all the questions correctly within the time allowed, the best possible score on this section is a 30. (I know that this sounds confusing and that you're accustomed to thinking of 100 as a top score. But with the Postal Service, you need to learn how to think unnaturally.) Since nobody knows the secret formula for the final exam score, the only way you can measure your performance on this section is to compare your score to the best possible score of 30.

Example: Looking back at the above sample, my score was a 24. The maximum number of points available is 30, and the best possible score is 30. How does my score compare? I captured 80% of the maximum number of points available.

Interpretation: So, does 24 sound like a good score? Well, it's not bad. You might even say it's pretty good. But if I really want to get a job, my goal is to achieve the highest possible score. So, even with a pretty good score, I better get with the program and do some practicing to improve my score as much as possible. And my 710 study guide (page 349) is just what you need to prepare. (Bear in mind that, since we don't have the final scoring formula, we are making an educated guess when interpreting your performance on this section.)

Turn the page and begin when you are prepared to time yourself for exactly 5 minutes.

21. 7582818	7588218	7582818
22. 47231 NE Lancaster	47231 NE Lancaster	47231 NE Lancaster
23. Rancho Largo, CA	Rancho Largo, CA	Rancho Larga, CA
24. Ellie McAlister	Ellie McAlester	Elli McAlister
25. 05462-2312	05462-2321	05462-2321
26. Doyne D. Smelser	Doyne C. Smelser	Doyne D. Smelser
27. Joel Grenier	Joe Grenier	Joel Grenier
28. 5800484	5800484	5800484
29. 2542 N 1349 W	2542 N 1349 W	2542 N 1394 W
30. PMR1623-PL	PMR1623-RL	PMR1623-PL
31. Malpaso, TX	Malpas, TX	Malpas, TX
32. Adeline, Margaret	Adelene, Margaret	Adeline, Margareta
33. 1488 Mailstop 32	1488 Mailbox 32	1488 Mailstop 32
34. Terminal C Gate 14A	Terminal C Gate 14A	Terminal C Gate 14A
35. Chuck E. Lester	Clark E. Lester	Chuck E. Lestor
36. 38579-1903	38579-1903	38589-1903
37. Loren A. Porter	Lauren A. Porter	Loren A. Porter
38. 39507	39570	39570
39. Champlain IL	Champlin IL	Champlin IL
40. Captain Zizzman	Capitan Zizzman	Captain Zizzmann
41. North Industrial Freeway	North Industrial Causeway	North Industrial Highway
42. Aurora Borealis, AK	Aurora Borealis, AK	Aurora Borealis, AR
43. DRP2330-4	DRP2303-4	DRP2330-4
44. Massapequa, NY	Massappequa, NY	Massapequa, NJ
45. 8354139	8354139	8354139
46. Boystown, DE	Boyston, DE	Boyston, DE
47. 74055-8971	74055-8971	70455-8971
48. Hartsdale, AZ	Hartsdale, AZ	Hartsdale, AZ
49. Algonquin, WI	Algonoquin, WI	Algonquin, WI
50. 94861-9669	94891-9669	94861-9696

End of Comparison Section

DIRECTIONS

In this section you are given 3 minutes to answer 20 questions. Each question gives you three possible ways - labeled A, B, and C - to spell a particular word. Answer choice D is "None of the above". You are to mark on the answer sheet either the answer choice with the correct spelling or answer choice D if you believe that none of the possible spellings are correct.

SCORING

Formula: To score all sections of exam 710, use the answer key at the end of the test to identify your correct and incorrect answers. Then count your correct answers, and that is your score. Your score for this section is simply your number of correct answers. Wrong answers do not figure into the formula for this section.

Example: Let's say that, out of the 20 questions, I answered 19 in the time allowed. And, of the 19 answered, 14 were correct, and 5 were wrong. My score is a 14 … the number of correct answers.

HOW TO INTERPRET YOUR SCORE

Process: If I answered all the questions correctly within the time allowed, the best possible score on this section is a 20. (I know that this sounds confusing and that you're accustomed to thinking of 100 as a top score. But with the Postal Service, you need to learn how to think unnaturally.) Since nobody knows the secret formula for the final exam score, the only way you can measure your performance on this section is to compare your score to the best possible score of 20.

Example: Looking back to the above sample, we figured my score to be a 14. When comparing my score to the best possible score of 20, it's obvious that my score is not nearly as good as it could have been. More specifically, there's a maximum of 20 points available on this section, and I was only able to capture 70% of them.

Interpretation: So, does 14 sound like a good score? No. It sounds like I need to do much better. If I want to excel on this section, I need to practice to master the skills and speed demanded. Where can you find the reviews, refreshers, and help needed to succeed? In my 710 study guide (page 349). (Bear in mind that, since we don't have the final scoring formula, we are basically making an educated guess when interpreting your performance on this section.)

Turn the page and begin when you are prepared to time yourself for exactly 3 minutes.

51. A) acuracy
    B) accuracy
    C) accurasy
    D) None of the above

52. A) possession
    B) posesion
    C) posession
    D) None of the above

53. A) begining
    B) beginning
    C) beginng
    D) None of the above

54. A) advertize
    B) advertise
    C) adveritise
    D) None of the above

55. A) excede
    B) exsede
    C) exceed
    D) None of the above

56. A) noticeable
    B) noticable
    C) noticeible
    D) None of the above

57. A) acheive
    B) acheivie
    C) achievie
    D) None of the above

58. A) permissable
    B) permisible
    C) permissible
    D) None of the above

59. A) mischeivous
    B) mischeivuos
    C) mischievous
    D) None of the above

60. A) decision
    B) decsion
    C) decistion
    D) None of the above

61. A) personel
    B) personnel
    C) personell
    D) None of the above

62. A) judgeing
    B) judgging
    C) judging
    D) None of the above

63. A) disatisfy
    B) dissatisfy
    C) disatissfy
    D) None of the above

64. A) ocurring
    B) ocuring
    C) ocureing
    D) None of the above

65. A) paralell
    B) parellel
    C) paralel
    D) None of the above

66. A) sophomore
    B) sophmore
    C) sophomor
    D) None of the above

67. A) fasinate
    B) facinate
    C) fascinate
    D) None of the above

68. A) auxilery
    B) auxillary
    C) auxiliary
    D) None of the above

69. A) vengence
    B) vengeance
    C) veangence
    D) None of the above

70. A) laboratory
    B) labratory
    C) labaratory
    D) None of the above

End of Spelling Section

DIRECTIONS

In this section you have 8 minutes to answer 15 math questions. You must solve the problems using pencil and paper. No calculators are allowed! Do your calculations in the margins or blank areas on the page with the questions. For each question, answer choices A, B, C, and D are possible solutions to the math problem. Answer choice E is "none of the above". You are to mark on your answer sheet either the answer choice with the correct solution or answer choice D if you believe that none of the possible solutions is correct.

SCORING

Formula: To score all sections of exam 710, use the answer key at the end of the test to identify your correct and incorrect answers. Then count your correct answers, and that is your score. Your score for this section is simply your number of correct answers. Wrong answers do not figure into the formula for this section.

Example: Let's say that, out of the 15 questions, I answered 12 in the time allowed. And, of the 12 answered, 10 were correct, and 2 were wrong. My score is a 10 ... the number of correct answers.

HOW TO INTERPRET YOUR SCORE

Process: If I answered all the questions correctly within the time allowed, the best possible score on this section is a 15. (I know that this sounds confusing and that you're accustomed to thinking of 100 as a top score. But with the Postal Service, you need to learn how to think unnaturally.) Since nobody knows the secret formula for the final exam score, the only way you can measure your performance on this section is to compare your score to the best possible score of 15.

Example: Looking back to the above sample, we figured my score to be a 10. When comparing my score to the best possible score of 15, it's obvious that my score is not nearly as good as it could have been. More specifically, there's a maximum of 15 points available on this section, and I was only able to capture 67% of them.

Interpretation: So, is 10 a good score? No, it's a terrible score. I need to do much better. If I want to excel on this section, I need to practice to master the skills and speed demanded. And my 710 study guide (page 349) provides the Math reviews and practice you need. (Bear in mind that, since we don't have the final scoring formula, we are basically making an educated guess when interpreting your performance on this section.)

Turn the page and begin when you are prepared to time yourself for exactly 8 minutes.

71) 1/8 of 36 =
A) 4.5
B) 6.4
C) 5.6
D) 4.0
E) None of the above

72) 33.45 + 82.23 =
A) 108.26
B) 124.22
C) 112.08
D) 116.68
E) None of the above

73) 32 x 24.5 =
A) 642
B) 728
C) 784
D) 802
E) None of the above

74) 83 + 118 =
A) 211
B) 201
C) 212
D) 193
E) None of the above

75) 12.5% of 12 =
A) 2.6
B) 3.5
C) 4.0
D) 1.5
E) None of the above

76) 122 − 79 =
A) 43
B) 57
C) 63
D) 45
E) None of the above

77) 39 x 7 =
A) 321
B) 293
C) 301
D) 273
E) None of the above

78) 504 / 12 =
A) 42
B) 68
C) 36
D) 54
E) None of the above

79) 57.86 − 22.34 =
A) 32.52
B) 35.52
C) 28.06
D) 27.02
E) None of the above

80) 137 + 7% =
A) 152.14
B) 144.52
C) 159.79
D) 147.59
E) None of the above

81) $15.20 − 15% =
A) $12.92
B) $13.80
C) $11.35
D) $14.15
E) None of the above

82) 137 + 35 =
A) 175
B) 170
C) 168
D) 172
E) None of the above

83) 3/4 of 824 =
A) 618
B) 704
C) 580
D) 642
E) None of the above

84) 231 ÷ 33 =
A) 23
B) 11
C) 9
D) 7
E) None of the above

85) 232 x .175 =
A) 35.8
B) 44.4
C) 40.6
D) 36.4
E) None of the above

The second part of the exam, Verbal Abilities, has 55 questions broken down into 3 sections. You work through all 3 of the sections in a single 50 minute period without pausing between sections. Following are instructions for all 3 sections and scoring information that applies to all 3 sections.

FOLLOWING WRITTEN INSTRUCTIONS

There are 20 questions in the Following Written Instructions section. Each question is a set of instructions that causes you create a letter-number combination. After creating a letter-number combination, you look it up on a Look-Up Table, which enables you to convert it into an answer choice. The answer choices are A, B, C, D, and E. You answer the questions by darkening your answer choices on the answer sheet.

I'm stepping away from my policy of only providing realistic instructions for a moment because the above directions are about as clear as mud. And it won't be much better at the real exam either. So, to help you understand, I'm going to explain a bit and give you a sample.

And by the way, this really is what the Following Written Instructions section is actually like. I'm not making this up. The questions are very similar to the below sample and to the questions on this sample test, and there is a Look-Up Table just like in the below sample and in the sample test.

As described earlier, to answer a question correctly you must accomplish three steps:

- First, you create a preliminary answer based upon the wording of the question. The preliminary answer will be a letter-number combination like this: T 5
- Then, you find the preliminary answer on a Look-Up Table provided on the exam to discover the answer choice (A, B, C, D, or E) that it correlates to.
- Finally, you darken the proper answer choice (A, B, C, D, or E) on your answer sheet.

That maybe helped a little, but not much. So let's look at a sample to clear things up.

LOOK-UP TABLE

	P	Q	R	S	T
1	A	B	C	D	E
2	B	C	D	E	A
3	C	D	E	A	B
4	D	E	A	B	C
5	E	A	B	C	D
6	A	B	C	D	E
7	B	C	D	E	A
8	C	D	E	A	B
9	D	E	A	B	C
10	E	A	B	C	D

Draw a line under each letter that appears only once below. Write the letter "R" and the number of lines you drew here: ___ ___

   S   T   R   Q   P   Q   T   P   T

Since "S" and "R" are the only letters that appear only once, we draw lines under the one "S" and the one "R". Then, as instructed, we write the letter "R" and the number of lines we drew (2 lines - 1 under the "S" and 1 under the "R") in the blanks like this: R 2 . We have our letter-number combination ... R2. Next we go to the Look-Up Table to find our R2 letter-number combination. We look across the top of the table to find the letter "R", and then we follow the "R" column down to the "2" row. Answer choice "D" appears where the "R" column and the "2" row meet. This is our answer ... "D". So, for this question, we darken the answer "D" on our answer sheet. (I highlighted the "R" column and the "2" row so you could see exactly how to use the Look-Up Table.)

Really ... I'm not lying ... That's exactly what it's like. Remember when I questioned the sanity of the people who write these tests? Perhaps you're beginning to understand what I mean.

Directions for the final two Verbal Abilities sections and scoring information on the next page.

GRAMMAR, USAGE & PUNCTUATION

This section has 20 questions dealing with the proper use of grammar, words, and punctuation. Each question gives you 4 similar sentences labeled A, B, C, and D. You are to choose which is structured most appropriately with respect to grammar, usage, and punctuation. Mark the letter for the best choice (A, B, C, or D) as your answer on the answer sheet.

VOCABULARY & READING COMPREHENSION

This section consists of 15 questions - 5 Vocabulary and 10 Reading Comprehension. It is really two smaller sections merged together. Each type of question is discussed below.

Vocabulary Questions

Each Vocabulary question is a sentence with a particular word highlighted. Under this sentence is a list of four words labeled A, B, C, and D. You are to choose which of the four listed words most nearly means the same as the highlighted word in the sentence. Mark your answer by darkening your answer choice on the answer sheet.

Reading Comprehension Questions

Each Reading Comprehension question is a paragraph followed by four sentences labeled A, B, C, and D. You are to choose which sentence best summarizes the paragraph. Mark your answer by darkening your answer choice on the answer sheet.

SCORING

Formula: To score all sections of exam 710, use the answer key at the end of the test to identify your correct and incorrect answers. Then count your correct answers, and that is your score. Your score for each section is simply your number of correct answers. Wrong answers do not figure into the formula for this section.

Note: Even though the Verbal Abilities half of the test is divided into three sections, it is taken as one single session. We will therefore, group the three sections together as we discuss scoring.

Example: Let's say that, when taking the Verbal Abilities portion of the test, I was able to answer all the questions within the time allowed. After all, as explained earlier, speed is not such an issue on this part of the test. But, of course, I answered some of these questions incorrectly. The below table shows my results. Per the scoring formula, my score in each case is simply my number of correct answers.

Section	Max Score	My Questions Answered	My Correct Answers	My Incorrect Answers	My Score	My Points Captured
Following Written Instructions	20	20	17	3	17	85%
Grammar, Usage & Punctuation	20	20	15	5	15	75%
Vocabulary & Reading Comprehension	15	15	13	2	13	87%

HOW TO INTERPRET YOUR SCORE

Process: Looking back at the table, we see how my scores compare to the maximum possible score in each case and how my scores translate into a percentage of the maximum number of points available in each case.

Example: Per the table, my comparisons worked out as follows:

Following Written Instructions – I captured 85% of the available points.

Grammar, Usage & Punctuation – I captured 75% of the available points.

Vocabulary & Reading Comprehension – I captured 87% of the available points.

Interpretation: So, how did I do? These scores are fair, but they are certainly not great. What does this mean to me? It means that if I really want a job, I need to get serious about test preparation to assure a good enough score. Where can you find the help needed to master these skills and speed? My 710 guide (page 349) has the tips and practice needed for success on all three of these sections. (Bear in mind that, since we don't have the final scoring formula, we are making an educated guess when interpreting your performance on this section.)

Turn the page and begin when you are prepared to time yourself for exactly 50 minutes.

Use the below list of letter-number combinations for questions 1 – 10.

P8　　T6　　Q9　　S1　　S4　　R3　　P8　　Q2　　T5　　Q7

LOOK-UP TABLE

	P	Q	R	S	T
1	A	B	C	D	E
2	B	C	D	E	A
3	C	D	E	A	B
4	D	E	A	B	C
5	E	A	B	C	D
6	A	B	C	D	E
7	B	C	D	E	A
8	C	D	E	A	B
9	D	E	A	B	C
10	E	A	B	C	D

1. There is one combination that appears twice in the list. Write the combination that appears twice here: _____ _____

2. There is one letter that appears three times. Write that letter and the number from the last combination in the list here: _____ _____

3. There is one letter that appears only once in the series of combinations. Write the combination that contains the letter that only appears once here: _____ _____

4. Add all the numbers together that appear in the list with the letter S. Write the letter S and the total of all the numbers that appear in the list with the letter S here: _____ _____

5. Write the letter from the second combination in the list and the number from the third combination in the list here: _____ _____

6. Circle the eighth combination in the list. Write the combination you circled here: _____ _____

7. Draw a line under the combination in the list with the largest number. Write the combination you drew a line under here: _____ _____

8. Subtract the number in the last combination from the number in the first combination. Write the letter from the first combination and the result you get when subtracting the number in the last combination from the number in the first combination here: _____ _____

9. Draw a square around the second combination from the right in the list. Write the combination you drew a square around here: _____ _____

10. Add the numbers together from the fourth, fifth, and sixth letter-number combinations in the list. Write the letter T and the total you get when adding the numbers together from the fourth, fifth, and sixth combinations here: _____ _____

11. Circle the third letter and the third number in the below list. Write the letter you circled and the number you circled here: _____ _____
　　　　2　　7　　S　　9　　T　　R　　5　　P　　4　　Q　　S　　4

12. Look back at the list of letters and numbers in question eleven. Write the first letter in the list and the smallest number in the list here: _____ _____

13. Look again at the list of letters and numbers in question eleven. There is one letter that appears twice in the list and one number that appears twice in the list. Write the letter that appears twice and the number that appears twice here: _____ _____

continued on next page

14. Look at the words listed below. Add the number of letters in the first three words. Subtract the number of letters in the last word from the total number of letters in the first three words. Write the last letter in the first word and the result you found when subtracting the number of letters in the last word from the total number of letters in the first three words here: ___ ___

tar   sit   tip   roast

15. Look back at the words listed in question fourteen. Find the first letter of the last word and count the number of letters in the second word. Write the first letter of the last word and the number of letters in the second word here: ____ ____

LOOK-UP TABLE

	P	Q	R	S	T
1	A	B	C	D	E
2	B	C	D	E	A
3	C	D	E	A	B
4	D	E	A	B	C
5	E	A	B	C	D
6	A	B	C	D	E
7	B	C	D	E	A
8	C	D	E	A	B
9	D	E	A	B	C
10	E	A	B	C	D

16. Look again at the words in question fourteen. Find the first letter of the second word and add the number of letters in the second and third words. Write the first letter of the second word and the total number of letters in the second and third words here: ____ ____

17. Look at the states listed below. Circle the name of the state with the most letters. Write the last letter and the number of letters in the name of the state your circled here: ____ ____

Texas   Illinois   Kansas

18. Look at the states in question seventeen again. Subtract the number of letters in the name of the first state from the number of letters in the name of the last state. Write the first letter in the name of the first state and the result you got when subtracting the number of letters in the name of the first state from the number of letters in the name of the last state here: ____ ____

19. Look back again at the states in question seventeen. Count the number of letters in the names of all three states put together. Write the letter Q and the number 7 here: ____ ____

20. Look at the letters listed below. Circle the sixth letter in the list. Write the letter you circled and the number 6 here: ____ ____

LOOKUPTABLELOOKUPTABLELOOKUPTABLE

21. A) An extensive collection of ancient Egyptian artifacts is on display at the museum.
     B) An extensive collection of ancient Egyptian artifacts are on display at the museum.
     C) An extensive collections of ancient Egyptian artifacts are on display at the museum.
     D) An extensive collection of ancient Egyptian artifact are on display at the museum.

22. A) Every soldier must maintain their own equipment.
     B) All soldiers must maintain his own equipment.
     C) Every soldier must maintain his own equipment.
     D) Every soldier must maintain his own equipment himself.

23. A) The school principle lectured us on the principals upon which our country was founded.
     B) The school principal lectured us on the principles upon which our country was founded.
     C) The school principal lectured us on the principals upon which our country was founded.
     D) The school principle lectured us on the principles upon which our country was founded.

24. A) We signed the contract, and our interests will be protected.
     B) We signed the contract, our interests will be protected.
     C) We signed the contract; and our interests will be protected.
     D) We signed the contract: our interests will be protected.

25. A) The cash will be divided among us two, and residuals will be divided among all the others.
     B) The cash will be divided among us two, and residuals will be divided between all the others.
     C) The cash will be divided between us two, and residuals will be divided between all the others.
     D) The cash will be divided between us two, and residuals will be divided among all the others.

26. A) When Sue first saw Meredith, she squealed with delight.
     B) When Sue and Meredith first saw each other, she squealed with delight.
     C) When Sue first saw Meredith and Meredith saw Sue, she squealed with delight.
     D) Sue squealed with delight when she first saw Meredith.

27. A) The committee's first report on possible expansion plans for the Andrews facility.
     B) The committee's first possible expansion plans for the Andrews facility report.
     C) The committee's possible expansion plans for the Andrews facility first report.
     D) The committee's first report was on possible expansion plans for the Andrews facility.

28. A) We counted seventy-three at the first meeting and 142 at the second one.
     B) We counted 73 at the first meeting and 142 at the second one.
     C) We counted 73 at the first meeting and one hundred forty-two at the second one.
     D) We counted seventy-three at the first meeting and one hundred forty-two at the second one.

29. A) The award was a complete surprise to Mark and me.
     B) The award was a complete surprise to Mark and I.
     C) The award was a complete surprise to me and Mark.
     D) The award was a complete surprise to I and Mark.

30. A) Neither Mr. Clark nor Mr. Adams is qualified for this position.
     B) Neither Mr. Clark nor Mr. Adams are qualified for this position.
     C) Neither Mr. Clark is qualified nor Mr. Adams is qualified for this position.
     D) Neither Mr. Clark and Mr. Adams are qualified for this position.

continued on next page

continued

31.   A) The two of them were to late to catch the train.
      B) The two of them were too late to catch the train.
      C) The too of them were to late to catch the train.
      D) The to of them were to late to catch the train.

32.   A) As ordered, Private Jones didn't say nothing to them.
      B) As ordered, Private Jones did not say nothing to them.
      C) As ordered, Private Jones didn't say nothing at all to them.
      D) As ordered, Private Jones said nothing to them.

33.   A) The coach says that Larry plays tennis real good.
      B) The coach says that Larry plays tennis real goodly.
      C) The coach says that Larry plays tennis really good.
      D) The coach says that Larry plays tennis really well.

34.   A) I'm not feeling good at the moment.
      B) I'm not feeling well at the moment.
      C) I don't feel good at the moment.
      D) I do not feel good at the moment.

35.   A) The detective wishes to speak to you in regards to this case.
      B) The detective wishes to speak to you with regards to this case.
      C) The detective wishes to speak to you in regard to this case.
      D) The detective wishes to speak to you with regard to this case.

36.   A) Please check on our dog every so often while we are out of town.
      B) Please check on our dog sometimes while we are out of town.
      C) Please check on our dog occasionally sometimes while we are out of town.
      D) Please check on our dog occasionally while we are out of town.

37.   A) My car is parked besides yours.
      B) My car is parked right next to yours.
      C) My car is parked beside yours.
      D) My car is parked along side yours.

38.   A) Paul is hardly ever invited to their parties.
      B) Paul is rarely invited to their parties.
      C) Paul is almost never invited to their parties.
      D) Paul doesn't hardly ever get invited to their parties.

39.   A) When going through the airport security gate, try not to lose your lose change.
      B) When going through the airport security gate, try not to lose your loose change.
      C) When going through the airport security gate, try not to loose your lose change.
      D) When going through the airport security gate, try not to loose your loose change.

40.   A) The moral of this little story is to make sure that your troops maintain their moral.
      B) The morale of this little story is to make sure that your troops maintain their moral.
      C) The morale of this little story is to make sure that your troops maintain their morale.
      D) The moral of this little story is to make sure that your troops maintain their morale.

End of Grammar, Usage, and Punctuation

41. Her blind date had a **bland** personality.
    bland most nearly means
    A) hopeless
    B) spicy
    C) boring
    D) fragile

42. He made an **earnest** attempt to resolve the controversy.
    earnest most nearly means
    A) hypocritical
    B) feeble
    C) humorous
    D) sincere

43. The last element should be added to the mixture in a **gradual** fashion.
    gradual most nearly means
    A) rapid
    B) careful
    C) slow
    D) expedient

44. Many believe that the judge was too **lenient** when sentencing the convict.
    lenient most nearly means
    A) tolerant
    B) careless
    C) harsh
    D) vindictive

45. **Migratory** laborers frequently do the harvesting.
    migratory most nearly means
    A) experienced
    B) immigrant
    C) contract
    D) transient

46. After World War II, the city of Berlin was divided into East Berlin and West Berlin. The Soviet Union controlled East Berlin, and West Berlin was allied with democratic western countries. In 1961, Soviet East Germany erected a wall of concrete, steel, and barbed wire to separate East Berlin from West Berlin. Called the Berlin Wall, it was twenty-seven miles long, had twelve official crossing points, and was constantly patrolled. This barrier to peaceful relations was finally dismantled in 1989.

    This paragraph best supports the statement that the separation of East and West Berlin
    A) is a permanent situation.
    B) was radically defined from 1961 to 1989 by a twenty-seven mile wall.
    C) is the result of Communist aggression.
    D) is but a political formality.

continued on next page

47. Although Ulysses S. Grant improved relations with Britain during his two terms as president, his stay in office is remembered for graft, failure to annex Santo Domingo, and failure to enforce the Force Acts. The Force Acts were designed to assure Negro civil and voting rights. Mr. Grant's major problem was appointing friends rather than capable men to key government positions.

This paragraph best supports the statement that President Grant's terms of office
A) are remembered for failure rather than success.
B) resulted in depressed economic conditions.
C) were regarded as failures because of Grant's lack of leadership abilities.
D) destroyed Mr. Grant's reputation.

48. Michel de Nostradamus was court physician to Charles IX of France. He was made famous by his prediction of the death of Henry II. He published his prophesies in verse in a book entitled *Centuries* in 1555. His prophesies are generally considered vague.

This paragraph best supports the statement that Nostradamus
A) made his fame as a physician to Charles IX.
B) was an astrologer.
C) published a book of prophesies.
D) is respected to this day for his predictions.

49. The Mau Mau, a Kenyan Kikuyu terrorist organization, ran a campaign of sabotage and murder from 1952 until 1960. Their aim was to drive out the British. The Mau Mau lost over 11,000 members in their crusade. They killed an estimated 100 Europeans and 2,000 natives who refused to join the organization. In excess of 20,000 Mau Mau were finally detained.

This paragraph best supports the statement that the Mau Mau uprising in Kenya
A) resulted in the British relinquishing control in that country.
B) resulted in over 10,000 deaths.
C) swept through several African countries.
D) was successful.

50. Many basic examinations test applicants' graph reading skills. When reading a graph, one must first ascertain the zero point on the vertical axis. Many errors occur when graph readers assume the zero value to be at the origin, when in fact it is not. Another common error occurs when the graph reader does not accurately determine the units of measurement on the horizontal and vertical axes. Educators agree that graph reading is an important skill that should be acquired before a student completes high school, but unfortunately this does not always happen.

This paragraph best supports the statement that graph reading skills
A) are easily acquired.
B) are usually mastered by high school age.
C) require one to identify the zero value and the units of measure along each axis.
D) require a certain amount of background work in advanced mathematics.

continued on next page

51. The tragedies of war are not always confined to the time frame in which battles are fought. A widely known example is the side effects of Agent Orange, the chemical used to defoliate jungles in Vietnam. This herbicide was found to contain a lethal dioxin. The use of Agent Orange was discontinued due to a high rate of birth defects among infants in Vietnam. After the war, many veterans were found to have suffered ill effects from Agent Orange as well.

This paragraph best supports the statement that Agent Orange
A) had immediate as well as long term negative effects on those exposed to it.
B) was a lethal poison used in chemical warfare.
C) has not been proven to be the cause of birth defects.
D) is manufactured from a lethal dioxin.

52. Many people think that Cyrano De Bergerac is but the romantic hero of Edmund Rostand's play which also bears the name "Cyrano De Bergerac". But, before the play immortalized the man and his nose, De Bergerac was a French author of plays and prose. He gave up a military career to satirize the society of his day in fantasies about voyages to the sun and the moon.

This paragraph best supports the statement that Cyrano De Bergerac was a
A) man of many varied talents.
B) romantic who made the writing of love poems his life's work.
C) military man whose satires were posthumously published in Edmund Rostand's play.
D) man who existed before Rostand's play.

53. When it comes to employment exams, there are arguments both for and against test preparation. Some insist that such exams are aptitude tests for which one cannot study or prepare. However, the facts dispute this opinion. It has been repeatedly demonstrated that those who study exam content, learn test-taking tips, and practice with realistic sample tests do indeed score higher.

This paragraph best supports the statement that preparing for employment exams
A) is not beneficial.
B) guarantees one a job.
C) only helps in certain situations.
D) has been proven to improve scores.

54. People often complain about their jobs. These complaints may be about the job itself, about wages, about benefits, about managers, about co-workers, or about the commute. Those voicing these comments usually feel that they have no choice but to keep their unrewarding jobs. Others believe that we do have choices, that quality of life is more important than standard of living, and that life is too short to choose a demeaning career. These people feel that, even if one chooses a job with lesser wages or status, it can be more rewarding than a career that diminishes one's quality of life.

This paragraph best supports the statement that when seeking employment, you should
A) always choose the job with the highest wages.
B) not accept a job if the commute is over thirty minutes.
C) consider how various aspects of the job will affect your quality of life.
D) get to know the manager first to see if you can get along with him or her.

continued on next page

55.   Computer technology has dramatically improved today's business operations. Many functions that were formerly tedious and expensive are now accomplished rapidly and efficiently. As a matter of fact, it is not unusual for a firm to be so dependent upon this technology that a computer system crash can almost put the firm out of business. To avoid such a disaster, experts recommend that critical electronic files be routinely backed-up and that businesses invest in redundant systems to fall back upon in the event of a crash.

This paragraph best supports the statement that a business should
A) take steps to assure continued operations in the event of a computer crash.
B) not become dependent upon computers.
C) use computers only for certain non-sensitive functions.
D) not back-up computerized records unless its system crashes.

End of Vocabulary & Reading Comprehension

EXAM 710 ANSWER SHEET

Clerical Abilities - Part A

Sequencing	Comparison	Spelling	Mathematics
1 Ⓐ Ⓑ Ⓒ Ⓓ Ⓔ	21 Ⓐ Ⓑ Ⓒ Ⓓ Ⓔ	51 Ⓐ Ⓑ Ⓒ Ⓓ	71 Ⓐ Ⓑ Ⓒ Ⓓ Ⓔ
2 Ⓐ Ⓑ Ⓒ Ⓓ Ⓔ	22 Ⓐ Ⓑ Ⓒ Ⓓ Ⓔ	52 Ⓐ Ⓑ Ⓒ Ⓓ	72 Ⓐ Ⓑ Ⓒ Ⓓ Ⓔ
3 Ⓐ Ⓑ Ⓒ Ⓓ Ⓔ	23 Ⓐ Ⓑ Ⓒ Ⓓ Ⓔ	53 Ⓐ Ⓑ Ⓒ Ⓓ	73 Ⓐ Ⓑ Ⓒ Ⓓ Ⓔ
4 Ⓐ Ⓑ Ⓒ Ⓓ Ⓔ	24 Ⓐ Ⓑ Ⓒ Ⓓ Ⓔ	54 Ⓐ Ⓑ Ⓒ Ⓓ	74 Ⓐ Ⓑ Ⓒ Ⓓ Ⓔ
5 Ⓐ Ⓑ Ⓒ Ⓓ Ⓔ	25 Ⓐ Ⓑ Ⓒ Ⓓ Ⓔ	55 Ⓐ Ⓑ Ⓒ Ⓓ	75 Ⓐ Ⓑ Ⓒ Ⓓ Ⓔ
6 Ⓐ Ⓑ Ⓒ Ⓓ Ⓔ	26 Ⓐ Ⓑ Ⓒ Ⓓ Ⓔ	56 Ⓐ Ⓑ Ⓒ Ⓓ	76 Ⓐ Ⓑ Ⓒ Ⓓ Ⓔ
7 Ⓐ Ⓑ Ⓒ Ⓓ Ⓔ	27 Ⓐ Ⓑ Ⓒ Ⓓ Ⓔ	57 Ⓐ Ⓑ Ⓒ Ⓓ	77 Ⓐ Ⓑ Ⓒ Ⓓ Ⓔ
8 Ⓐ Ⓑ Ⓒ Ⓓ Ⓔ	28 Ⓐ Ⓑ Ⓒ Ⓓ Ⓔ	58 Ⓐ Ⓑ Ⓒ Ⓓ	78 Ⓐ Ⓑ Ⓒ Ⓓ Ⓔ
9 Ⓐ Ⓑ Ⓒ Ⓓ Ⓔ	29 Ⓐ Ⓑ Ⓒ Ⓓ Ⓔ	59 Ⓐ Ⓑ Ⓒ Ⓓ	79 Ⓐ Ⓑ Ⓒ Ⓓ Ⓔ
10 Ⓐ Ⓑ Ⓒ Ⓓ Ⓔ	30 Ⓐ Ⓑ Ⓒ Ⓓ Ⓔ	60 Ⓐ Ⓑ Ⓒ Ⓓ	80 Ⓐ Ⓑ Ⓒ Ⓓ Ⓔ
11 Ⓐ Ⓑ Ⓒ Ⓓ Ⓔ	31 Ⓐ Ⓑ Ⓒ Ⓓ Ⓔ	61 Ⓐ Ⓑ Ⓒ Ⓓ	81 Ⓐ Ⓑ Ⓒ Ⓓ Ⓔ
12 Ⓐ Ⓑ Ⓒ Ⓓ Ⓔ	32 Ⓐ Ⓑ Ⓒ Ⓓ Ⓔ	62 Ⓐ Ⓑ Ⓒ Ⓓ	82 Ⓐ Ⓑ Ⓒ Ⓓ Ⓔ
13 Ⓐ Ⓑ Ⓒ Ⓓ Ⓔ	33 Ⓐ Ⓑ Ⓒ Ⓓ Ⓔ	63 Ⓐ Ⓑ Ⓒ Ⓓ	83 Ⓐ Ⓑ Ⓒ Ⓓ Ⓔ
14 Ⓐ Ⓑ Ⓒ Ⓓ Ⓔ	34 Ⓐ Ⓑ Ⓒ Ⓓ Ⓔ	64 Ⓐ Ⓑ Ⓒ Ⓓ	84 Ⓐ Ⓑ Ⓒ Ⓓ Ⓔ
15 Ⓐ Ⓑ Ⓒ Ⓓ Ⓔ	35 Ⓐ Ⓑ Ⓒ Ⓓ Ⓔ	65 Ⓐ Ⓑ Ⓒ Ⓓ	85 Ⓐ Ⓑ Ⓒ Ⓓ Ⓔ
16 Ⓐ Ⓑ Ⓒ Ⓓ Ⓔ	36 Ⓐ Ⓑ Ⓒ Ⓓ Ⓔ	66 Ⓐ Ⓑ Ⓒ Ⓓ	
17 Ⓐ Ⓑ Ⓒ Ⓓ Ⓔ	37 Ⓐ Ⓑ Ⓒ Ⓓ Ⓔ	67 Ⓐ Ⓑ Ⓒ Ⓓ	
18 Ⓐ Ⓑ Ⓒ Ⓓ Ⓔ	38 Ⓐ Ⓑ Ⓒ Ⓓ Ⓔ	68 Ⓐ Ⓑ Ⓒ Ⓓ	
19 Ⓐ Ⓑ Ⓒ Ⓓ Ⓔ	39 Ⓐ Ⓑ Ⓒ Ⓓ Ⓔ	69 Ⓐ Ⓑ Ⓒ Ⓓ	
20 Ⓐ Ⓑ Ⓒ Ⓓ Ⓔ	40 Ⓐ Ⓑ Ⓒ Ⓓ Ⓔ	70 Ⓐ Ⓑ Ⓒ Ⓓ	
	41 Ⓐ Ⓑ Ⓒ Ⓓ Ⓔ		
	42 Ⓐ Ⓑ Ⓒ Ⓓ Ⓔ		
	43 Ⓐ Ⓑ Ⓒ Ⓓ Ⓔ		
	44 Ⓐ Ⓑ Ⓒ Ⓓ Ⓔ		
	45 Ⓐ Ⓑ Ⓒ Ⓓ Ⓔ		
	46 Ⓐ Ⓑ Ⓒ Ⓓ Ⓔ		
	47 Ⓐ Ⓑ Ⓒ Ⓓ Ⓔ		
	48 Ⓐ Ⓑ Ⓒ Ⓓ Ⓔ		
	49 Ⓐ Ⓑ Ⓒ Ⓓ Ⓔ		
	50 Ⓐ Ⓑ Ⓒ Ⓓ Ⓔ		

Verbal Abilities - Part B

Following Instructions		Grammar, Usage & Punctuation		Vocabulary & Reading
1 Ⓐ Ⓑ Ⓒ Ⓓ Ⓔ	11 Ⓐ Ⓑ Ⓒ Ⓓ Ⓔ	21 Ⓐ Ⓑ Ⓒ Ⓓ	31 Ⓐ Ⓑ Ⓒ Ⓓ	41 Ⓐ Ⓑ Ⓒ Ⓓ
2 Ⓐ Ⓑ Ⓒ Ⓓ Ⓔ	12 Ⓐ Ⓑ Ⓒ Ⓓ Ⓔ	22 Ⓐ Ⓑ Ⓒ Ⓓ	32 Ⓐ Ⓑ Ⓒ Ⓓ	42 Ⓐ Ⓑ Ⓒ Ⓓ
3 Ⓐ Ⓑ Ⓒ Ⓓ Ⓔ	13 Ⓐ Ⓑ Ⓒ Ⓓ Ⓔ	23 Ⓐ Ⓑ Ⓒ Ⓓ	33 Ⓐ Ⓑ Ⓒ Ⓓ	43 Ⓐ Ⓑ Ⓒ Ⓓ
4 Ⓐ Ⓑ Ⓒ Ⓓ Ⓔ	14 Ⓐ Ⓑ Ⓒ Ⓓ Ⓔ	24 Ⓐ Ⓑ Ⓒ Ⓓ	34 Ⓐ Ⓑ Ⓒ Ⓓ	44 Ⓐ Ⓑ Ⓒ Ⓓ
5 Ⓐ Ⓑ Ⓒ Ⓓ Ⓔ	15 Ⓐ Ⓑ Ⓒ Ⓓ Ⓔ	25 Ⓐ Ⓑ Ⓒ Ⓓ	35 Ⓐ Ⓑ Ⓒ Ⓓ	45 Ⓐ Ⓑ Ⓒ Ⓓ
6 Ⓐ Ⓑ Ⓒ Ⓓ Ⓔ	16 Ⓐ Ⓑ Ⓒ Ⓓ Ⓔ	26 Ⓐ Ⓑ Ⓒ Ⓓ	36 Ⓐ Ⓑ Ⓒ Ⓓ	46 Ⓐ Ⓑ Ⓒ Ⓓ
7 Ⓐ Ⓑ Ⓒ Ⓓ Ⓔ	17 Ⓐ Ⓑ Ⓒ Ⓓ Ⓔ	27 Ⓐ Ⓑ Ⓒ Ⓓ	37 Ⓐ Ⓑ Ⓒ Ⓓ	47 Ⓐ Ⓑ Ⓒ Ⓓ
8 Ⓐ Ⓑ Ⓒ Ⓓ Ⓔ	18 Ⓐ Ⓑ Ⓒ Ⓓ Ⓔ	28 Ⓐ Ⓑ Ⓒ Ⓓ	38 Ⓐ Ⓑ Ⓒ Ⓓ	48 Ⓐ Ⓑ Ⓒ Ⓓ
9 Ⓐ Ⓑ Ⓒ Ⓓ Ⓔ	19 Ⓐ Ⓑ Ⓒ Ⓓ Ⓔ	29 Ⓐ Ⓑ Ⓒ Ⓓ	39 Ⓐ Ⓑ Ⓒ Ⓓ	49 Ⓐ Ⓑ Ⓒ Ⓓ
10 Ⓐ Ⓑ Ⓒ Ⓓ Ⓔ	20 Ⓐ Ⓑ Ⓒ Ⓓ Ⓔ	30 Ⓐ Ⓑ Ⓒ Ⓓ	40 Ⓐ Ⓑ Ⓒ Ⓓ	50 Ⓐ Ⓑ Ⓒ Ⓓ
				51 Ⓐ Ⓑ Ⓒ Ⓓ
				52 Ⓐ Ⓑ Ⓒ Ⓓ
				53 Ⓐ Ⓑ Ⓒ Ⓓ
				54 Ⓐ Ⓑ Ⓒ Ⓓ
				55 Ⓐ Ⓑ Ⓒ Ⓓ

Clerical Abilities

Sequencing	Comparison		Spelling	Mathematics
1. B	21. C	36. B	51. B	71. A
2. D	22. A	37. C	52. A	72. E
3. A	23. B	38. D	53. B	73. C
4. D	24. E	39. D	54. B	74. B
5. B	25. D	40. E	55. C	75. D
6. A	26. C	41. E	56. A	76. A
7. C	27. C	42. B	57. D	77. D
8. E	28. A	43. C	58. C	78. A
9. B	29. B	44. E	59. C	79. B
10. E	30. C	45. A	60. A	80. E
11. A	31. D	46. D	61. B	81. A
12. E	32. E	47. B	62. C	82. D
13. C	33. C	48. A	63. B	83. A
14. C	34. A	49. C	64. D	84. D
15. B	35. E	50. E	65. D	85. C
16. A			66. A	
17. A			67. C	
18. A			68. C	
19. D			69. D	
20. D			70. A	

Verbal Abilities

Following Written Instructions		Grammar, Usage & Punctuation		Vocab & Reading
1. C	11. A	21. A	31. B	41. C
2. C	12. E	22. C	32. D	42. D
3. E	13. B	23. B	33. D	43. C
4. C	14. A	24. A	34. B	44. A
5. C	15. E	25. D	35. C	45. D
6. C	16. D	26. D	36. D	46. B
7. E	17. A	27. D	37. C	47. A
8. A	18. E	28. B	38. B	48. C
9. D	19. C	29. A	39. B	49. B
10. B	20. A	30. A	40. D	50. C
				51. A
				52. D
				53. D
				54. C
				55. A

End of Exam 710 Sample Test

About Exam Exam 916

Exam 916 is used to fill fulltime career custodial jobs (page 35). Custodians clean and maintain buildings and grounds. Postal policy states that this exam is restricted to preference eligible military veterans (page 345). If you're a preference eligible military veteran, read on. If not, you might as well skip this section and move on to other possible jobs and/or exams.

No revisions to exam 916 are expected in the foreseeable future. However, there is a long term plan to convert all Postal exams from paper to electronic over a period of years. So, even though the 916 is now a paper exam, it will eventually become a computerized test. Just to be safe, make sure to check Pathfinder Perks (page 19) for any updates if you plan to take exam 916.

Exam 916 consists of four sections as detailed below:

Vocabulary & Reading
This section tests your ability to read and understand written materials as in reading product label instructions and warnings, material safety data sheets (MSDS), equipment operating instructions, and cleaning route sheets.

Basic Safety
This section tests your knowledge of basic safety principles and practices such as proper lifting techniques, use of personal protective equipment, and awareness of electrical, chemical, and other health hazards in the area of cleaning and building maintenance.

General Cleaning
This section tests your knowledge of general cleaning and disinfecting materials, techniques, equipment, and tools commonly used by custodians.

Following Written Instructions
The Postal Service claims that this section tests your ability to understand instructions similar to those you might receive on the job. However, we cannot believe that any sane human being would ever give you instructions as strange, convoluted, and confusing as these questions. In order to answer a question correctly, you must accomplish three steps:

1. First you must create a preliminary answer based upon the wording of the question. The preliminary answer will be a letter and a number put together like this: T 5

2. Then, you must look up the preliminary answer on a table provided on the exam to find its correlating answer choice (A, B, C, D, or E).

3. Finally, you darken the proper answer choice (A, B, C, D, or E) on your answer sheet.

How to Prepare for Exam 916

Since I'm not a military veteran, I'm not qualified to take this exam, which means that I'm not qualified to write a study guide for it. As mentioned earlier, I refuse to publish a study guide for an exam until personally taking that exam numerous times so that I can guarantee absolute accuracy and realism. My information on exam 916 presented here is based upon extensive research and is quite accurate. But there's just no such thing as writing a study guide based exclusively upon research. If I haven't been there and done it, I can't write it.

Are there any study guides out there for the 916? Only a few, and I cannot personally vouch for any of them since I've never been able to take the test. However, based upon experience and research, I can share a few points with you about preparing for exam 916:

- I've heard from a number of sources that it may not be necessary – or even possible – to prepare for the 916 because it is simply a common sense test. After seeing some sample questions on the next several pages, you may be inclined to agree. To me, most sections of this exam don't appear very challenging unless the applicant has a problem understanding English. This language problem, however, could be a real issue for many because over the last several years a rapidly growing portion of exam applicants claim English as their second language.

- Another reason that there are so few study guides is that custodian jobs and the 916 exam are just not very popular. There are simply not that many people who (1) want this type job and (2) meet the military veteran qualification. The bottom line is that, if the exam is not popular, there will be limited demand for the study guide. And major publishers will not publish a book unless it is justified by a reasonable level of projected sales.

- Consequently, the few guides out there are only available from self-published authors and small publishing companies. They are not available from the larger publishing firms who dominate the book industry, whose books are more likely to be available via wholesalers, and whose books are therefore more likely to be found in stores and libraries. (By the way, I am most certainly not knocking self-published authors and small publishers. I am one of these little guys myself. The only difference is that my sales history has earned me a position in the book distribution system that most the other little guys cannot attain.)

- If you cannot find 916 guides at bookstores or libraries, where can you get one? The few guides that exist are usually only available on the web. Here's my suggestion ... Mix and match the below search terms to search for a guide online. When you find a guide, customer reviews can give you a good idea of what it has to offer.

| Postal Exam 916 | Custodian | USPS |
| Study Guide | Custodial | US Postal Service |

Turn to the next page for sample 916 test questions.

DIRECTIONS

This section consists of the two types of questions discussed below:

Vocabulary Questions

Each Vocabulary question is a sentence with a particular word highlighted. Under this sentence is a list of five words labeled A, B, C, D, and E. You are to choose which of the five listed words most nearly means the same as the highlighted word in the sentence. Answers are marked by darkening answer choices on an answer sheet.

Reading Questions

Each Reading Comprehension question is a paragraph followed by five sentences labeled A, B, C, D, and E. You are to choose which sentence best supports or summarizes the paragraph. Answers are marked by darkening answer choices on an answer sheet.

NOTE

The section of exam 916 is very similar to the Vocabulary and Reading Comprehension section of exam 710. The only real differences are that on exam 916 the reading selections and vocabulary words revolve around custodial topics and there are five answer choices rather than four. See the discussion on exam 710 (page 143) for details.

Turn to the next page for sample Reading & Vocabulary questions.

SAMPLE QUESTIONS

After applying, you will be sent a scheduling packet that provides several sample questions for each section of the test. Included in the scheduling packet are four sample Vocabulary & Reading questions very similar to those below. Mark your answers by darkening bubbles on the Sample Answer Sheet at the bottom of this page.

1. Due to possible <u>fumes</u>, use this product in a well ventilated area. <u>Fumes</u> most nearly means:
   A) Leaks
   B) Spills
   C) Gases
   D) Chemicals
   E) Poisons

2. The contents of this load are <u>hazardous</u> and require special handling. <u>Hazardous</u> most nearly means:
   A) Fragile
   B) Dangerous
   C) Worthless
   D) Valuable
   E) Sharp

3. Safety gloves are <u>mandatory</u> when handling caustic products. <u>Mandatory</u> most nearly means:
   A) Essential
   B) Discouraged
   C) Encouraged
   D) Unnecessary
   E) Optional

4. "Bleach is a strong oxidizer. Flush drains before and after using bleach. Do not use or mix bleach with other chemicals, cleaners, rust removers, acids, or ammonia containing products. Using or mixing bleach with such products may release hazardous gases. Prolonged contact with bleach may cause metals to pit or become discolored."

   <u>This quotation best supports the statement that:</u>
   A) Bleach should not be used indoors.
   B) Bleach should only be mixed with non-acidic solutions.
   C) Bleach should not be stored in metal containers.
   D) Bleach should be used with caution due to its caustic nature.
   E) Bleach should be mixed with other chemicals only in a well ventilated area.

SAMPLE ANSWER SHEET

1.	○ A	○ B	○ C	○ D	○ E
2.	○ A	○ B	○ C	○ D	○ E
3.	○ A	○ B	○ C	○ D	○ E
4.	○ A	○ B	○ C	○ D	○ E

The correct answers are 1-C, 2-B, 3-A, and 4-D.

End of Vocabulary & Reading

DIRECTIONS

In this section, each question asks about a particular safety issue. Under each question is a list of five answer choices labeled A, B, C, D, and E. You are to choose the most appropriate answer and mark your answer choice by darkening it on an answer sheet.

SAMPLE QUESTIONS

After applying, you will be sent a scheduling packet that provides several sample questions for each section of the test. Included in the scheduling packet are four sample Basic Safety questions very similar to those below. Mark your answers by darkening bubbles on the Sample Answer Sheet at the bottom of this page.

1. Which of the following addresses the hazards of servicing equipment while it is in operation?
   A) Lockout/tagout fact sheet
   B) National Electric Code (NEC)
   C) National Building Code (NBC)
   D) Better Business Bureau (BBB)
   E) Material Safety Data Sheet (MSDS)

2. Extension cords should not be placed where?
   A) Across areas where there is vehicle and personnel traffic.
   B) Above and over heavily traveled vehicle and personnel routes.
   C) Across non-metal supports.
   D) Across moving machinery.
   E) Both A and D

3. What is the cause of most accidents related to manual lifting or handling of materials?
   A) Using the wrong equipment
   B) Buddy lifting
   C) Wet, icy, or slippery floors
   D) Unsafe practices
   E) Not wearing steel-toed boots

4. OSHA states that a rope should be able to support at least how many times the intended load?
   A) 2
   B) 4
   C) 6
   D) 8
   E) 10

SAMPLE ANSWER SHEET

1.	○ A	○ B	○ C	○ D	○ E
2.	○ A	○ B	○ C	○ D	○ E
3.	○ A	○ B	○ C	○ D	○ E
4.	○ A	○ B	○ C	○ D	○ E

The correct answers are 1-A, 2-E, 3-D, and 4-C.

End of Basic Safety

DIRECTIONS

In this section, each question asks about a particular cleaning practice. Under each question is a list of five answer choices labeled A, B, C, D, and E. You are to choose the most appropriate answer and mark your answer choice by darkening it on an answer sheet.

SAMPLE QUESTIONS

After applying, you will be sent a scheduling packet that provides several sample questions for each section of the test. Included in the scheduling packet are four sample General Cleaning questions very similar to those below. Mark your answers by darkening bubbles on the Sample Answer Sheet at the bottom of this page.

1. Which of these is used to clean splattered residue off a finished surface such as a wall or a floor?
   A) Sponge
   B) Spatula
   C) Scraper
   D) Wire brush
   E) Drop cloth

2. Which of these uses a high efficiency particulate air filter to trap fine airborne particles while cleaning?
   A) Treated dust cloth
   B) Bowl brush
   C) Chamois cloth
   D) Feather duster
   E) HEPA vacuum

3. What is the primary function of bleach in cleaning?
   A) Freshen air
   B) Prevent fires
   C) Polish metals
   D) Stain fabrics
   E) Disinfect surfaces

4. Which of the following is a textile mounted on a handle used in cleaning?
   A) Push broom
   B) Sponge cloth
   C) Floor stripper
   D) Counter brush
   E) Mop

SAMPLE ANSWER SHEET

1. ○ A	○ B	○ C	○ D	○ E
2. ○ A	○ B	○ C	○ D	○ E
3. ○ A	○ B	○ C	○ D	○ E
4. ○ A	○ B	○ C	○ D	○ E

The correct answers are 1-B, 2-E, 3-E, and 4-E.

End of General Cleaning

DIRECTIONS

Each question in this section is a set of instructions that causes you create a letter-number combination. After creating a letter-number combination, you look it up on a Look-Up Table, which enables you to convert it into an answer choice. The answer choices are A, B, C, D, and E. You answer the questions by darkening your answer choices on an answer sheet.

I'm stepping away from my policy of only providing realistic instructions for a moment because the above directions are about as clear as mud. And it won't be much better at the real exam either. So, to help you understand, I'm going to explain a bit and give you a sample.

And by the way, this really is what the Following Written Instructions section is actually like. I'm not making this up. The questions are very similar to the below sample and to the questions on this sample test, and there is a Look-Up Table just like in the below sample and in the sample test.

As described earlier, to answer a question correctly you must accomplish three steps:

- First, you create a preliminary answer based upon the wording of the question. The preliminary answer will be a letter-number combination like this: T 5

- Then, you find the preliminary answer on a Look-Up Table provided on the exam to discover the answer choice (A, B, C, D, or E) that it correlates to.

- Finally, you darken the proper answer choice (A, B, C, D, or E) on your answer sheet.

That maybe helped a little, but not much. So let's look at a sample to clear things up.

LOOK-UP TABLE

	P	Q	R	S	T
1	A	B	C	D	E
2	B	C	D	E	A
3	C	D	E	A	B
4	D	E	A	B	C
5	E	A	B	C	D
6	A	B	C	D	E
7	B	C	D	E	A
8	C	D	E	A	B
9	D	E	A	B	C
10	E	A	B	C	D

Draw a line under each letter that appears only once below. Write the letter "R" and the number of lines you drew here: ___ ___

     S   T   R   Q   P   Q   T   P   T

Since "S" and "R" are the only letters that appear only once, we draw lines under the one "S" and the one "R". Then, as instructed, we write the letter "R" and the number of lines we drew (2 lines - 1 under the "S" and 1 under the "R") in the blanks like this: R 2. We have our letter-number combination ... R2. Next we go to the Look-Up Table to find our R2 letter-number combination. We look across the top of the table to find the letter "R", and then we follow the "R" column down to the "2" row. Answer choice "D" appears where the "R" column and the "2" row meet. This is our answer ... "D". So, for this question, we darken the answer "D" on our answer sheet. (I highlighted the "R" column and the "2" row so you could see exactly how to use the Look-Up Table.)

Really ... I'm not lying ... That's exactly what it's like. Remember when I questioned the sanity of the people who write these tests? Perhaps you're beginning to understand what I mean.

SAMPLE QUESTIONS

After applying, you will be sent a scheduling packet that provides several sample questions for each section of the test. Included in the scheduling packet are four sample Following Instructions questions very similar to those on the next page. Mark your answers by darkening bubbles on the Sample Answer Sheet at the bottom of the next page page.

Turn to the next page for sample Following Written Instructions questions.

Mark your answers by darkening bubbles on the Sample Answer Sheet at the bottom of this page.

SAMPLE QUESTIONS

LOOK-UP TABLE

	P	Q	R	S	T
1	A	B	C	D	E
2	B	C	D	E	A
3	C	D	E	A	B
4	D	E	A	B	C
5	E	A	B	C	D
6	A	B	C	D	E
7	B	C	D	E	A
8	C	D	E	A	B
9	D	E	A	B	C
10	E	A	B	C	D

1. There is one combination that appears twice in the below list. Write the combination that appears twice here: ____ ____

   P8   T6   Q9   S1   S4   R3   P8   Q2   T5   Q7

2. Look at the states listed below. Circle the name of the state with the most letters. Write the last letter and the number of letters in the name of the state your circled here: ____ ____

   Texas   Illinois   Kansas

3. Look at the letters listed below. Circle the sixth letter in the list. Write the letter you circled and the number 6 here: ____ ____

   LOOKUPTABLELOOKUPTABLELOOKUPTABLE

4. Circle the third letter and the third number in the below list. Write the letter you circled and the number you circled here: ____ ____

   2   7   S   9   T   R   5   P   4   Q   S   4

SAMPLE ANSWER SHEET

1.	○ A	○ B	○ C	○ D	○ E
2.	○ A	○ B	○ C	○ D	○ E
3.	○ A	○ B	○ C	○ D	○ E
4.	○ A	○ B	○ C	○ D	○ E

The correct answers are 1-C, 2-A, 3-A, and 4-A.

End of Following Written Instructions

196

About Exam 943/944

This is another case of exams that are so closely linked that we need to discuss them together. Exams 943 and 944 are technical exams that deal exclusively with automotive maintenance and repair. These tests consist of multiple choice questions with answer choices of A, B, C, or D.

Exam 943 is used to hire career Automotive Mechanics (page 33) who are responsible for more routine types of maintenance and repair.

Exam 944 is used to hire career Automotive Technicians (page 33) who are responsible for more complex types of maintenance and repair.

As might be assumed from the above descriptions, the questions on exam 944 are more complex and challenging than those on exam 943.

Here's the odd part of this situation, to get an Auto Mechanic job, you take one exam - the 943. To get an Auto Technician job, you take two exams - both the 943 and the 944 - together. As a matter of fact, when referring to the Auto Technician test, you will often see the exam titles merged together like this: 943/944, 943/44, 9434, etc.

Exams 943 and 944 were recently converted from paper to electronic computerized tests. For this reason you may occasionally see them referred to as the 943E and 944E, but for the most part they are still simply called the 943 and 944. No additional revisions are expected in the foreseeable future, but just to be safe, make sure to check Pathfinder Perks (page 19) for any updates if you plan to take exam 943/944.

How to Prepare for Exam 943/944

How do you prepare for exams 943 and 944? To my knowledge, there are no guides specifically published for these exams, so I cannot suggest any particular form of test preparation. There are many auto repair books in bookstores and libraries, and there are even books to prepare for auto service and repair certification tests. You might look into some of these books if you feel the need, but none of them are directly related to Postal exams 943 and 944.

On the subject test preparation, while researching exams 943 and 944, I interviewed a number of people who had taken these tests. The interview results almost exactly echoed the outcome of my research into the exams for jobs like Electronic Technician, Mail Processing Equipment Mechanic, etc. In every case, I was told that years of experience and training are required to pass these tests and that, if you do not have such a knowledgeable background, you probably cannot make up for it by trying to study or prepare before the exam. I was told in addition that, since even professional mechanics find these tests to be challenging, casual or handyman type mechanics may have real trouble with them.

Applicants for exam 943 are sent a few sample questions to familiarize them with the format of the test. Applicants for exam 944 receive the same 943 sample questions plus a few sample questions from the 944. If you apply, these few sample questions will likely be the only advance information you will find for exams 943 and 944.

About Exam 955/955E & How to Prepare

Electronic test 955/955E was recently launched to replace old paper exams 931, 932, and 933. (The E stands for electronic.) You may see it called the 955 or 955E, but either way it's the same test. Exam 955 is used to fill maintenance jobs such as Building Equipment Mechanic (page 30), Maintenance Mechanic (page 30), Electronic Technician (page 31) Mail Processing Equipment Mechanic (page 32), etc. Stay tuned to Pathfinder Perks (page 19) for any updates.

Note: As of the publish date of this book, the Postal Service website had not yet been updated to reflect this change. References to old exams 931, 932, and 933 were still included on the site. If this is still true when you visit their site, do not be alarmed. If you apply for any of the jobs formerly filled from these old exams, you will find that my information on exam 955 is 100% accurate.

It was logical to use a single exam to replace the three prior tests because the old tests were very similar and were used to fill similar jobs. As a matter of fact, the content of the three old exams was 90% identical. **Reviewing info on retired exams 931, 932, and 933 (page 227) would be beneficial since they cover technical fields considered important by the Postal Service.**

One reason for replacing the old tests is that they had such unbelievably high failure rates. At least 95% of all applicants typically failed exams 931, 932, and 933. With such high failure rates, they found it almost impossible to fill their maintenance jobs. Compounding this problem, as Postal operations become more automated, there is an ever increasing demand for technical maintenance employees. In fact, maintenance is expected to be one of the highest growth Postal employment fields within the foreseeable future. Finding it impossible to satisfy employment demands due to the high failure rates, they had to do something. That's why they replaced the old exams.

Do you have the background necessary to succeed on this test? Nobody can answer that but you. This decision should be based upon your knowledge and experience in the technical fields listed as we discuss exam content in a few pages. To succeed, you must have extensive education, training, and/or experience in the fields covered on this test. People without such background really have no business applying for exam 955. One reason for the high failure rates on the old tests was that many people who took the exams were simply not qualified and never should have applied.

So, how do you prepare for exam 955? Since this exam is so new, as of the publish date of this book, there were no study guides available for it. There may eventually be guides available for this test, but publishing a study guide for exam 955 presents unique challenges as detailed below.

I have thoroughly researched exam 955 and interviewed experts in most of the technical fields it covers. **The experts unanimously agree that it would be difficult, if not impossible, to prepare for exam 955.** The problem is that the exam covers 21 technical fields broken down into over 100 topics. A guide that adequately covers that many technical topics would be thousands of pages long, and it's simply not possible to publish a book of that monstrous size. And, it's not possible for an applicant to bone up on that many different topics. If an applicant already has a strong background in most of these areas and only needs to brush up on a few topics, that may be possible. But if the applicant does not already have a background in most or all these areas … if the applicant needs to bone up on all of these different topics … that's virtually impossible.

Exam 955 is broken down into two sessions. Session 1 is an online Personal Characteristics & Experience Inventory test that you take on your own. Session two is the technical portion of the exam that you take via computer as well, but it is taken at a supervised testing site. Session two is broken down into two sections – Multicraft and Spatial Relations. We will look at each session and/or section individually over the next several pages.

Session 1 is a self-administered Personal Characteristics & Experience Inventory test. You take this session on your own without supervision. Most people take this online test at home using their own computer, but you can take it anywhere using whatever computer is convenient for you (at a library, borrow a friend's computer, etc.). This is a psychological test that is used to identify the best potential employees. Basically, this part of the exam builds a profile of your personality. In this session, you are given 75 minutes to answer 120 multiple-choice questions. (Note: Session 1 of exam 955 is almost identical to Session 1 of exam 473E discussed on page 51. The only difference is that, for unknown reasons, Session 1 of exam 473E has 30 more questions and allows you 15 more minutes than Session 1 of exam 955.)

It is not possible to prepare for this Personal Characteristics & Experience Inventory test. The only safe way to take this test is to answer honestly and sincerely. Attempting to manipulate – to answer is a fashion that you think they want to hear – is a sure route to failure. As part of my research, I interviewed psychologists and representatives from the company that created this part of the exam for the Postal Service. The most important thing I learned is that there are built-in traps that expose any attempt at manipulation. The computers that score the exam look for certain types of inconsistent replies that indicate manipulation. When evidence of manipulation is indicated, your score plummets. If you attempt to manipulate, you _will_ get caught, and your score _will_ suffer. You may think that you can outsmart them, but you simply cannot. Your best and only course is to answer honestly and sincerely.

Session 2 is an online electronic test as well, but it taken at a testing site in a strictly supervised environment. This testing site is a facility with a quantity of computers where a number of people can take computerized tests simultaneously. **Session 2 consists of two sections as follows:**

The **Multicraft section** consists of 60 multiple choice questions to be answered in 60 minutes. This is the true technical part of the test. The Postal Service says that this section tests your mechanical and electrical skills, but in reality it covers many more technical topics than just those two fields.

The **Spatial Relations section** is broken down into two segments – Matching Parts & Figures and Spatial Visualization. As I write these words, there is confusion about the timing for and number of questions in the Spatial Relations section. The Postal Service publishes two conflicting stories. Plus, exam 955 had only been offered a few times as of the publish date of this book, but people who had taken the test reported another entirely different story as detailed below:

Questions	Time	Source
68	40 minutes	Postal Service
65	60 minutes	Postal Service
65	40 minutes	Test Takers

So, exam 955 is supposed to be less challenging than the old tests it replaced, but is it? Yes and no. People who had taken some of the few 955 tests offered as of the publish date of this book reported that (1) the technical section is still quite challenging – about the same as before, (2) the Spatial Relations section is not so bad, so it helps bring the scores up, (3) the net result is that some people who failed the old tests are passing the 955 exam with pretty good scores. If you have the proper background and a grasp of spatial relations, hopefully you will have similar success.

Beginning on the next page is a complete sample test for session 1 of exam 955. Following this sample test we will discuss the content of session 2, the technical portion of exam 955.

DIRECTIONS

The Personal Characteristics & Experience Inventory (PCEI) is the first session that you take on your own without supervision. The PCEI is both simple and confusing at the same time. It is simple in that you read a question/statement and then respond by simply stating how it applies to you. It is confusing in that both the questions and the answers can seem ambiguous. And you will notice that they ask about the same topic multiple times. They ask in different ways each time, but the topic (frustration, stress, temper, organization, tolerance, motivation, safety, etc.) is the same.

In this session, you have 75 minutes to answer 120 questions. Unlike all other exams/sections, the time allowed for the PCEI is generous. This is a rare Postal exam situation where speed is not an issue. Most people finish before the 75 minutes run out. However, do set some type of a timer for 75 minutes to make sure that you don't exceed the specified allotment of time.

All PCEI questions are multiple choice. The number and type of answer choices vary as follows:

In the first portion consisting of 70 questions, there are two different series of answer choices ...
- Strongly Agree, Agree, Disagree, and Strongly Disagree
- Very Often, Often, Sometimes, and Rarely or Never

For the final portion, the questions can have from four to nine answer choices, and the answer choices are worded differently for each question.

Regardless of how many answer choices are presented or how the answer choices are worded, you are only supposed to mark one answer choice per question. Even if two or more choices seem appropriate, you must choose only one.

The format of this paper sample test varies from the real electronic exam in only two significant ways. On the real test, there is only one PCEI question per page/screen. If I followed that format here, this one section of the test alone would be 120 pages long. To prevent this book from being a zillion pages long, I included as many PCEI sample questions as possible on each page.

The second difference has to do with answer choices. The answer choices appear under each question just like on the actual exam. But since this is a paper test, you must choose answers by darkening them with a pencil rather than clicking them with a mouse. On every section of the real electronic exam except this one, you choose an answer by clicking on a typical small round radio button. On the PCEI section only, there are large square buttons rather than small round ones. However, to save space/pages on this paper sample test as described in the above paragraph, I used small round radio buttons instead of the large square ones.

SCORING

There are no right or wrong answers on this section. Whatever answer choice best describes you is the right answer for you. They somehow convert your answers into a numerical score, but they will not share any details about how this is accomplished. Since there are no official right or wrong answers and since there is no formula we can give you for scoring the PCEI, we have not included an answer key for this section. Since you cannot score yourself in this case, it will not be possible for you to interpret how your performance on this section of the sample test might contribute to your final exam score. I have given you this PCEI sample test simply for you experience it.

Turn the page and begin when you are prepared to time yourself for exactly 75 minutes.

1) After finishing one task, you automatically move on to other duties without having to be told to do so.
   - A) Strongly Agree
   - B) Agree
   - C) Disagree
   - D) Strongly Disagree

2) You are valued as an employee for not having to be continually managed.
   - A) Strongly Agree
   - B) Agree
   - C) Disagree
   - D) Strongly Disagree

3) You are offended if a customer is not satisfied with the service you provide.
   - A) Strongly Agree
   - B) Agree
   - C) Disagree
   - D) Strongly Disagree

4) You can easily and comfortably associate with almost everyone.
   - A) Strongly Agree
   - B) Agree
   - C) Disagree
   - D) Strongly Disagree

5) You like to learn new concepts that can be helpful personally or professionally.
   - A) Strongly Agree
   - B) Agree
   - C) Disagree
   - D) Strongly Disagree

6) Even if you don't enjoy a particular duty, you complete it without having to be prompted.
   - A) Strongly Agree
   - B) Agree
   - C) Disagree
   - D) Strongly Disagree

7) Multitasking is one of your strongest skills.
   - A) Strongly Agree
   - B) Agree
   - C) Disagree
   - D) Strongly Disagree

8) You strongly believe in the adage "A job worth doing is a job worth doing well".
   - A) Strongly Agree
   - B) Agree
   - C) Disagree
   - D) Strongly Disagree

203

Continued on next page …

9) You believe that occasionally being a little late for work is okay.
- A) Strongly Agree
- B) Agree
- C) Disagree
- D) Strongly Disagree

10) You prefer a job that offers challenges more than a job that is routine.
- A) Strongly Agree
- B) Agree
- C) Disagree
- D) Strongly Disagree

11) You are willing to bypass safety procedures sometimes to get a job finished faster.
- A) Strongly Agree
- B) Agree
- C) Disagree
- D) Strongly Disagree

12) You are more productive and efficient that most of the people you work with.
- A) Strongly Agree
- B) Agree
- C) Disagree
- D) Strongly Disagree

13) You are willing to learn exactly what you need to know to do your job but no more.
- A) Strongly Agree
- B) Agree
- C) Disagree
- D) Strongly Disagree

14) It is difficult for you to focus on one thing for an extended amount of time.
- A) Strongly Agree
- B) Agree
- C) Disagree
- D) Strongly Disagree

15) You're always willing to start a new task but sometimes have trouble completing it.
- A) Strongly Agree
- B) Agree
- C) Disagree
- D) Strongly Disagree

16) People enjoy being with you.
- A) Strongly Agree
- B) Agree
- C) Disagree
- D) Strongly Disagree

Continued on next page …

17) When you are frustrated it affects your relationships and your performance on the job.
   - ○ A) Strongly Agree
   - ○ B) Agree
   - ○ C) Disagree
   - ○ D) Strongly Disagree

18) You can deal with frustration on the job better than most of your co-workers.
   - ○ A) Strongly Agree
   - ○ B) Agree
   - ○ C) Disagree
   - ○ D) Strongly Disagree

19) You do not need to own up to mistakes if nobody else catches them and they do not affect anyone.
   - ○ A) Strongly Agree
   - ○ B) Agree
   - ○ C) Disagree
   - ○ D) Strongly Disagree

20) Safety is a priority in everything you do.
   - ○ A) Strongly Agree
   - ○ B) Agree
   - ○ C) Disagree
   - ○ D) Strongly Disagree

21) If a co-worker is very busy, pointing out a safety concern to him or her may be counterproductive.
   - ○ A) Strongly Agree
   - ○ B) Agree
   - ○ C) Disagree
   - ○ D) Strongly Disagree

22) If a customer treats you unfairly, you should not be expected to treat the customer any better.
   - ○ A) Strongly Agree
   - ○ B) Agree
   - ○ C) Disagree
   - ○ D) Strongly Disagree

23) You arrive at work early more often than late.
   - ○ A) Strongly Agree
   - ○ B) Agree
   - ○ C) Disagree
   - ○ D) Strongly Disagree

24) Organization is essential for success.
   - ○ A) Strongly Agree
   - ○ B) Agree
   - ○ C) Disagree
   - ○ D) Strongly Disagree

Continued on next page …

25) You always keep a promise.
○ A) Strongly Agree
○ B) Agree
○ C) Disagree
○ D) Strongly Disagree

26) It is not necessary to point out a problem at work if nobody else is aware of it.
○ A) Strongly Agree
○ B) Agree
○ C) Disagree
○ D) Strongly Disagree

27) Deadlines are usually flexible.
○ A) Strongly Agree
○ B) Agree
○ C) Disagree
○ D) Strongly Disagree

28) You have a variety of friends from different ethnic backgrounds.
○ A) Strongly Agree
○ B) Agree
○ C) Disagree
○ D) Strongly Disagree

29) You like working with customers on a daily basis.
○ A) Strongly Agree
○ B) Agree
○ C) Disagree
○ D) Strongly Disagree

30) When assigned a job, you begin promptly and continue until it is complete.
○ A) Strongly Agree
○ B) Agree
○ C) Disagree
○ D) Strongly Disagree

31) Some people are difficult for anyone to get along with.
○ A) Strongly Agree
○ B) Agree
○ C) Disagree
○ D) Strongly Disagree

32) You find that assisting people on the job is personally rewarding.
○ A) Strongly Agree
○ B) Agree
○ C) Disagree
○ D) Strongly Disagree

Continued on next page …

33) You enjoy expanding your horizons.
- ○ A) Strongly Agree
- ○ B) Agree
- ○ C) Disagree
- ○ D) Strongly Disagree

34) You are known for accomplishing more in less time than your fellow employees.
- ○ A) Strongly Agree
- ○ B) Agree
- ○ C) Disagree
- ○ D) Strongly Disagree

35) Friends know that they can depend on you when they need help.
- ○ A) Strongly Agree
- ○ B) Agree
- ○ C) Disagree
- ○ D) Strongly Disagree

36) You welcome suggestions that may help you personally or professionally.
- ○ A) Very Often
- ○ B) Often
- ○ C) Sometimes
- ○ D) Rarely or Never

37) You complete all assignments even if some do not seem very important to you.
- ○ A) Very Often
- ○ B) Often
- ○ C) Sometimes
- ○ D) Rarely or Never

38) Stress can distract your focus.
- ○ A) Very Often
- ○ B) Often
- ○ C) Sometimes
- ○ D) Rarely or Never

39) You adhere to the safety practice of lifting with your legs, not your back.
- ○ A) Very Often
- ○ B) Often
- ○ C) Sometimes
- ○ D) Rarely or Never

40) Even in a tense situation when everyone else is irritated, you control your temper.
- ○ A) Very Often
- ○ B) Often
- ○ C) Sometimes
- ○ D) Rarely or Never

Continued on next page …

continued

41) Completing tasks seems to take you more time than it should.
- ○ A) Very Often
- ○ B) Often
- ○ C) Sometimes
- ○ D) Rarely or Never

42) You make a great first impression.
- ○ A) Very Often
- ○ B) Often
- ○ C) Sometimes
- ○ D) Rarely or Never

43) You are willing to listen to someone's opinion even if you don't agree.
- ○ A) Very Often
- ○ B) Often
- ○ C) Sometimes
- ○ D) Rarely or Never

44) You immediately offer to help when you see a fellow employee in need of assistance.
- ○ A) Very Often
- ○ B) Often
- ○ C) Sometimes
- ○ D) Rarely or Never

45) You first create a prioritized plan when beginning an assignment.
- ○ A) Very Often
- ○ B) Often
- ○ C) Sometimes
- ○ D) Rarely or Never

46) You share new information with fellow employees if it will improve their job performance.
- ○ A) Very Often
- ○ B) Often
- ○ C) Sometimes
- ○ D) Rarely or Never

47) People look to you for resolving tense situations.
- ○ A) Very Often
- ○ B) Often
- ○ C) Sometimes
- ○ D) Rarely or Never

48) You employ safety precautions when doing odd jobs at home.
- ○ A) Very Often
- ○ B) Often
- ○ C) Sometimes
- ○ D) Rarely or Never

Continued on next page ...

49) You get aggravated by people reminding you of safety precautions.
- ○ A) Very Often
- ○ B) Often
- ○ C) Sometimes
- ○ D) Rarely or Never

50) You maintain thorough records on the job.
- ○ A) Very Often
- ○ B) Often
- ○ C) Sometimes
- ○ D) Rarely or Never

51) You respond respectfully regardless of how another person treats you.
- ○ A) Very Often
- ○ B) Often
- ○ C) Sometimes
- ○ D) Rarely or Never

52) Fellow employees say that you are calm even in stressful situations.
- ○ A) Very Often
- ○ B) Often
- ○ C) Sometimes
- ○ D) Rarely or Never

53) When you discover a better system or practice on the job, you tell fellow employees about it.
- ○ A) Very Often
- ○ B) Often
- ○ C) Sometimes
- ○ D) Rarely or Never

54) You react quickly without always considering the results of your actions.
- ○ A) Very Often
- ○ B) Often
- ○ C) Sometimes
- ○ D) Rarely or Never

55) You practice the adage: "Do unto others as you would have them do unto you".
- ○ A) Very Often
- ○ B) Often
- ○ C) Sometimes
- ○ D) Rarely or Never

56) You do not readily accept suggestions for improvement without proof the suggestions are valid.
- ○ A) Very Often
- ○ B) Often
- ○ C) Sometimes
- ○ D) Rarely or Never

Continued on next page ...

57) Your fellow employees can tell very easily when you are in a bad mood.
   ○ A)   Very Often
   ○ B)   Often
   ○ C)   Sometimes
   ○ D)   Rarely or Never

58) You must be reminded of appointments and schedules.
   ○ A)   Very Often
   ○ B)   Often
   ○ C)   Sometimes
   ○ D)   Rarely or Never

59) You treat people respectfully even when they treat you disrespectfully.
   ○ A)   Very Often
   ○ B)   Often
   ○ C)   Sometimes
   ○ D)   Rarely or Never

60) People get angry at you because you refuse to consider their suggestions.
   ○ A)   Very Often
   ○ B)   Often
   ○ C)   Sometimes
   ○ D)   Rarely or Never

61) You maintain an optimistic outlook in discouraging circumstances.
   ○ A)   Very Often
   ○ B)   Often
   ○ C)   Sometimes
   ○ D)   Rarely or Never

62) You are more careful when driving in inclement weather than most other people.
   ○ A)   Very Often
   ○ B)   Often
   ○ C)   Sometimes
   ○ D)   Rarely or Never

63) You overcome any obstructions to assure that an assignment is completed.
   ○ A)   Very Often
   ○ B)   Often
   ○ C)   Sometimes
   ○ D)   Rarely or Never

64) You offer to assist fellow employees after completing your own tasks.
   ○ A)   Very Often
   ○ B)   Often
   ○ C)   Sometimes
   ○ D)   Rarely or Never

                                    Continued on next page ...

continued

65) You do what is expected of you plus a little more.
- ○ A) Very Often
- ○ B) Often
- ○ C) Sometimes
- ○ D) Rarely or Never

66) You complete assignments on schedule.
- ○ A) Very Often
- ○ B) Often
- ○ C) Sometimes
- ○ D) Rarely or Never

67) You do not take a risk without completely understanding the possible results.
- ○ A) Very Often
- ○ B) Often
- ○ C) Sometimes
- ○ D) Rarely or Never

68) When working with a team, you encourage input from all teammates.
- ○ A) Very Often
- ○ B) Often
- ○ C) Sometimes
- ○ D) Rarely or Never

69) You give people your respect even if they have not earned it.
- ○ A) Very Often
- ○ B) Often
- ○ C) Sometimes
- ○ D) Rarely or Never

70) You get more done on the job than others.
- ○ A) Very Often
- ○ B) Often
- ○ C) Sometimes
- ○ D) Rarely or Never

71) When there is a problem on the job, who or what is usually at fault?
- ○ A) Management
- ○ B) Equipment
- ○ C) Other employees
- ○ D) Insufficient scheduling
- ○ E) Something you did or did not do
- ○ F) Something else
- ○ G) I don't know.

Continued on next page ...

72) How do you handle stressful circumstances on the job?
- ○ A) My performance is better under stressful circumstances.
- ○ B) Stressful circumstances don't affect me one way or the other.
- ○ C) I don't enjoy stressful circumstances, but I can endure it.
- ○ D) I do not handle stressful circumstances very well.
- ○ E) I don't know.

73) What motivates you the most at this point in your life?
- ○ A) Status and prestige
- ○ B) Wages, benefits, and job security
- ○ C) Generating new concepts and ideas
- ○ D) Personal freedom
- ○ E) Helping those in need
- ○ F) Something else
- ○ G) I don't know.

74) How frequently have you voluntarily stayed late after work or school to finish a special project?
- ○ A) Never
- ○ B) Less than five times
- ○ C) Five to ten times
- ○ D) More than ten times
- ○ E) I don't know.

75) How frequently do you establish personal goals or objectives that are virtually unachievable?
- ○ A) All the time
- ○ B) Frequently
- ○ C) Occasionally
- ○ D) Not very often
- ○ E) Not at all
- ○ F) I don't know.

76) What rating were you given in your latest performance review?
- ○ A) Excellent
- ○ B) Superior
- ○ C) Satisfactory
- ○ D) Unsatisfactory
- ○ E) I've never had a performance review.
- ○ F) I don't know.

77) How would you feel about having to work several nights every week?
- ○ A) I prefer working at night.
- ○ B) I would do it but would not like it.
- ○ C) I would refuse to work at night.
- ○ D) I don't know.

Continued on next page …

continued

78) If you were in an assembly of 100 diverse people, how would others rank your talent for getting along?
- A) #1
- B) In the top 10
- C) In the top 25
- D) In the top 50
- E) I'm not interested in getting along with other types of people.
- F) I don't know.

79) Of the below factors, which would make your job the most unpleasant or unacceptable?
- A) Not being given a specific job description
- B) Not having the freedom to call my own shots
- C) Having to perform repetitive tasks over and over
- D) Having to frequently explain why I did something
- E) All of these factors would make my job difficult.
- F) None of the factors would bother me.
- G) I don't know.

80) Which of these have you been responsible for?
- A) Locking and securing a facility at the end of the day
- B) Balancing the books, accounts, etc.
- C) Managing cash, receipts, etc.
- D) Two of the above
- E) All of the above
- F) None of the above
- G) I don't know.

81) Have you met with more or less success than other people with similar education?
- A) Much less success
- B) Less success
- C) About the same success
- D) More success
- E) Much more success
- F) I don't know.

82) Which of the below management circumstances bothers you the most?
- A) Not having the freedom to do the work my way
- B) Being told what to do all the time
- C) Having a manager who is willing to consider my suggestions
- D) None of the above circumstances bother me.
- E) I don't know.

83) How are you at learning new procedures?
- A) Much better and quicker than my co-workers
- B) A little better and quicker than my co-workers
- C) About the same as everybody else
- D) A little slower than my co-workers
- E) I don't know.

Continued on next page ...

84) How would you handle it if a fellow employee's personal habits really bothered you?
- ○ A) Try to ignore it and hope that it stops
- ○ B) Drop hints about the problem
- ○ C) Confront him or her and demand that it stop
- ○ D) Submit a complaint to management
- ○ E) Try something else
- ○ F) I don't know.

85) How do you prefer to schedule tasks at work?
- ○ A) Concentrate on one thing at a time
- ○ B) At the most, handle two or three things at the same time
- ○ C) Multitask several assignments simultaneously
- ○ D) I don't know.

86) If you resigned from your most recent job, how much notice did you give?
- ○ A) None
- ○ B) One week or less
- ○ C) More than one week
- ○ D) Does not apply

87) If you have changed jobs in the past, what was your greatest motivation for the change?
- ○ A) More challenging work
- ○ B) Better co-workers
- ○ C) Better wages
- ○ D) Better use of your skills, education, etc.
- ○ E) None of the above
- ○ F) I've never had a job or never changed jobs.

88) How did you get along with your teachers in high school?
- ○ A) Much better than my classmates
- ○ B) A little better than my classmates
- ○ C) About the same as my classmates
- ○ D) Not as good as my classmates
- ○ E) I did not get along with my teachers at all.
- ○ F) Does not apply

89) At this point in your life, which of the below factors is most important when seeking a new job?
- ○ A) Better wages
- ○ B) Greater status
- ○ C) Relocation
- ○ D) Less stress
- ○ E) Better hours
- ○ F) More challenging work
- ○ G) None of the above

90) Which of the below items best describes your management experience?
- ○ A) I have been self-managed.
- ○ B) I have managed one other employee.
- ○ C) I have managed two or more other employees.
- ○ D) None of the above

Continued on next page …

91) How much experience do you have working in a manufacturing environment?
   - ○ A) More than ten years
   - ○ B) Five to ten years
   - ○ C) One to five years
   - ○ D) Less than one year
   - ○ E) I have no manufacturing experience.

92) Which of the below items would be easiest for you?
   - ○ A) Trying to assist a someone who has a limited grasp of your native language
   - ○ B) Prompting a fellow employee to be more productive
   - ○ C) Pacifying an irritated customer
   - ○ D) A public speaking engagement for a large group
   - ○ E) Convincing a manager to consider your suggestions
   - ○ F) All of these items would be easy for me.
   - ○ G) None of these items would be easy for me.
   - ○ H) I don't know.

93) Which of the below situations bothers you most at work?
   - ○ A) Your suggestion is misunderstood
   - ○ B) Your suggestion is ignored
   - ○ C) A fellow employee criticizes your work
   - ○ D) A manager tells you to complete a job left unfinished by another employee
   - ○ E) All of these situations bother me.
   - ○ F) None of these situations bother me.
   - ○ G) I don't know.

94) Have you ever wanted to quit a job because of a management problem?
   - ○ A) No
   - ○ B) Yes, one time
   - ○ C) Yes, several times
   - ○ D) Yes, quite a number of times
   - ○ E) I don't remember.

95) Does it bother you to work under many strict rules and regulations?
   - ○ A) Yes, quite a lot
   - ○ B) Yes, somewhat
   - ○ C) No, not much
   - ○ D) No, not at all

96) How would your latest manager rate your dependability?
   - ○ A) Better than anyone else
   - ○ B) Better than most
   - ○ C) The same as most
   - ○ D) Less than most
   - ○ E) Not dependable at all
   - ○ F) I don't know.

97) Compared to others, how frequently are you asked to take on a special project?
- A) Much more frequently than others
- B) More frequently than others
- C) The same as others
- D) Less frequently than others
- E) Never
- F) I don't know.

98) How long does it take to calm your temper enough to work normally when you become angry?
- A) I never lose my temper.
- B) A few minutes
- C) A few hours
- D) One day
- E) More than one day
- F) I don't know.

99) How do you handle fellow employees that are having family or personal problems?
- A) Tell them to leave their problems at home and leave you alone
- B) Offer your help if they would like it
- C) Be compassionate and encouraging
- D) Suggest how they could take care of their problems
- E) Force them to discuss it with you
- F) Ignore them
- G) None of the above

100) In which of the below school functions did you excel?
- A) Class participation
- B) Team projects
- C) Papers or reports
- D) Test taking
- E) None of the above

101) How would you describe your ability to function as a member of a team?
- A) Not as good as most
- B) About the same as most
- C) Better than most
- D) I don't know.

102) As a team leader, how are you at convincing others to follow your instructions?
- A) Not as good as most
- B) About the same as most
- C) Better than most
- D) I've never been a team leader.
- E) I don't know.

Continued on next page …

continued

103) In what area do you really stand out?
- ○ A) Helping people
- ○ B) Keeping records
- ○ C) Prioritizing
- ○ D) Setting goals
- ○ E) None of the above

104) How much of a risk taker are you?
- ○ A) I take risks frequently.
- ○ B) I occasionally take small risks.
- ○ C) I never take risks.
- ○ D) None of the above
- ○ E) I don't know.

105) How much experience do you have working at a facility that runs 24 hours a day?
- ○ A) None
- ○ B) Less than 1 month
- ○ C) 1 to 12 months
- ○ D) 1 to 5 years
- ○ E) Over 5 years

106) Which type duty do you enjoy more?
- ○ A) Manual labor
- ○ B) Customer service
- ○ C) Record keeping
- ○ D) None of the above

107) How quickly do you finish assignments?
- ○ A) Slower than most
- ○ B) About the same as most
- ○ C) Faster than most
- ○ D) I don't know.

108) Which of these job situations bothers you the most?
- ○ A) Being asked to begin additional assignments before current ones are completed
- ○ B) Having to revise a project repeatedly before it is approved
- ○ C) Helping disrespectful or rude people
- ○ D) Being overwhelmed with more assignments than one person should be expected to handle
- ○ E) None of the above
- ○ F) I don't know.

109) How frequently would your high school teachers say you participated in class discussions?
- ○ A) More than most
- ○ B) About the same as most
- ○ C) Less than most
- ○ D) Never
- ○ E) I don't know.

                                Continued on next page ...

110) While in high school, how frequently were you in fights or physical confrontations?
- A) Daily
- B) Weekly
- C) Monthly
- D) Once or twice
- E) Never

111) What is your opinion of working nights?
- A) I enjoy working nights.
- B) I will work nights if required.
- C) I avoid working nights.
- D) I refuse to work nights.
- E) I don't know.

112) Which word best describes you?
- A) Motivated
- B) Tolerant
- C) Reliable
- D) Intelligent
- E) Pleasant
- F) None of the above
- G) I don't know.

113) As an employee, what level of management do you require?
- A) More than most
- B) About the same as most
- C) Less than most
- D) Almost none

114) How do you feel when being introduced to a stranger?
- A) Relaxed
- B) Okay
- C) Nervous
- D) I don't know.

115) How much input should employees have in supervisory decisions?
- A) None
- B) Employee suggestions should be considered.
- C) Employees should play a key role in the decision making process.
- D) I don't know.

116) What type goals are easier for you to achieve?
- A) Organizational goals
- B) Team goals
- C) Personal goals
- D) None of the above

117) Which duty as a team member is easier for you?
- ○ A) Prioritizing
- ○ B) Record keeping
- ○ C) Mediating
- ○ D) Communicating
- ○ E) None of the above

118) Which of these employment factors means the most to you?
- ○ A) Wages
- ○ B) Job security
- ○ C) Status
- ○ D) Advancement

119) Which employment factor(s) would be the worst for you personally?
- ○ A) Low wages
- ○ B) Lack of communication
- ○ C) Inferior working conditions
- ○ D) Disrespectful supervisor
- ○ E) Vague job description
- ○ F) All the above

120) What type management do you prefer?
- ○ A) General and occasional
- ○ B) Consistent and sensible
- ○ C) Constant and detailed
- ○ D) None of the above

End of Personal Characteristics & Experience Inventory

As explained earlier, Session 2 of exam 955 is taken on a computer at a supervised testing site. **Session 2 consists of below two sections.**

The **Multicraft section** is truly a test of technical knowledge and skills. We will discuss the topics covered on this section of the test beginning on the next page.

As described earlier, the **Spatial Relations section** is broken into two segments. We will discuss this section in detail immediately after covering the Multicraft section.

Before discussing the content of the Session 2, we need to talk about scoring. As with all other exams, the Postal Service will not release the scoring formula used to create the final overall exam score. But we do know one thing about scoring of Session 2... your score depends upon how many questions you answer correctly. In other words, they score you by simply counting your correct answers. Looking at it that way, incorrect answers and unanswered questions do not seem to figure into the scoring formula. But in fact, incorrect answers and unanswered questions are very important. You see, in order to achieve your highest possible score, you need to capture every single point possible. Incorrect and blank answers represent points that you desperately needed but failed to capture. Since they won't release the formula, we know lots of things that it is _not_, but unfortunately we do not know what it _is_. For instance, the overall score is not a simple percentage. More specifically, just because you answered 85% of the questions correctly does not mean that your score is an 85.

Should you guess? YES! Never leave a question blank. If you don't know the answer, just guess. This is true for all of Session 2 – for both the Multicraft and Spatial Relations sections. Look at it this way: If you don't know the answer to some questions and you leave them blank, you lost all the points that those questions had to offer. And, again, you need to capture every single point possible in order to achieve your highest possible score. So, what if you guess on questions you don't know instead of leaving them blank? Well, statistically many of your guesses are likely to be wrong, which means that you lost the points that those questions had to offer. That's no loss to you … you were going to lose those points anyway by leaving the questions blank … it make's no difference whether you lost them because they were wrong or because they were blank. But what about the questions where you guessed correctly? Here's where you come out ahead. If you had left those questions blank, you would have lost all those points. But by guessing correctly, you captured those points by blind luck. Never leave a question blank. Guess! You have nothing to lose and everything to gain.

How do they score the test if it covers so many different fields and fills different jobs? When you take this exam, even though you only took one test, you get multiple scores. There is one score for each job, each score is different, and it is possible that some of scores will be great while others are terrible. Different jobs call for different skills. For instance, an Electronic Technician is expected to have more expertise in electronics than heating systems, and just the opposite is true for a Building Equipment Mechanic. There is a different scoring formula for each job, and the different formulas are weighted to place more emphasis on the skills needed for that particular job. So, the Electronic Technician formula places more emphasis on electronic questions, the Building Equipment Mechanic formula emphasizes heating system questions more, and so on.

Reminder: The above scoring info applies to all of Session 2, but not to Session 1 – the Personal Characteristics & Experience Inventory section. As explained previously, they will not release any information about how is Session 1 is scored.

The Postal Service says that this part of exam 955 assesses your mechanical and electrical skills, but it actually goes much farther. Listed in alphabetical order below and on the next page are the 21 technical fields covered on the test and the numerous topics that each of the fields is broken down into.

Basic AC/DC Theory
- Capacitance
- Current Calculation
- Inductance
- Ohm's Law
- RC Networks
- Resistance Calculation
- Simple Circuits

Combustion
- Analyzers
- Control Systems
- Furnaces, Boilers & Heating Systems

Computer & PLC
- Addressing
- Input/Output
- Keyboard
- Registers
- Symbols

Controls
- AC
- DC
- Devices

Digital Electronics
- Adders
- And/or
- Counters
- Exclusive/or
- Nand/nor
- Shift Registers

Electrical Maintenance
- Failure Analysis
- Prevention
- Troubleshooting

Hydraulics
- Control Valves
- Filters
- Fluids
- Hydraulic Actuators
- Piping & Sealing
- Pressure Regulation
- Pumps
- Servo Valves

Lubrication
- Dry Lubricants
- Grease
- Oils
- Principles

Mechanical Maintenance
- Bulk Storage
- Prevention
- Recording
- Troubleshooting

Motors
- AC
- Control
- DC
- Generator
- Maintenance

Piping
- Accessories
- Heat Exchanger
- Metallic
- Non-metallic
- Specialized Valves
- Steam
- Strainers, Filters & Traps
- Tubing, Hoses & Fittings

Pneumatics
- Air Compressors
- Air Dryers
- Air Lubricators
- Air Motors
- Air Supply Systems
- Cylinders
- Regulation & Control
- System Maintenance
- Valves

Power Distribution

Fuses
Kilovars
Kilowatts
Metering
Oil & Air Circuit Breakers
Overload
Overvoltage
Phase Loss Relays
Transformers
Voltage Loss

Power Supply

Basic Transformer Theory
Filtering
Gating
Rectifiers
SCR's
Zener Diode

Power Transmission

Alignment
Bearings
Belt Drives
Brakes
Cables & Sheaves
Chains & Sprockets
Clutches, Cams & Couplings
Gears
Motors
Speed Changers / Reducers

Pumps

Alignment
Centrifugal
Horizontal
Positive Displacement
Seals
Thrust
Vertical

Rigging

Cranes & Hoists
Fiber Rope & Knots
Levers, Jacks & Screws
Scaffolds & Ladders
Wire Rope & Chains

Schematics & Print Reading

Assembly Drawings
Electrical Symbols
Mechanical Drawing
Relay Logic
Schematics - Basic
Schematics - Complex Piping
Schematics - Complex Welding
Solid State Logic

Shop Machines, Tools & Equipment

Breaks
Drill Press
Flame Tools
Grinder
Pipe Cutting & Threading Machines
Pneumatic Tools
Presses
Saws

Test Instruments

Ammeter
Basic Analyzer (VOM)
Brush Recorder
High Voltage Test Equipment
Megger
Oscilloscope
Voltmeter

Welding

Air-arcing
Arc Welding
Brazing & Gas Welding
Cutting Torch
Electrodes

Reviewing the above list of technical fields and topics correctly gives the impression that exam 955 is an intimidating test. But, you will not see every single one of these items on the particular test you take. There's a total of 60 Multicraft questions. Simple math tells us that it is not possible for each and every one of the above 131 items to be covered with only 60 questions. If there's only 60 questions, only 60 of the items can be covered at the very most. But, there's no way to predict which items will appear on your particular test. There are many different versions of the test, and each version has different questions. The bottom line is that you need to be prepared to answer questions about as many of the above items as possible because any of them could appear on your test.

The Spatial Relations section is an aptitude test, not a knowledge test. It tests your inherent ability (or at least your capacity to learn) to visualize how parts and pieces come together to form the "big picture" ... to visualize the end product represented by a drawing or schematic ... to visualize the assembly of a piece of equipment using illustrated instructions ... etc. Spatial ability is essential for success in a job that deals with mechanics and maintenance, so the Postal Service views the Spatial Relations test as an important tool when recruiting for the jobs filled from exam 955. We will discuss the two segments of the Spatial Relations section individually below.

In the **Matching Parts & Figures** segment, you are to visualize what shape would result from fitting two or more 2D flat pieces together. Each question gives you drawings of two or more 2D flat pieces. For answer choices, you are given drawings of four larger shapes, each consisting of multiple pieces. Your job is to figure out which of these four options shows how the original two or more pieces can be fitted together without gaps or overlapping. You will usually have to turn the original pieces around, over, etc. in your mind in order to see how they might fit together to form one of the answer options. The below sample question may help you understand better ...

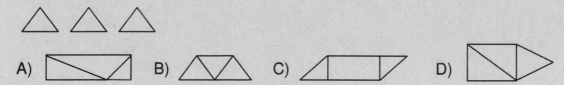

This sample question gives us three triangles. Looking at the answer options, do any of them seem to include all three of our triangles fitted perfectly together? Option A has three triangles, but they are definitely not shaped like our original ones. Option C cannot be right because it has two triangles and a rectangle. Option D has three triangles, but two of them don't look like our originals. If you turn one of our original triangles upside-down, option B looks like all three of our original triangles fitted perfectly together. That's our answer ... Option B.

In the **Spatial Visualization** segment, each question gives you the top, front, and right side views of an object. Then you are given four figures, one of which is the object represented by the original three views. You are to choose which of the four objects is indeed the one represented by the original three views. See the below sample for a better understanding ...

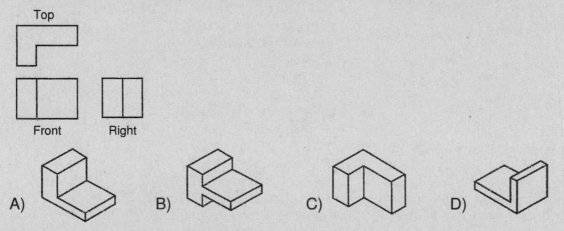

The correct answer is C. Option C is the only one that fits our three original views.

End of sample questions and exam content for exam 955/955E.

226

Important Information on Prior Exams 931, 932, and 933

As explained earlier, paper exams 931, 932, and 933 were retired and replaced by new exam 955 (page 199). **This replacement was effective immediately for public applicants, but not for internal applicants … current Postal employees hoping to move into higher paying technical maintenance positions.**

As of the publish date of this book, the Postal Service's internal system had not yet been updated for new exam 955. **This meant that internal applicants would continue to take old exams 931, 932, or 933 for an unknown period of time.** The internal system will eventually be updated, but internal applicants will continue to take the old tests until this update is implemented.

➢ If you applied for a maintenance job and **you are _not_ presently a Postal employee,** you will take exam 955 (page 199). However, reviewing the content of old exams 931, 932, and 933 will benefit you because these exams cover the technical fields they consider important.

➢ **If you _are_ a current Postal employee** who plans to take an internal exam for maintenance jobs, double check to confirm whether you will be taking one of the old tests or new exam 955. If you will take new exam 955 (page 199), reviewing the old tests will still benefit you as noted above. If you are sure that you will be taking one of the old tests, read on for valuable info…

If you believe that you will be taking one of the old paper tests (931, 932, or 933), following is important information for you. **However, make very sure to check Pathfinder Perks (page 19) online for any updates on this situation.**

We will discuss exams 931, 932, and 933 together rather than separately for several reasons. The most important reason is that that are so similar. The content of these three tests is 90% identical. And these three exams are used to fill similar technical maintenance jobs as detailed below:

• Exam 931 is used to fill various career building and equipment maintenance jobs (page 30).

• Exam 932 is used to fill career Electronic Technician jobs (page 31).

• Exam 933 is used to fill career Mail Processing Equipment Mechanic jobs (page 32).

These are the same reasons that, when the old exams were publicly retired (and will eventually be retired internally as well), they were replaced by one single new test.

When applying for any of these three exams, applicants receive a message saying:

> You should apply for this exam only if you have technical maintenance training or experience.

Take this message seriously! The failure rate on these three deeply technical exams is over 95%. One reason for the high failure rate is that these exams are so incredibly difficult. Another reason is that many people who take these tests are just not qualified. Many applicants simply do not have the necessary technical background and should have never even applied for these tests in the first place. A person literally has no business taking these tests unless he/she has thorough training, education, and/or experience in an extensive range of technical fields to be discussed shortly.

And experience alone, even many years of experience, may not be enough to get you by on these exams. They go far beyond matters of practical experience. They go into theories, principles, and formulas that are typically known only to those with technical training to go along with experience. As a matter of fact, applicants who have the necessary training but completed it long ago may be in trouble. I've heard from many people who failed even though they had extensive training years ago and have been working in technical fields since. These people have vast practical experience, but they've forgotten the theories, principles, and formulas that were important in school but are rarely – if ever – used on the job.

Like many of you, I'm a decent handyman, but I do not have extensive technical expertise. My general electrical, plumbing, carpentry, and mechanical skills are as good as most and better than some. I'm not bad with a computer either. But handyman skills are not good enough. For that matter, many professional contractors, electricians, HVAC technicians, computer technicians, etc. routinely fail these exams because their experience is limited to particular fields and due to lack of training/education.

I've done a great deal of research on these three exams over the last few years. As part of this research, I arranged for several college instructors to take these tests to get their feedback. We're talking about highly educated professors who teach the technical fields covered on these tests. If anybody was ever qualified to take these exams, it would definitely be these guys. Guess what happened … One of the instructors failed two of the tests and barely passed the third one. The other instructors passed all three tests with scores in the 70's and 80's, but none of them were able to score in the 90's. They were all astonished at the depth of these tests and amazed that the Postal Service uses employment exams that are so incredibly challenging. They also wondered how in the world the Postal Service can recruit new technical maintenance employees if nobody can even pass the necessary exams – which leads me directly into my next topic.

In recent years, the Postal Service has been desperate to fill their technical maintenance jobs. Two factors contribute to this situation:

• As Postal operations become more automated and sophisticated, there is an ever increasing demand for technical maintenance employees. In fact, maintenance is expected to be one of the highest growth Postal employment fields within the foreseeable future.

• However, even though there is increasing demand for these jobs, it has been very difficult to fill the jobs because nobody could pass their tests.

And these are the very reasons that exams 931, 932, and 933 were retired and replaced by new test 955. Supposedly exam 955 tests applicants for basic mechanical knowledge and aptitude without expecting the applicant to be a rocket scientist. In short, the new test is supposedly less challenging, which means that more applicants should be able to pass, which in turn hopefully means that they should be able to satisfy the increasing demand for maintenance jobs. Notice, however, that I use the words "supposedly" and "hopefully". Since it is so new, the verdict is not yet in on exam 955.

Beginning on the next page we will discuss what's on exam 931, 932, and 933. Buckle your seat belt and hold on tight because some of what you're going to hear may blow your mind.

Exams 931, 932, and 933 all consist of two sections as detailed below:

The first section on all three exams, Following Oral Instructions, is a series of questions presented verbally either by the test administrator or via a recording. Each question is actually a set of instructions that prompt you to find the correct answer or answers.

There are 20 questions/answers, and this section lasts as long as it takes for the questions to be presented verbally. There is not a specified time limit.

> Note: Although the Following Oral Instructions section was included on old exams 931, 932, and 933, it does not appear on new exam 955. The info on this section is therefore only important to you if you are absolutely sure that you will be taking one of these old tests. (See page 227.)

You must overcome four obstacles to succeed on the Following Oral Instructions section:

* The questions are intentionally long, tedious, and terribly confusing. Some of the questions deal with technical topics, but most do not.

* You must answer exclusively based upon what you hear. Answering verbal questions rather than written ones is much more difficult than you might imagine.

* You only have a few seconds after each question to find and mark the correct answers. Some questions have multiple answers that must be found and marked during this brief pause.

* Answers are marked on the answer sheet in a most unusual fashion that does not correlate with the numbers of the questions. Postal contacts tell me that over 60% of all applicants fail this section because they never really understand where and how to mark their answers.

The second part on all three tests is the KSA section. (Here come the mysterious KSA's again.) KSA is an acronym that stands for **K**nowledge, **S**kills, and **A**bilities. This is the killer technical part of the test that even college professors and rocket scientists have trouble passing.

The Postal Service uses the term KSA to refer to a particular technical field or a particular skill-set. In this case of these exams, when they say KSA, they are referring to a particular technical field that is tested on that exam.

You are given three hours to answer 150 questions in the KSA section. If you finish before time is called, they usually allow you to leave early. For most people, the time allowed is generous, and speed is not an issue. Most applicants fit one of two categories … Either they are unable to answer the questions regardless of how much time allowed, so they give up and leave long before time is called … Or they leave early because they knew the material well enough to answer all the questions long before time was called. Unfortunately, most people fit into the first category. But there are always a few people still plugging away when time is called. These are the applicants who don't know the material well, but they know enough to give it a good shot. Since they know the material to some degree, a few of these folks will pass, but most of them will end up failing.

The KSA section on each of these three exams covers sixteen technical fields. Fourteen of these fields are common to all three tests. Only two of these fields vary from one exam to another. Let me repeat that to make sure you fully understand. Fourteen of the technical fields are repeated on all three exams. Of the sixteen fields tested, only two change as you move from one test to another. Now you see what I meant when saying that the content of these tests is 90% identical.

How do you prepare for exams 931, 932, and 933? That's a very good question. I would like to try to answer it point by point:

Preparing for Following Oral Instructions Section

It is indeed possible to prepare for the Following Oral Instructions section. In fact, unless your grasp of English is limited, this section is not so bad once you understand how you're supposed to answer the questions. If you have trouble understanding English, however, there's really nothing that I or anyone else can do to help you. The questions are presented aloud in English, and you simply cannot answer the questions if you don't understand them.

As a matter of fact, I am going to fully prepare you for the Following Oral Instructions section here in this book. It will only take me 39 pages to offer full preparation including six complete practice tests, so I've provided everything you need. I mentioned earlier that this book would be thousands of pages long if I tried to include full preparation for all the exams, and this is indeed true. But adding only 39 more pages should not break anybody's back, so I slipped them in beginning on page 233 immediately after our discussion on the KSA section content – which begins below ...

Preparing for the KSA / Technical Section

However, preparing for the technical section of these exams is a whole different story. My research into the KSA sections of exams 931, 932, and 933 led to results very similar to my discussion on new exam 955. Allow me to share some of what I discovered in this research:

I thoroughly researched exams 931, 932, and 933, and I interviewed experts in all the technical fields covered on these tests. And, remember the college instructors who took these tests for me? They had many insights to share. **These experts and instructors all agree that it would be difficult, if not impossible, to prepare for the KSA sections of exam 931, 932, and 933.** The problem is that these tests cover 16 technical fields listed on the following two pages. A guide that adequately covers that many technical fields would be thousands of pages long, and it's simply not possible to publish a book of that size. And, it's not possible for an applicant to bone up on that many different fields. If an applicant already has a strong background in most of these fields and only needs to brush up on a few, that may be possible. But if the applicant does not already have a background in most or all these fields ... if the applicant needs to bone up on all of these different fields ... that's virtually impossible.

Do you have the background necessary to succeed on these tests? Nobody can answer that question but you. This decision should primarily be based upon your knowledge and experience in the technical fields listed on the following two pages.

On the next two pages is a table listing all the fields covered on all three of these exams. Notice that the first fourteen fields listed on the first page appear on all three of these exams. Of the last six fields listed on the second page, two are on the 931 only, two are on the 932 only, and two are on the 933 only.

KSA / Field Tested	Exam
Knowledge of basic mechanics refers to the theory of operation, terminology, usage, and characteristics of basic mechanical principles as they apply to such things as gears, pulleys, cams, pawls, power transmissions, linkages, fasteners, chains, sprockets, and belts; and including hoisting, rigging, roping, pneumatics, and hydraulic devices.	931 932 933
Knowledge of basic electricity refers to the theory, terminology, usage, and characteristics of basic electrical principles such as Ohm's Law, Kirchoff's Law, and magnetism, as they apply to such things as AC-DC circuitry and hardware, relays, switches, and circuit breakers.	931 932 933
Knowledge of basic electronics refers to the theory, terminology, usage, and characteristics of basic electronic principles concerning such things as solid state devices, vacuum tubes, coils, capacitors, resistors, and basic logic circuitry.	931 932 933
Knowledge of safety procedures and equipment refers to the knowledge of industrial hazards (e.g., mechanical, chemical, electrical, electronic) and procedures and techniques established to avoid injuries to self and others such as lock-out devices, protective clothing, and waste disposal techniques.	931 932 933
Ability to perform basic mathematical computations refers to the ability to perform basic calculations such as addition, subtraction, multiplication and division with whole numbers, fractions and decimals.	931 932 933
Ability to perform more complex mathematics refers to the ability to perform calculations such as basic algebra, geometry, scientific notation, and number conversions, as applied to mechanical, electrical and electronic applications.	931 932 933
Ability to apply theoretical knowledge to practical applications refers to the ability to recall specific theoretical knowledge and apply it to mechanical, electrical, electronic, or computerized maintenance applications such as inspection, troubleshooting, equipment repair and modification, preventive maintenance, and installation of electrical equipment; and isolating combinational (hardware/software) or interactive problems.	931 932 933
Ability to detect patterns refers to the ability to observe and analyze qualitative factors such as number progressions, spatial relationships, and auditory and visual patterns. This includes combining information and determining how a given set of numbers, objects, or sounds are related to each other.	931 932 933
Ability to use written reference materials refers to the ability to locate, read, and comprehend text material such as handbooks, manuals, bulletins, directives, checklists and route sheets.	931 932 933
Ability to follow instructions refers to the ability to comprehend and execute written and oral instructions such as work orders, checklists, route sheets, and verbal directions and instructions.	931 932 933
Ability to use hand tools refers to the knowledge of, and proficiency with, various hand tools. This ability involves the safe and efficient use and maintenance of such tools as screwdrivers, wrenches, hammers, pliers, chisels, punches, taps, dies, rules, gauges, and alignment tools.	931 932 933
Ability to use technical drawings refers to the ability to read and comprehend technical materials such as diagrams, schematics, flow charts, and blueprints.	931 932 933
Ability to use test equipment refers to the knowledge of, and proficiency with, various types of mechanical, electrical and electronic test equipment such as VOMS, oscilloscopes, circuit tracers, amprobes, and RPM meters.	931 932 933
Ability to solder refers to the knowledge of, and ability to safely and effectively apply, the appropriate soldering techniques.	931 932 933

continued on next page

continued form previous page

KSA / Field Tested	Exam
Knowledge of refrigeration refers to the theory, terminology, usage, and characteristics of refrigeration principles as they apply to such things as the refrigeration cycle, compressors, condensers, receivers, evaporators, metering devices, and refrigerant coils.	931
Knowledge of heating, ventilation, and air conditioning (HVAC) equipment operation refers to the knowledge of equipment operation such as safety considerations, start-up, shut-down, and mechanical/electrical operating characteristics of HVAC equipment (e.g., chillers, direct expansion units, window units, heating equipment). This does not include the knowledge of refrigeration.	931
Knowledge of digital electronics refers to the terminology, characteristics, symbololgy, and operation of digital components as used in such things as logic gates, registers, adders, counters, memories, encoders and decoders.	932
Knowledge of basic computer concepts refers to the terminology, usage, and characteristics of digital memory storage/processing devices such as core memory, input-output peripherals, and familiarity with programming concepts; and computer operating systems and utilities.	932
Knowledge of lubrication materials and procedures refers to the terminology, characteristics, storage, preparation, disposal, and usage techniques involved with lubrication materials such as oils, greases, and other types of lubricants.	933
Ability to use portable power tools refers to the knowledge of, and proficiency with, various power tools. This ability involves the safe and efficient use and maintenance of power tools such as drills, saws, sanders and grinders.	933

Before leaving the KSA's behind, I would like to elaborate on two of them:

The **"Ability to Follow Instructions"** KSA is actually the Following Oral Instructions section, the first section, on each of these exams. We discussed this section a couple of pages back, and beginning on the next page I will give you full preparation and six complete sample tests for the Following Oral Instructions section.

The **"Ability to Use Written Reference Materials"** questions that appear on all three exams are very similar to the Vocabulary and Reading Comprehension section of the 710 exam (page 143). The only real difference is that the vocabulary words and reading selections on exams 931, 932, and 933 are technical in nature.

Preparation for the Following Oral Instructions Section

As previously mentioned, I am able to include full preparation for the Following Oral Instructions section of exam 931, 932, and 933 in this book because it will only take me 39 pages to do so. Over the next few pages, I will share important test-taking tips with you. Then you will be given six complete practice tests to take so that you can master what you've learned.

On this part of the test, you will be looking at a page containing circles, squares, lines, words, numbers, letters, etc. The instructions, which will be presented verbally, direct you to select or mark certain items on the page. The selections/marks you make, coupled with the instructions you hear, will lead you to the correct answer. Note the below examples:

Sample 1.   _____ A   _____ B   _____ C   _____ D   _____ E

For a question like this sample, you may be told to write the number "67" on the line beside the third letter from the left, and then to mark on your answer sheet the number-letter combination you just created. Accordingly, you would write the number "67" beside the letter "C", which is the third letter from the left. Then you would darken item "67-C" on your answer sheet.

Sample 2.   [___ 45]   [___ 14]   [___ 73]   [___ 57]   [___ 38]

On this question, you may be instructed to write the letter "D" on the line inside the box with the largest number, and then to mark the number-letter combination you just made on your answer sheet. So, you would write the letter "D" on the line inside the box containing the number "73", which is the largest number. The number-letter combination you created by writing the letter "D" beside the number "73" is "73-D". Accordingly, you will darken item "73-D" on the answer sheet.

If you are at least partially sane, these samples probably only confused you. Here's some tips that should give you a better understanding of this section:

Following Oral Instructions Tip #1 | **Number-Letter Combination.** A clear understanding of this term is essential. Most the questions will cause you to create a number-letter combination, which is simply a number and a letter paired together. For instance, a particular question may instruct you to write the letter B beside the number 18 and then to mark this number-letter combination on your answer sheet. The number-letter combination you created is 18-B. The answer to this question is 18-B. To mark the answer, go to number 18 on the answer sheet and darken the letter B.

The problem is that you may be answering question number 3, yet you are marking an answer at item 18 on the answer sheet. This goes against everything we have ever learned about taking tests. Up until this point in our lives, we have always marked the answer to question 3 at item 3 on the answer sheet, marked the answer to question 18 at answer sheet item 18, and so on. Herein lies the problem. For this section, we must unlearn our orderly approach toward test taking.

On the Following Oral Instructions section, the number of the question will never have anything whatsoever to do with where you mark your answer. The one and only thing that dictates where you mark your answer is the number-letter combination. If the number-letter combination for question 13 is 77-D, you mark the letter D at item number 77 on the answer sheet. The fact that this is question number 13 does not matter at all. If the number-letter combination for question number 25 is 4-C, you mark the letter C at item number 4 on the answer sheet.

Occasionally you will be instructed to simply darken a certain letter at a particular number on the answer sheet without having first created a number-letter combination. For instance, for question 23, you may simply be told to darken the letter A at item number 6 on the answer sheet. There was no number-letter combination involved. But, for the most part, a number-letter combination will be involved and will dictate where you mark your answer.

Following Oral Instructions Tip #2 **Multiple Answers.** There will be instructions that cause you to create several number-letter combinations for a single question. This causes great confusion for most people when they are told to mark their answers. Being orderly test takers, we expect only one answer for each question. Again, we must unlearn our orderly approach. There will indeed be several questions that have multiple answers, and you are indeed expected to mark all of them.

Following Oral instructions Tip #3 **Timing.** The questions will be presented verbally at a rather slow and deliberate rate of approximately 75 words per minute. There will be a pause for about five seconds between the questions for you to mark answers. Do so rapidly and be ready to listen to the next question. If the question has multiple answers, mark them quickly so you will be ready for the next question. The verbal presentation of the questions will start again in about five seconds whether you are ready or not. And, how can you possibly answer the next question correctly if you do not hear the complete question?

Following Oral Instructions Tip #4 **If you become confused on a particular question**, should you [1] continue worrying with it and trying to salvage it while the Exam Administrator moves on to the next question or [2] **skip it and be ready to listen to the next question**? If you didn't get it, then you didn't get it. Let it go. Why miss the next question (maybe even the next two or three questions) worrying over the one you already lost. It makes much more sense to let it go and be prepared to capture the next point(s).

Following Oral Instructions Tip #5 **You _can_ make marks and notes during this section** of the exam. As a matter of fact, you are specifically directed to do so in the instructions you hear.

Following Oral Instructions Tip #6 **Guessing, where possible, on this section is acceptable**. This section is scored by simply counting your correct answers. So, why not guess? You may pick up a few extra points. But, there is a problem with guessing in this case. Where do you guess? Since the question number has nothing to do with where you mark the answer, how do you know where to mark your guess? You cannot guess unless you understood at least enough of the question to know where to make a guess.

Following Oral Instructions Tip #7 The key to success is to **listen closely to the instructions and then to follow them explicitly.** Do not allow you mind to wander or to try to make some type of rational sense out of what you are hearing. Simply listen and do exactly what you are told to do. Just to trip you up, included in some of the questions will be completely irrelevant information that has nothing to do with the answer. And you will only hear each question once. You cannot ask for a question to be repeated.

Following Oral Instructions Tip #8 **The majority rules!** Some questions will instruct you to mark a certain answer if a particular item of information is true or accurate. They will then follow up by instructing you to mark a different answer if that particular item of information is not true or accurate. For instance, a question might say: "If 82 is greater than 55 and 14 is less than 18, mark the number-letter combination 77-B on your answer sheet. If not, mark 25-D." In this case, the information read to you is accurate, so you would mark 77-B. Bear in mind however, that most such questions will more challenging than this rather simple example.

Pay attention to the other test takers around you when answering such questions. Let's assume, for instance, that you're in the middle such a question. Let's assume further that you feel that the first item of information given is not true, so you decide not to mark the first answer choice. Instead, you plan to mark the second answer choice that you're about to hear. But, as you wait for the second answer choice, you hear scribbling noises all across the room as the majority of your neighbors mark the first answer choice. What's more, with your peripheral vision, you notice a great deal of frantic movement as your neighbors mark the first answer.

Stop and think ... Is it more likely that you are the only one who properly understood the question and that all your neighbors are complete idiots? Or, is it perhaps more probable that the majority of your neighbors understood the question better than you did and that you are about to answer incorrectly? I propose that the majority understood better than you did and that you will be ahead of the game to follow their lead. _The majority rules!_

Just the opposite, if you begin marking the first answer choice but notice that no one around you is marking anything, again I suggest that you stop and think. It would likely be best to choose the second answer choice as the majority of your neighbors seem to have done.

Following Oral Instructions Tip #9 **Make notes.** Frequently, the question will provide identifying information about items displayed on your test booklet page. Such a question may sound like this:

> "Look at the five boxes in question number 8. Starting from the left side, the first box has mail for Jackson and Canton. The second box has mail for Greenville and Glendale. The third box has mail for Kingsville and San Marcos. The fourth box has mail for Houston and Dallas. The fifth box has mail for Lawerenceburg and Auburn. Write the letter "D" as in dog on the blank line beside the number in the box that has mail for Greenville and Glendale. Write the letter "A" as in apple on the line beside the number in the box that has mail for Houston and Dallas. Now, mark your number-letter combinations on the answer sheet."

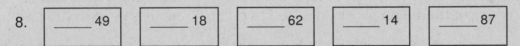

8. _____ 49   _____ 18   _____ 62   _____ 14   _____ 87

By the time you have listened to this long and confusing question, how in the world can you recall which box is which in order to mark the correct answer? The solution is for you to make brief notes as you hear the question. Remember, you can mark in your test booklet on this section of the exam. So, as you hear identifying information about particular items, make notes accordingly. In this case, you could have written the respective city names (probably in an abbreviated form) beside each box for later recognition.

Following Oral Instructions Tip #10 **Converting time of day into numbers.** Several questions will instruct you to convert time of day into a number. You may be told to find the first two numbers of the time 5:30 PM on the answer sheet and then to darken the letter B. The first two numbers in the time of 5:30 PM are a 5 and a 3. Put together, they make the number 53. So, we would find 53 on the answer sheet and darken the letter B. Or, you may be told to find the last two numbers of this time and to darken the letter A. So, you would find the number 30 and darken the letter A. If you were told to find the first number, it would be the number 5. As previously discussed, simply do as you are instructed. Don't waste time trying to make sense of it.

Following Oral Instructions Tip #11 To **practice realistically**, you must have someone read the questions from the following six practice tests aloud to you. _Do not read the questions yourself!_ If you want to succeed, you must practice the same way that the questions are presented on the real exam – by having the questions read to you out loud.

DIRECTIONS

On this section of the test, the verbally presented questions will direct you to write or mark certain items in your test booklet, which in turn will lead you to the correct answer(s). Then you will be instructed to mark the correct answer(s) on an answer sheet. The below practice test items are included over the next several pages:

- Beginning the very next page are practice test booklet pages on which you write or mark as verbally instructed in order to find what answer(s) to mark on an answer sheet.

- Following these pages are practice answer sheets where you are to mark your answers. You will need to either tear out the answer sheet pages or make copies of them so that you will have loose answers sheets at hand for marking answers. Note that for each practice test there are many more answer spots available then there are questions. As explained previously, (1) the verbal questions will instruct you where to mark answers on the answer sheet, (2) where you mark answers will not correlate with the question numbers, and (3) you will only use a portion of the available answer spots.

- After the answer sheets, you will find the printed questions that must be read aloud to you. You will need to either tear out these pages or make copies of them so that someone can read the questions to you while you take the practice tests here in the book.

- The final item found after the printed questions is the answer key that you will use as directed below to score your practice tests.

Even though each practice test has less than 20 questions, you will mark exactly 20 answers if you answer all the questions correctly. This is because some questions have multiple answers. Also, these questions are not technical in nature, but a few questions on the real test may be technical.

SCORING

Formula: They will not release the formula used to calculate the final scores for this exam, but we do know how to score the individual sections. To score each Following Oral Instructions practice test, use the answer key to identify your correct and incorrect answers. Then count your correct answers, and that is your score. The score for this section is simply your number of correct answers.

Example: Let's say that, out of the 20 questions, I answered 19. And, of the 19 that I answered, 16 were correct, and 3 were wrong. My score is simply a 16 … the number of correct answers.

HOW TO INTERPRET YOUR SCORE

Process: If I answered all the questions correctly, the best possible score on this section is a 20. The only way you can measure your performance on this section is to compare your score to the best possible score of 20.

Example: Looking at the above sample, we figured my score to be a 16. There's a maximum of 20 points available on this section, and I was only able to capture 80% of them.

Interpretation: So, does 16 sound like a good score? Well, it sounds fair, but not great. If I want to excel on this section, I need to practice to master the skills and speed demanded. (Bear in mind that, since we don't have the final scoring formula, we are basically making an educated guess when interpreting your performance on this section.)

1.   3_____

2.   7   3   9   5

3.   1   C   5   E

4.   3   6   8   9   1

5.   C   D   E   G

6.   [A____]   [C____]   [D____]   [E____]

7.   33____   39____   45____   58____   69____

8.   [10__]   (6__)   [15__]   (2__)

9.   C____   A____   E____   D____

10.   [12 __]   [8 __]   [19 __]   [72 __]

11.   [77 __]   (11 __)   [13 __]   (16)

12.   C____   D____   C____   B____   A____

13.   (B 1:30)   (C 12:30)   (D 1:10)   (E 6:30)   (F 8:45)

14.   [A]   (B)   [C]   (D)

15.   [1:15 __]   [1:45 __]   [2:45 __]   [3:25 __]

16.   [32 __]   [28 __]   [39 __]   [62 __]

17.   (72)   (11)   (54)   (13)

1.   7   11   14   22

2.   A   D   E   S   B

3.   A   12   14   C   3   D

4.   78   82   52   12

5.   R____   D____   A____   C____

6.   [6____]   [8____]   [5____]   [10____]

7.   27   36   52   87

8.   [7__]   (4__)   (9__)   [6__]

9.   [22____]   [12____]   [71____]   [9____]

10.   ____E   ___C   ____D   ____B   ____A

11.   (1)   (3)   [7]   [2]

12.   62____   47____   94____   13____   51____

13.   D A Y S

     __   __   __   __

14.   [2:20 PM ____]   [12:05 AM ____]   [6:10 PM ____]   [9:45 AM ____]   [1:15 PM ____]

continued on next page

continued

15. _____

16.

| 9____ | 32____ | 57____ | 64____ |

17.

| Chicago 91 | Dallas 52 | Denver 12 | Akron 72 |

18.

| 12:00 AM | 3:00 PM | 6:00 AM |

1.   12   26   37   42

2.   [9____]   [11____]   [17____]   [16____]

3.   A   E   D   C

4.   [73____]   [41____]   [37____]   [62____]

5.   [C__]   [D__]   [E__]   [A__]

6.   (4:30 AM)   (3:00 PM)   (7:15 AM)   (12:05 PM)

7.   Wednesday   Thursday   Monday   Tuesday   Friday

8.   [81]   [79]   [74]   [72]

9.   [Monday 9:00 AM]   [Monday 4:45 PM]   [Monday 8:00 AM]   [Monday 12:00 AM]

10.   [7]   (12)   (2)   [72]   [81]

11.   34   27

12.   C   D   A   E   B

13.   29   11   61   71

14.   [____]   [____]   ____   ____

1.   B   C   A   E   D

2.   (__B)   (__E)   (__C)   (__A)

3.   81   28   57   66   30   43   27   15   41

4.   A   D   E   B   C

5.   (19___)   (21___)   [37___]   [15___]

6.   (7:00 ___)   (7:10 ___)   (6:51 ___)   (6:47 ___)   (5:10 ___)

7.   (14___)   (37___)   (21___)   ABE   DIE   CAB

8.   [85___]   [78___]

9.   OOX   XOO   XXO   XOX   XXO

10.   12___   18___   47___   52___   32___   31__   26___

11.   42   51   73   86   19   23   16

12.   [67___]   [43___]   [64___]

1. (76___) (37___) (18___)   EMMA   CUD   BOB

2. | 12___ | | 84___ | | 71___ |

3. | Biloxi 48_____ | | Utica 17_____ | | Rutland 38_____ | | San Jose 44_____ |

4.   12   29   41   11   58   67   83   36   87

5.   ABBA   BAAB   BBAB   AABA   BBBA

6. | ___C | (___A) | ___E | (___D)

7. | 19___ | | 38___ | | 27___ | | 78___ |

8. | Chicago 51_____ | | Atlanta 62_____ | | Portland 33_____ |

9.   ___A   ___B   ___C   ___D   ___E

10.   3   8   20   32   57   17   14   15

1.   C   D   A   B   E   A   D   E

2.

___E   ___D   ___A   ___C   ___B

3. | 28___ | 26___ | 33___ | 37___ |

4.   XYXY   YXXY   XXYY   XXYX   YYXX

5.   30   58   14   28   42   80   24

6.   (6:50 ___)   (7:15 ___)   (8:05 ___)   (7:35 ___)   (7:00 ___)

7.   ____E   ____C

8.   (63___)   (79___)   (61___)   B a b e   A b l e   C a d

9. | 85___ | 49___ |

10.   (Gulfport 35___)   (Biloxi 17___)   (Waveland 88___)

PRACTICE TEST 1

1 Ⓐ Ⓑ Ⓒ Ⓓ Ⓔ	19 Ⓐ Ⓑ Ⓒ Ⓓ Ⓔ	37 Ⓐ Ⓑ Ⓒ Ⓓ Ⓔ	55 Ⓐ Ⓑ Ⓒ Ⓓ Ⓔ	73 Ⓐ Ⓑ Ⓒ Ⓓ Ⓔ
2 Ⓐ Ⓑ Ⓒ Ⓓ Ⓔ	20 Ⓐ Ⓑ Ⓒ Ⓓ Ⓔ	38 Ⓐ Ⓑ Ⓒ Ⓓ Ⓔ	56 Ⓐ Ⓑ Ⓒ Ⓓ Ⓔ	74 Ⓐ Ⓑ Ⓒ Ⓓ Ⓔ
3 Ⓐ Ⓑ Ⓒ Ⓓ Ⓔ	21 Ⓐ Ⓑ Ⓒ Ⓓ Ⓔ	39 Ⓐ Ⓑ Ⓒ Ⓓ Ⓔ	57 Ⓐ Ⓑ Ⓒ Ⓓ Ⓔ	75 Ⓐ Ⓑ Ⓒ Ⓓ Ⓔ
4 Ⓐ Ⓑ Ⓒ Ⓓ Ⓔ	22 Ⓐ Ⓑ Ⓒ Ⓓ Ⓔ	40 Ⓐ Ⓑ Ⓒ Ⓓ Ⓔ	58 Ⓐ Ⓑ Ⓒ Ⓓ Ⓔ	76 Ⓐ Ⓑ Ⓒ Ⓓ Ⓔ
5 Ⓐ Ⓑ Ⓒ Ⓓ Ⓔ	23 Ⓐ Ⓑ Ⓒ Ⓓ Ⓔ	41 Ⓐ Ⓑ Ⓒ Ⓓ Ⓔ	59 Ⓐ Ⓑ Ⓒ Ⓓ Ⓔ	77 Ⓐ Ⓑ Ⓒ Ⓓ Ⓔ
6 Ⓐ Ⓑ Ⓒ Ⓓ Ⓔ	24 Ⓐ Ⓑ Ⓒ Ⓓ Ⓔ	42 Ⓐ Ⓑ Ⓒ Ⓓ Ⓔ	60 Ⓐ Ⓑ Ⓒ Ⓓ Ⓔ	78 Ⓐ Ⓑ Ⓒ Ⓓ Ⓔ
7 Ⓐ Ⓑ Ⓒ Ⓓ Ⓔ	25 Ⓐ Ⓑ Ⓒ Ⓓ Ⓔ	43 Ⓐ Ⓑ Ⓒ Ⓓ Ⓔ	61 Ⓐ Ⓑ Ⓒ Ⓓ Ⓔ	79 Ⓐ Ⓑ Ⓒ Ⓓ Ⓔ
8 Ⓐ Ⓑ Ⓒ Ⓓ Ⓔ	26 Ⓐ Ⓑ Ⓒ Ⓓ Ⓔ	44 Ⓐ Ⓑ Ⓒ Ⓓ Ⓔ	62 Ⓐ Ⓑ Ⓒ Ⓓ Ⓔ	80 Ⓐ Ⓑ Ⓒ Ⓓ Ⓔ
9 Ⓐ Ⓑ Ⓒ Ⓓ Ⓔ	27 Ⓐ Ⓑ Ⓒ Ⓓ Ⓔ	45 Ⓐ Ⓑ Ⓒ Ⓓ Ⓔ	63 Ⓐ Ⓑ Ⓒ Ⓓ Ⓔ	81 Ⓐ Ⓑ Ⓒ Ⓓ Ⓔ
10 Ⓐ Ⓑ Ⓒ Ⓓ Ⓔ	28 Ⓐ Ⓑ Ⓒ Ⓓ Ⓔ	46 Ⓐ Ⓑ Ⓒ Ⓓ Ⓔ	64 Ⓐ Ⓑ Ⓒ Ⓓ Ⓔ	82 Ⓐ Ⓑ Ⓒ Ⓓ Ⓔ
11 Ⓐ Ⓑ Ⓒ Ⓓ Ⓔ	29 Ⓐ Ⓑ Ⓒ Ⓓ Ⓔ	47 Ⓐ Ⓑ Ⓒ Ⓓ Ⓔ	65 Ⓐ Ⓑ Ⓒ Ⓓ Ⓔ	83 Ⓐ Ⓑ Ⓒ Ⓓ Ⓔ
12 Ⓐ Ⓑ Ⓒ Ⓓ Ⓔ	30 Ⓐ Ⓑ Ⓒ Ⓓ Ⓔ	48 Ⓐ Ⓑ Ⓒ Ⓓ Ⓔ	66 Ⓐ Ⓑ Ⓒ Ⓓ Ⓔ	84 Ⓐ Ⓑ Ⓒ Ⓓ Ⓔ
13 Ⓐ Ⓑ Ⓒ Ⓓ Ⓔ	31 Ⓐ Ⓑ Ⓒ Ⓓ Ⓔ	49 Ⓐ Ⓑ Ⓒ Ⓓ Ⓔ	67 Ⓐ Ⓑ Ⓒ Ⓓ Ⓔ	85 Ⓐ Ⓑ Ⓒ Ⓓ Ⓔ
14 Ⓐ Ⓑ Ⓒ Ⓓ Ⓔ	32 Ⓐ Ⓑ Ⓒ Ⓓ Ⓔ	50 Ⓐ Ⓑ Ⓒ Ⓓ Ⓔ	68 Ⓐ Ⓑ Ⓒ Ⓓ Ⓔ	86 Ⓐ Ⓑ Ⓒ Ⓓ Ⓔ
15 Ⓐ Ⓑ Ⓒ Ⓓ Ⓔ	33 Ⓐ Ⓑ Ⓒ Ⓓ Ⓔ	51 Ⓐ Ⓑ Ⓒ Ⓓ Ⓔ	69 Ⓐ Ⓑ Ⓒ Ⓓ Ⓔ	87 Ⓐ Ⓑ Ⓒ Ⓓ Ⓔ
16 Ⓐ Ⓑ Ⓒ Ⓓ Ⓔ	34 Ⓐ Ⓑ Ⓒ Ⓓ Ⓔ	52 Ⓐ Ⓑ Ⓒ Ⓓ Ⓔ	70 Ⓐ Ⓑ Ⓒ Ⓓ Ⓔ	88 Ⓐ Ⓑ Ⓒ Ⓓ Ⓔ
17 Ⓐ Ⓑ Ⓒ Ⓓ Ⓔ	35 Ⓐ Ⓑ Ⓒ Ⓓ Ⓔ	53 Ⓐ Ⓑ Ⓒ Ⓓ Ⓔ	71 Ⓐ Ⓑ Ⓒ Ⓓ Ⓔ	
18 Ⓐ Ⓑ Ⓒ Ⓓ Ⓔ	36 Ⓐ Ⓑ Ⓒ Ⓓ Ⓔ	54 Ⓐ Ⓑ Ⓒ Ⓓ Ⓔ	72 Ⓐ Ⓑ Ⓒ Ⓓ Ⓔ	

PRACTICE TEST 2

1 Ⓐ Ⓑ Ⓒ Ⓓ Ⓔ	19 Ⓐ Ⓑ Ⓒ Ⓓ Ⓔ	37 Ⓐ Ⓑ Ⓒ Ⓓ Ⓔ	55 Ⓐ Ⓑ Ⓒ Ⓓ Ⓔ	73 Ⓐ Ⓑ Ⓒ Ⓓ Ⓔ
2 Ⓐ Ⓑ Ⓒ Ⓓ Ⓔ	20 Ⓐ Ⓑ Ⓒ Ⓓ Ⓔ	38 Ⓐ Ⓑ Ⓒ Ⓓ Ⓔ	56 Ⓐ Ⓑ Ⓒ Ⓓ Ⓔ	74 Ⓐ Ⓑ Ⓒ Ⓓ Ⓔ
3 Ⓐ Ⓑ Ⓒ Ⓓ Ⓔ	21 Ⓐ Ⓑ Ⓒ Ⓓ Ⓔ	39 Ⓐ Ⓑ Ⓒ Ⓓ Ⓔ	57 Ⓐ Ⓑ Ⓒ Ⓓ Ⓔ	75 Ⓐ Ⓑ Ⓒ Ⓓ Ⓔ
4 Ⓐ Ⓑ Ⓒ Ⓓ Ⓔ	22 Ⓐ Ⓑ Ⓒ Ⓓ Ⓔ	40 Ⓐ Ⓑ Ⓒ Ⓓ Ⓔ	58 Ⓐ Ⓑ Ⓒ Ⓓ Ⓔ	76 Ⓐ Ⓑ Ⓒ Ⓓ Ⓔ
5 Ⓐ Ⓑ Ⓒ Ⓓ Ⓔ	23 Ⓐ Ⓑ Ⓒ Ⓓ Ⓔ	41 Ⓐ Ⓑ Ⓒ Ⓓ Ⓔ	59 Ⓐ Ⓑ Ⓒ Ⓓ Ⓔ	77 Ⓐ Ⓑ Ⓒ Ⓓ Ⓔ
6 Ⓐ Ⓑ Ⓒ Ⓓ Ⓔ	24 Ⓐ Ⓑ Ⓒ Ⓓ Ⓔ	42 Ⓐ Ⓑ Ⓒ Ⓓ Ⓔ	60 Ⓐ Ⓑ Ⓒ Ⓓ Ⓔ	78 Ⓐ Ⓑ Ⓒ Ⓓ Ⓔ
7 Ⓐ Ⓑ Ⓒ Ⓓ Ⓔ	25 Ⓐ Ⓑ Ⓒ Ⓓ Ⓔ	43 Ⓐ Ⓑ Ⓒ Ⓓ Ⓔ	61 Ⓐ Ⓑ Ⓒ Ⓓ Ⓔ	79 Ⓐ Ⓑ Ⓒ Ⓓ Ⓔ
8 Ⓐ Ⓑ Ⓒ Ⓓ Ⓔ	26 Ⓐ Ⓑ Ⓒ Ⓓ Ⓔ	44 Ⓐ Ⓑ Ⓒ Ⓓ Ⓔ	62 Ⓐ Ⓑ Ⓒ Ⓓ Ⓔ	80 Ⓐ Ⓑ Ⓒ Ⓓ Ⓔ
9 Ⓐ Ⓑ Ⓒ Ⓓ Ⓔ	27 Ⓐ Ⓑ Ⓒ Ⓓ Ⓔ	45 Ⓐ Ⓑ Ⓒ Ⓓ Ⓔ	63 Ⓐ Ⓑ Ⓒ Ⓓ Ⓔ	81 Ⓐ Ⓑ Ⓒ Ⓓ Ⓔ
10 Ⓐ Ⓑ Ⓒ Ⓓ Ⓔ	28 Ⓐ Ⓑ Ⓒ Ⓓ Ⓔ	46 Ⓐ Ⓑ Ⓒ Ⓓ Ⓔ	64 Ⓐ Ⓑ Ⓒ Ⓓ Ⓔ	82 Ⓐ Ⓑ Ⓒ Ⓓ Ⓔ
11 Ⓐ Ⓑ Ⓒ Ⓓ Ⓔ	29 Ⓐ Ⓑ Ⓒ Ⓓ Ⓔ	47 Ⓐ Ⓑ Ⓒ Ⓓ Ⓔ	65 Ⓐ Ⓑ Ⓒ Ⓓ Ⓔ	83 Ⓐ Ⓑ Ⓒ Ⓓ Ⓔ
12 Ⓐ Ⓑ Ⓒ Ⓓ Ⓔ	30 Ⓐ Ⓑ Ⓒ Ⓓ Ⓔ	48 Ⓐ Ⓑ Ⓒ Ⓓ Ⓔ	66 Ⓐ Ⓑ Ⓒ Ⓓ Ⓔ	84 Ⓐ Ⓑ Ⓒ Ⓓ Ⓔ
13 Ⓐ Ⓑ Ⓒ Ⓓ Ⓔ	31 Ⓐ Ⓑ Ⓒ Ⓓ Ⓔ	49 Ⓐ Ⓑ Ⓒ Ⓓ Ⓔ	67 Ⓐ Ⓑ Ⓒ Ⓓ Ⓔ	85 Ⓐ Ⓑ Ⓒ Ⓓ Ⓔ
14 Ⓐ Ⓑ Ⓒ Ⓓ Ⓔ	32 Ⓐ Ⓑ Ⓒ Ⓓ Ⓔ	50 Ⓐ Ⓑ Ⓒ Ⓓ Ⓔ	68 Ⓐ Ⓑ Ⓒ Ⓓ Ⓔ	86 Ⓐ Ⓑ Ⓒ Ⓓ Ⓔ
15 Ⓐ Ⓑ Ⓒ Ⓓ Ⓔ	33 Ⓐ Ⓑ Ⓒ Ⓓ Ⓔ	51 Ⓐ Ⓑ Ⓒ Ⓓ Ⓔ	69 Ⓐ Ⓑ Ⓒ Ⓓ Ⓔ	87 Ⓐ Ⓑ Ⓒ Ⓓ Ⓔ
16 Ⓐ Ⓑ Ⓒ Ⓓ Ⓔ	34 Ⓐ Ⓑ Ⓒ Ⓓ Ⓔ	52 Ⓐ Ⓑ Ⓒ Ⓓ Ⓔ	70 Ⓐ Ⓑ Ⓒ Ⓓ Ⓔ	88 Ⓐ Ⓑ Ⓒ Ⓓ Ⓔ
17 Ⓐ Ⓑ Ⓒ Ⓓ Ⓔ	35 Ⓐ Ⓑ Ⓒ Ⓓ Ⓔ	53 Ⓐ Ⓑ Ⓒ Ⓓ Ⓔ	71 Ⓐ Ⓑ Ⓒ Ⓓ Ⓔ	
18 Ⓐ Ⓑ Ⓒ Ⓓ Ⓔ	36 Ⓐ Ⓑ Ⓒ Ⓓ Ⓔ	54 Ⓐ Ⓑ Ⓒ Ⓓ Ⓔ	72 Ⓐ Ⓑ Ⓒ Ⓓ Ⓔ	

PRACTICE TEST 3

1 Ⓐ Ⓑ Ⓒ Ⓓ Ⓔ   19 Ⓐ Ⓑ Ⓒ Ⓓ Ⓔ   37 Ⓐ Ⓑ Ⓒ Ⓓ Ⓔ   55 Ⓐ Ⓑ Ⓒ Ⓓ Ⓔ   73 Ⓐ Ⓑ Ⓒ Ⓓ Ⓔ
2 Ⓐ Ⓑ Ⓒ Ⓓ Ⓔ   20 Ⓐ Ⓑ Ⓒ Ⓓ Ⓔ   38 Ⓐ Ⓑ Ⓒ Ⓓ Ⓔ   56 Ⓐ Ⓑ Ⓒ Ⓓ Ⓔ   74 Ⓐ Ⓑ Ⓒ Ⓓ Ⓔ
3 Ⓐ Ⓑ Ⓒ Ⓓ Ⓔ   21 Ⓐ Ⓑ Ⓒ Ⓓ Ⓔ   39 Ⓐ Ⓑ Ⓒ Ⓓ Ⓔ   57 Ⓐ Ⓑ Ⓒ Ⓓ Ⓔ   75 Ⓐ Ⓑ Ⓒ Ⓓ Ⓔ
4 Ⓐ Ⓑ Ⓒ Ⓓ Ⓔ   22 Ⓐ Ⓑ Ⓒ Ⓓ Ⓔ   40 Ⓐ Ⓑ Ⓒ Ⓓ Ⓔ   58 Ⓐ Ⓑ Ⓒ Ⓓ Ⓔ   76 Ⓐ Ⓑ Ⓒ Ⓓ Ⓔ
5 Ⓐ Ⓑ Ⓒ Ⓓ Ⓔ   23 Ⓐ Ⓑ Ⓒ Ⓓ Ⓔ   41 Ⓐ Ⓑ Ⓒ Ⓓ Ⓔ   59 Ⓐ Ⓑ Ⓒ Ⓓ Ⓔ   77 Ⓐ Ⓑ Ⓒ Ⓓ Ⓔ
6 Ⓐ Ⓑ Ⓒ Ⓓ Ⓔ   24 Ⓐ Ⓑ Ⓒ Ⓓ Ⓔ   42 Ⓐ Ⓑ Ⓒ Ⓓ Ⓔ   60 Ⓐ Ⓑ Ⓒ Ⓓ Ⓔ   78 Ⓐ Ⓑ Ⓒ Ⓓ Ⓔ
7 Ⓐ Ⓑ Ⓒ Ⓓ Ⓔ   25 Ⓐ Ⓑ Ⓒ Ⓓ Ⓔ   43 Ⓐ Ⓑ Ⓒ Ⓓ Ⓔ   61 Ⓐ Ⓑ Ⓒ Ⓓ Ⓔ   79 Ⓐ Ⓑ Ⓒ Ⓓ Ⓔ
8 Ⓐ Ⓑ Ⓒ Ⓓ Ⓔ   26 Ⓐ Ⓑ Ⓒ Ⓓ Ⓔ   44 Ⓐ Ⓑ Ⓒ Ⓓ Ⓔ   62 Ⓐ Ⓑ Ⓒ Ⓓ Ⓔ   80 Ⓐ Ⓑ Ⓒ Ⓓ Ⓔ
9 Ⓐ Ⓑ Ⓒ Ⓓ Ⓔ   27 Ⓐ Ⓑ Ⓒ Ⓓ Ⓔ   45 Ⓐ Ⓑ Ⓒ Ⓓ Ⓔ   63 Ⓐ Ⓑ Ⓒ Ⓓ Ⓔ   81 Ⓐ Ⓑ Ⓒ Ⓓ Ⓔ
10 Ⓐ Ⓑ Ⓒ Ⓓ Ⓔ   28 Ⓐ Ⓑ Ⓒ Ⓓ Ⓔ   46 Ⓐ Ⓑ Ⓒ Ⓓ Ⓔ   64 Ⓐ Ⓑ Ⓒ Ⓓ Ⓔ   82 Ⓐ Ⓑ Ⓒ Ⓓ Ⓔ
11 Ⓐ Ⓑ Ⓒ Ⓓ Ⓔ   29 Ⓐ Ⓑ Ⓒ Ⓓ Ⓔ   47 Ⓐ Ⓑ Ⓒ Ⓓ Ⓔ   65 Ⓐ Ⓑ Ⓒ Ⓓ Ⓔ   83 Ⓐ Ⓑ Ⓒ Ⓓ Ⓔ
12 Ⓐ Ⓑ Ⓒ Ⓓ Ⓔ   30 Ⓐ Ⓑ Ⓒ Ⓓ Ⓔ   48 Ⓐ Ⓑ Ⓒ Ⓓ Ⓔ   66 Ⓐ Ⓑ Ⓒ Ⓓ Ⓔ   84 Ⓐ Ⓑ Ⓒ Ⓓ Ⓔ
13 Ⓐ Ⓑ Ⓒ Ⓓ Ⓔ   31 Ⓐ Ⓑ Ⓒ Ⓓ Ⓔ   49 Ⓐ Ⓑ Ⓒ Ⓓ Ⓔ   67 Ⓐ Ⓑ Ⓒ Ⓓ Ⓔ   85 Ⓐ Ⓑ Ⓒ Ⓓ Ⓔ
14 Ⓐ Ⓑ Ⓒ Ⓓ Ⓔ   32 Ⓐ Ⓑ Ⓒ Ⓓ Ⓔ   50 Ⓐ Ⓑ Ⓒ Ⓓ Ⓔ   68 Ⓐ Ⓑ Ⓒ Ⓓ Ⓔ   86 Ⓐ Ⓑ Ⓒ Ⓓ Ⓔ
15 Ⓐ Ⓑ Ⓒ Ⓓ Ⓔ   33 Ⓐ Ⓑ Ⓒ Ⓓ Ⓔ   51 Ⓐ Ⓑ Ⓒ Ⓓ Ⓔ   69 Ⓐ Ⓑ Ⓒ Ⓓ Ⓔ   87 Ⓐ Ⓑ Ⓒ Ⓓ Ⓔ
16 Ⓐ Ⓑ Ⓒ Ⓓ Ⓔ   34 Ⓐ Ⓑ Ⓒ Ⓓ Ⓔ   52 Ⓐ Ⓑ Ⓒ Ⓓ Ⓔ   70 Ⓐ Ⓑ Ⓒ Ⓓ Ⓔ   88 Ⓐ Ⓑ Ⓒ Ⓓ Ⓔ
17 Ⓐ Ⓑ Ⓒ Ⓓ Ⓔ   35 Ⓐ Ⓑ Ⓒ Ⓓ Ⓔ   53 Ⓐ Ⓑ Ⓒ Ⓓ Ⓔ   71 Ⓐ Ⓑ Ⓒ Ⓓ Ⓔ
18 Ⓐ Ⓑ Ⓒ Ⓓ Ⓔ   36 Ⓐ Ⓑ Ⓒ Ⓓ Ⓔ   54 Ⓐ Ⓑ Ⓒ Ⓓ Ⓔ   72 Ⓐ Ⓑ Ⓒ Ⓓ Ⓔ

PRACTICE TEST 4

1 Ⓐ Ⓑ Ⓒ Ⓓ Ⓔ   19 Ⓐ Ⓑ Ⓒ Ⓓ Ⓔ   37 Ⓐ Ⓑ Ⓒ Ⓓ Ⓔ   55 Ⓐ Ⓑ Ⓒ Ⓓ Ⓔ   73 Ⓐ Ⓑ Ⓒ Ⓓ Ⓔ
2 Ⓐ Ⓑ Ⓒ Ⓓ Ⓔ   20 Ⓐ Ⓑ Ⓒ Ⓓ Ⓔ   38 Ⓐ Ⓑ Ⓒ Ⓓ Ⓔ   56 Ⓐ Ⓑ Ⓒ Ⓓ Ⓔ   74 Ⓐ Ⓑ Ⓒ Ⓓ Ⓔ
3 Ⓐ Ⓑ Ⓒ Ⓓ Ⓔ   21 Ⓐ Ⓑ Ⓒ Ⓓ Ⓔ   39 Ⓐ Ⓑ Ⓒ Ⓓ Ⓔ   57 Ⓐ Ⓑ Ⓒ Ⓓ Ⓔ   75 Ⓐ Ⓑ Ⓒ Ⓓ Ⓔ
4 Ⓐ Ⓑ Ⓒ Ⓓ Ⓔ   22 Ⓐ Ⓑ Ⓒ Ⓓ Ⓔ   40 Ⓐ Ⓑ Ⓒ Ⓓ Ⓔ   58 Ⓐ Ⓑ Ⓒ Ⓓ Ⓔ   76 Ⓐ Ⓑ Ⓒ Ⓓ Ⓔ
5 Ⓐ Ⓑ Ⓒ Ⓓ Ⓔ   23 Ⓐ Ⓑ Ⓒ Ⓓ Ⓔ   41 Ⓐ Ⓑ Ⓒ Ⓓ Ⓔ   59 Ⓐ Ⓑ Ⓒ Ⓓ Ⓔ   77 Ⓐ Ⓑ Ⓒ Ⓓ Ⓔ
6 Ⓐ Ⓑ Ⓒ Ⓓ Ⓔ   24 Ⓐ Ⓑ Ⓒ Ⓓ Ⓔ   42 Ⓐ Ⓑ Ⓒ Ⓓ Ⓔ   60 Ⓐ Ⓑ Ⓒ Ⓓ Ⓔ   78 Ⓐ Ⓑ Ⓒ Ⓓ Ⓔ
7 Ⓐ Ⓑ Ⓒ Ⓓ Ⓔ   25 Ⓐ Ⓑ Ⓒ Ⓓ Ⓔ   43 Ⓐ Ⓑ Ⓒ Ⓓ Ⓔ   61 Ⓐ Ⓑ Ⓒ Ⓓ Ⓔ   79 Ⓐ Ⓑ Ⓒ Ⓓ Ⓔ
8 Ⓐ Ⓑ Ⓒ Ⓓ Ⓔ   26 Ⓐ Ⓑ Ⓒ Ⓓ Ⓔ   44 Ⓐ Ⓑ Ⓒ Ⓓ Ⓔ   62 Ⓐ Ⓑ Ⓒ Ⓓ Ⓔ   80 Ⓐ Ⓑ Ⓒ Ⓓ Ⓔ
9 Ⓐ Ⓑ Ⓒ Ⓓ Ⓔ   27 Ⓐ Ⓑ Ⓒ Ⓓ Ⓔ   45 Ⓐ Ⓑ Ⓒ Ⓓ Ⓔ   63 Ⓐ Ⓑ Ⓒ Ⓓ Ⓔ   81 Ⓐ Ⓑ Ⓒ Ⓓ Ⓔ
10 Ⓐ Ⓑ Ⓒ Ⓓ Ⓔ   28 Ⓐ Ⓑ Ⓒ Ⓓ Ⓔ   46 Ⓐ Ⓑ Ⓒ Ⓓ Ⓔ   64 Ⓐ Ⓑ Ⓒ Ⓓ Ⓔ   82 Ⓐ Ⓑ Ⓒ Ⓓ Ⓔ
11 Ⓐ Ⓑ Ⓒ Ⓓ Ⓔ   29 Ⓐ Ⓑ Ⓒ Ⓓ Ⓔ   47 Ⓐ Ⓑ Ⓒ Ⓓ Ⓔ   65 Ⓐ Ⓑ Ⓒ Ⓓ Ⓔ   83 Ⓐ Ⓑ Ⓒ Ⓓ Ⓔ
12 Ⓐ Ⓑ Ⓒ Ⓓ Ⓔ   30 Ⓐ Ⓑ Ⓒ Ⓓ Ⓔ   48 Ⓐ Ⓑ Ⓒ Ⓓ Ⓔ   66 Ⓐ Ⓑ Ⓒ Ⓓ Ⓔ   84 Ⓐ Ⓑ Ⓒ Ⓓ Ⓔ
13 Ⓐ Ⓑ Ⓒ Ⓓ Ⓔ   31 Ⓐ Ⓑ Ⓒ Ⓓ Ⓔ   49 Ⓐ Ⓑ Ⓒ Ⓓ Ⓔ   67 Ⓐ Ⓑ Ⓒ Ⓓ Ⓔ   85 Ⓐ Ⓑ Ⓒ Ⓓ Ⓔ
14 Ⓐ Ⓑ Ⓒ Ⓓ Ⓔ   32 Ⓐ Ⓑ Ⓒ Ⓓ Ⓔ   50 Ⓐ Ⓑ Ⓒ Ⓓ Ⓔ   68 Ⓐ Ⓑ Ⓒ Ⓓ Ⓔ   86 Ⓐ Ⓑ Ⓒ Ⓓ Ⓔ
15 Ⓐ Ⓑ Ⓒ Ⓓ Ⓔ   33 Ⓐ Ⓑ Ⓒ Ⓓ Ⓔ   51 Ⓐ Ⓑ Ⓒ Ⓓ Ⓔ   69 Ⓐ Ⓑ Ⓒ Ⓓ Ⓔ   87 Ⓐ Ⓑ Ⓒ Ⓓ Ⓔ
16 Ⓐ Ⓑ Ⓒ Ⓓ Ⓔ   34 Ⓐ Ⓑ Ⓒ Ⓓ Ⓔ   52 Ⓐ Ⓑ Ⓒ Ⓓ Ⓔ   70 Ⓐ Ⓑ Ⓒ Ⓓ Ⓔ   88 Ⓐ Ⓑ Ⓒ Ⓓ Ⓔ
17 Ⓐ Ⓑ Ⓒ Ⓓ Ⓔ   35 Ⓐ Ⓑ Ⓒ Ⓓ Ⓔ   53 Ⓐ Ⓑ Ⓒ Ⓓ Ⓔ   71 Ⓐ Ⓑ Ⓒ Ⓓ Ⓔ
18 Ⓐ Ⓑ Ⓒ Ⓓ Ⓔ   36 Ⓐ Ⓑ Ⓒ Ⓓ Ⓔ   54 Ⓐ Ⓑ Ⓒ Ⓓ Ⓔ   72 Ⓐ Ⓑ Ⓒ Ⓓ Ⓔ

PRACTICE TEST 5

1 Ⓐ Ⓑ Ⓒ Ⓓ Ⓔ	19 Ⓐ Ⓑ Ⓒ Ⓓ Ⓔ	37 Ⓐ Ⓑ Ⓒ Ⓓ Ⓔ	55 Ⓐ Ⓑ Ⓒ Ⓓ Ⓔ	73 Ⓐ Ⓑ Ⓒ Ⓓ Ⓔ
2 Ⓐ Ⓑ Ⓒ Ⓓ Ⓔ	20 Ⓐ Ⓑ Ⓒ Ⓓ Ⓔ	38 Ⓐ Ⓑ Ⓒ Ⓓ Ⓔ	56 Ⓐ Ⓑ Ⓒ Ⓓ Ⓔ	74 Ⓐ Ⓑ Ⓒ Ⓓ Ⓔ
3 Ⓐ Ⓑ Ⓒ Ⓓ Ⓔ	21 Ⓐ Ⓑ Ⓒ Ⓓ Ⓔ	39 Ⓐ Ⓑ Ⓒ Ⓓ Ⓔ	57 Ⓐ Ⓑ Ⓒ Ⓓ Ⓔ	75 Ⓐ Ⓑ Ⓒ Ⓓ Ⓔ
4 Ⓐ Ⓑ Ⓒ Ⓓ Ⓔ	22 Ⓐ Ⓑ Ⓒ Ⓓ Ⓔ	40 Ⓐ Ⓑ Ⓒ Ⓓ Ⓔ	58 Ⓐ Ⓑ Ⓒ Ⓓ Ⓔ	76 Ⓐ Ⓑ Ⓒ Ⓓ Ⓔ
5 Ⓐ Ⓑ Ⓒ Ⓓ Ⓔ	23 Ⓐ Ⓑ Ⓒ Ⓓ Ⓔ	41 Ⓐ Ⓑ Ⓒ Ⓓ Ⓔ	59 Ⓐ Ⓑ Ⓒ Ⓓ Ⓔ	77 Ⓐ Ⓑ Ⓒ Ⓓ Ⓔ
6 Ⓐ Ⓑ Ⓒ Ⓓ Ⓔ	24 Ⓐ Ⓑ Ⓒ Ⓓ Ⓔ	42 Ⓐ Ⓑ Ⓒ Ⓓ Ⓔ	60 Ⓐ Ⓑ Ⓒ Ⓓ Ⓔ	78 Ⓐ Ⓑ Ⓒ Ⓓ Ⓔ
7 Ⓐ Ⓑ Ⓒ Ⓓ Ⓔ	25 Ⓐ Ⓑ Ⓒ Ⓓ Ⓔ	43 Ⓐ Ⓑ Ⓒ Ⓓ Ⓔ	61 Ⓐ Ⓑ Ⓒ Ⓓ Ⓔ	79 Ⓐ Ⓑ Ⓒ Ⓓ Ⓔ
8 Ⓐ Ⓑ Ⓒ Ⓓ Ⓔ	26 Ⓐ Ⓑ Ⓒ Ⓓ Ⓔ	44 Ⓐ Ⓑ Ⓒ Ⓓ Ⓔ	62 Ⓐ Ⓑ Ⓒ Ⓓ Ⓔ	80 Ⓐ Ⓑ Ⓒ Ⓓ Ⓔ
9 Ⓐ Ⓑ Ⓒ Ⓓ Ⓔ	27 Ⓐ Ⓑ Ⓒ Ⓓ Ⓔ	45 Ⓐ Ⓑ Ⓒ Ⓓ Ⓔ	63 Ⓐ Ⓑ Ⓒ Ⓓ Ⓔ	81 Ⓐ Ⓑ Ⓒ Ⓓ Ⓔ
10 Ⓐ Ⓑ Ⓒ Ⓓ Ⓔ	28 Ⓐ Ⓑ Ⓒ Ⓓ Ⓔ	46 Ⓐ Ⓑ Ⓒ Ⓓ Ⓔ	64 Ⓐ Ⓑ Ⓒ Ⓓ Ⓔ	82 Ⓐ Ⓑ Ⓒ Ⓓ Ⓔ
11 Ⓐ Ⓑ Ⓒ Ⓓ Ⓔ	29 Ⓐ Ⓑ Ⓒ Ⓓ Ⓔ	47 Ⓐ Ⓑ Ⓒ Ⓓ Ⓔ	65 Ⓐ Ⓑ Ⓒ Ⓓ Ⓔ	83 Ⓐ Ⓑ Ⓒ Ⓓ Ⓔ
12 Ⓐ Ⓑ Ⓒ Ⓓ Ⓔ	30 Ⓐ Ⓑ Ⓒ Ⓓ Ⓔ	48 Ⓐ Ⓑ Ⓒ Ⓓ Ⓔ	66 Ⓐ Ⓑ Ⓒ Ⓓ Ⓔ	84 Ⓐ Ⓑ Ⓒ Ⓓ Ⓔ
13 Ⓐ Ⓑ Ⓒ Ⓓ Ⓔ	31 Ⓐ Ⓑ Ⓒ Ⓓ Ⓔ	49 Ⓐ Ⓑ Ⓒ Ⓓ Ⓔ	67 Ⓐ Ⓑ Ⓒ Ⓓ Ⓔ	85 Ⓐ Ⓑ Ⓒ Ⓓ Ⓔ
14 Ⓐ Ⓑ Ⓒ Ⓓ Ⓔ	32 Ⓐ Ⓑ Ⓒ Ⓓ Ⓔ	50 Ⓐ Ⓑ Ⓒ Ⓓ Ⓔ	68 Ⓐ Ⓑ Ⓒ Ⓓ Ⓔ	86 Ⓐ Ⓑ Ⓒ Ⓓ Ⓔ
15 Ⓐ Ⓑ Ⓒ Ⓓ Ⓔ	33 Ⓐ Ⓑ Ⓒ Ⓓ Ⓔ	51 Ⓐ Ⓑ Ⓒ Ⓓ Ⓔ	69 Ⓐ Ⓑ Ⓒ Ⓓ Ⓔ	87 Ⓐ Ⓑ Ⓒ Ⓓ Ⓔ
16 Ⓐ Ⓑ Ⓒ Ⓓ Ⓔ	34 Ⓐ Ⓑ Ⓒ Ⓓ Ⓔ	52 Ⓐ Ⓑ Ⓒ Ⓓ Ⓔ	70 Ⓐ Ⓑ Ⓒ Ⓓ Ⓔ	88 Ⓐ Ⓑ Ⓒ Ⓓ Ⓔ
17 Ⓐ Ⓑ Ⓒ Ⓓ Ⓔ	35 Ⓐ Ⓑ Ⓒ Ⓓ Ⓔ	53 Ⓐ Ⓑ Ⓒ Ⓓ Ⓔ	71 Ⓐ Ⓑ Ⓒ Ⓓ Ⓔ	
18 Ⓐ Ⓑ Ⓒ Ⓓ Ⓔ	36 Ⓐ Ⓑ Ⓒ Ⓓ Ⓔ	54 Ⓐ Ⓑ Ⓒ Ⓓ Ⓔ	72 Ⓐ Ⓑ Ⓒ Ⓓ Ⓔ	

PRACTICE TEST 6

1 Ⓐ Ⓑ Ⓒ Ⓓ Ⓔ	19 Ⓐ Ⓑ Ⓒ Ⓓ Ⓔ	37 Ⓐ Ⓑ Ⓒ Ⓓ Ⓔ	55 Ⓐ Ⓑ Ⓒ Ⓓ Ⓔ	73 Ⓐ Ⓑ Ⓒ Ⓓ Ⓔ
2 Ⓐ Ⓑ Ⓒ Ⓓ Ⓔ	20 Ⓐ Ⓑ Ⓒ Ⓓ Ⓔ	38 Ⓐ Ⓑ Ⓒ Ⓓ Ⓔ	56 Ⓐ Ⓑ Ⓒ Ⓓ Ⓔ	74 Ⓐ Ⓑ Ⓒ Ⓓ Ⓔ
3 Ⓐ Ⓑ Ⓒ Ⓓ Ⓔ	21 Ⓐ Ⓑ Ⓒ Ⓓ Ⓔ	39 Ⓐ Ⓑ Ⓒ Ⓓ Ⓔ	57 Ⓐ Ⓑ Ⓒ Ⓓ Ⓔ	75 Ⓐ Ⓑ Ⓒ Ⓓ Ⓔ
4 Ⓐ Ⓑ Ⓒ Ⓓ Ⓔ	22 Ⓐ Ⓑ Ⓒ Ⓓ Ⓔ	40 Ⓐ Ⓑ Ⓒ Ⓓ Ⓔ	58 Ⓐ Ⓑ Ⓒ Ⓓ Ⓔ	76 Ⓐ Ⓑ Ⓒ Ⓓ Ⓔ
5 Ⓐ Ⓑ Ⓒ Ⓓ Ⓔ	23 Ⓐ Ⓑ Ⓒ Ⓓ Ⓔ	41 Ⓐ Ⓑ Ⓒ Ⓓ Ⓔ	59 Ⓐ Ⓑ Ⓒ Ⓓ Ⓔ	77 Ⓐ Ⓑ Ⓒ Ⓓ Ⓔ
6 Ⓐ Ⓑ Ⓒ Ⓓ Ⓔ	24 Ⓐ Ⓑ Ⓒ Ⓓ Ⓔ	42 Ⓐ Ⓑ Ⓒ Ⓓ Ⓔ	60 Ⓐ Ⓑ Ⓒ Ⓓ Ⓔ	78 Ⓐ Ⓑ Ⓒ Ⓓ Ⓔ
7 Ⓐ Ⓑ Ⓒ Ⓓ Ⓔ	25 Ⓐ Ⓑ Ⓒ Ⓓ Ⓔ	43 Ⓐ Ⓑ Ⓒ Ⓓ Ⓔ	61 Ⓐ Ⓑ Ⓒ Ⓓ Ⓔ	79 Ⓐ Ⓑ Ⓒ Ⓓ Ⓔ
8 Ⓐ Ⓑ Ⓒ Ⓓ Ⓔ	26 Ⓐ Ⓑ Ⓒ Ⓓ Ⓔ	44 Ⓐ Ⓑ Ⓒ Ⓓ Ⓔ	62 Ⓐ Ⓑ Ⓒ Ⓓ Ⓔ	80 Ⓐ Ⓑ Ⓒ Ⓓ Ⓔ
9 Ⓐ Ⓑ Ⓒ Ⓓ Ⓔ	27 Ⓐ Ⓑ Ⓒ Ⓓ Ⓔ	45 Ⓐ Ⓑ Ⓒ Ⓓ Ⓔ	63 Ⓐ Ⓑ Ⓒ Ⓓ Ⓔ	81 Ⓐ Ⓑ Ⓒ Ⓓ Ⓔ
10 Ⓐ Ⓑ Ⓒ Ⓓ Ⓔ	28 Ⓐ Ⓑ Ⓒ Ⓓ Ⓔ	46 Ⓐ Ⓑ Ⓒ Ⓓ Ⓔ	64 Ⓐ Ⓑ Ⓒ Ⓓ Ⓔ	82 Ⓐ Ⓑ Ⓒ Ⓓ Ⓔ
11 Ⓐ Ⓑ Ⓒ Ⓓ Ⓔ	29 Ⓐ Ⓑ Ⓒ Ⓓ Ⓔ	47 Ⓐ Ⓑ Ⓒ Ⓓ Ⓔ	65 Ⓐ Ⓑ Ⓒ Ⓓ Ⓔ	83 Ⓐ Ⓑ Ⓒ Ⓓ Ⓔ
12 Ⓐ Ⓑ Ⓒ Ⓓ Ⓔ	30 Ⓐ Ⓑ Ⓒ Ⓓ Ⓔ	48 Ⓐ Ⓑ Ⓒ Ⓓ Ⓔ	66 Ⓐ Ⓑ Ⓒ Ⓓ Ⓔ	84 Ⓐ Ⓑ Ⓒ Ⓓ Ⓔ
13 Ⓐ Ⓑ Ⓒ Ⓓ Ⓔ	31 Ⓐ Ⓑ Ⓒ Ⓓ Ⓔ	49 Ⓐ Ⓑ Ⓒ Ⓓ Ⓔ	67 Ⓐ Ⓑ Ⓒ Ⓓ Ⓔ	85 Ⓐ Ⓑ Ⓒ Ⓓ Ⓔ
14 Ⓐ Ⓑ Ⓒ Ⓓ Ⓔ	32 Ⓐ Ⓑ Ⓒ Ⓓ Ⓔ	50 Ⓐ Ⓑ Ⓒ Ⓓ Ⓔ	68 Ⓐ Ⓑ Ⓒ Ⓓ Ⓔ	86 Ⓐ Ⓑ Ⓒ Ⓓ Ⓔ
15 Ⓐ Ⓑ Ⓒ Ⓓ Ⓔ	33 Ⓐ Ⓑ Ⓒ Ⓓ Ⓔ	51 Ⓐ Ⓑ Ⓒ Ⓓ Ⓔ	69 Ⓐ Ⓑ Ⓒ Ⓓ Ⓔ	87 Ⓐ Ⓑ Ⓒ Ⓓ Ⓔ
16 Ⓐ Ⓑ Ⓒ Ⓓ Ⓔ	34 Ⓐ Ⓑ Ⓒ Ⓓ Ⓔ	52 Ⓐ Ⓑ Ⓒ Ⓓ Ⓔ	70 Ⓐ Ⓑ Ⓒ Ⓓ Ⓔ	88 Ⓐ Ⓑ Ⓒ Ⓓ Ⓔ
17 Ⓐ Ⓑ Ⓒ Ⓓ Ⓔ	35 Ⓐ Ⓑ Ⓒ Ⓓ Ⓔ	53 Ⓐ Ⓑ Ⓒ Ⓓ Ⓔ	71 Ⓐ Ⓑ Ⓒ Ⓓ Ⓔ	
18 Ⓐ Ⓑ Ⓒ Ⓓ Ⓔ	36 Ⓐ Ⓑ Ⓒ Ⓓ Ⓔ	54 Ⓐ Ⓑ Ⓒ Ⓓ Ⓔ	72 Ⓐ Ⓑ Ⓒ Ⓓ Ⓔ	

Provided on the next several pages are the questions for all six Following Oral Instructions practice tests. In order to practice realistically, these questions must be read out loud to you, and you must answer exclusively based upon what you hear. If you read the questions yourself, you are cheating yourself out of any benefits that these practice tests have to offer. The questions should be read at a rather slow and deliberate rate of approximately 75 words per minute and with proper diction. It is important also that the reader pause occasionally according to the specific directions given in the wording of the questions.

Once you complete a practice test, you should then review the questions you missed in order to determine what caused you to miss them. This review should enable you to be more successful on similar questions next time.

PRACTICE TEST 1

Look at Sample 1. (Pause slightly.) Sample 1 has a number with a line beside it. (Pause slightly.) Write the letter E as in egg on the line. (Pause 2 seconds.) Now, on the Answer Sheet, find number 22 and darken the space for the letter you wrote on the line. (Pause 5 seconds.)

Look at Sample 2. (Pause slightly.) There are four numbers. Circle the smallest number. (Pause 2 seconds.) Now, on the Answer Sheet, find that number, and darken the letter C as in cat. (Pause 5 seconds.)

Look at Sample 3. (Pause slightly.) There are two letters and two numbers. (Pause slightly.) Underline the second number and the last letter. (Pause 3 seconds.) On the Answer Sheet, darken the number-letter combination you just underlined. (Pause 5 seconds.)

Look at Sample 4. (Pause slightly.) There are five numbers. Draw a line under the third number. (Pause 3 seconds.) Now, find the number you underlined on the Answer Sheet, and darken the letter A. (Pause 5 seconds.)

Look at Sample 5. (Pause slightly.) Circle the second letter. (Pause 2 seconds.) Now, on the Answer Sheet, find number 67, and darken the letter you just circled. (Pause 5 seconds.)

Look at the four boxes in Sample 6. (Pause slightly.) Each box has a letter with a line beside it. (Pause slightly.) Find the box with the letter E as in egg, and write the number 21 on the line beside it. (Pause 3 seconds.) On the Answer sheet, darken the number-letter combination you just made. (Pause 5 seconds.)

Look at Sample 7. (Pause slightly.) There are five numbers. (Pause slightly.) If one of the numbers is greater than 42 and less than 57, write an A as in apple on the line beside it. (Pause 5 seconds.) Now find that number on the Answer Sheet, and darken the letter A. (Pause 4 seconds.) If there is not a number greater than 42 and less than 57, darken the letter C on line 23 of the Answer Sheet. (Pause 5 seconds.)

Look at Sample 8. (Pause slightly.) There are two boxes and two circles of different sizes with a number in each. (Pause slightly.) Write the letter D as in dog in the larger box. (Pause 2 seconds.) Now, on the Answer Sheet, darken the number-letter combination in the box. (Pause 5 seconds.)

Look at the letters in Sample 9. (Pause slightly.) Find the letter D as in dog, and write a 7 beside it. (Pause 3 seconds.) On the Answer Sheet, darken the number-letter combination you just made. (Pause 5 seconds.)

Look at Sample 10. (Pause slightly.) There are four different size boxes with a number in each. (Pause slightly.) Write the letter E as in egg on the line in the largest box. (Pause 4 seconds.) On the Answer Sheet, darken the number-letter combination for the box in which you just wrote. (Pause 5 seconds.)

Look at Sample 11. (Pause slightly.) There are two squares and two circles. (Pause slightly.) If 4 is greater than 7 and 6 is less than 9, write the letter D as in dog in the smaller circle. (Pause 5 seconds.) Otherwise, write the letter A as in apple in the larger square. (Pause 4 seconds.) On the answer sheet, darken the number-letter combination for the circle or square in which you just wrote. (Pause 5 seconds.)

continued on next page

PRACTICE TEST 1
continued

Look at the five letters in Sample 12. (Pause slightly.) If there are two letters that are the same, write the number 59 next to the letter A. (Pause 3 seconds.) Otherwise, write the number 33 by the last letter. (Pause 3 seconds.) On the Answer Sheet, darken the number-letter combination you have made. (Pause 5 seconds.)

Look at Sample 13. (Pause slightly.) There are five circles with a time and a letter in each. On the line in the second circle, write the last two numbers of the time in that circle. (Pause 4 seconds.) On the Answer Sheet, darken the number-letter combination for the circle in which you just wrote. (Pause 5 seconds.)

Look at Sample 14. (Pause slightly.) There are two squares and two circles of different sizes with a letter in each. (Pause 3 seconds.) If 2 is greater than 1 and 9 is less than 11, write the number 78 in the larger square. (Pause 3 seconds.) Otherwise, write the number 32 in the smaller circle. (Pause 3 seconds.) On the Answer Sheet, darken the number-letter combination you have made. (Pause 5 seconds.)

Look at the four letters in Sample 14 again. (Pause slightly.) Draw a line under the first letter if that letter is a B as in boy. (Pause 3 seconds.) Otherwise, draw a line under the last letter. (Pause 3 seconds.) Now, on the Answer Sheet, find the number 88, and darken the letter under which you drew a line. (Pause 5 seconds.)

Look at Sample 14 again. (Pause slightly.) If A comes before B and 7 is greater than 5, draw a line under the third letter. (Pause 3 seconds.) Otherwise, draw a line under the second letter. (Pause 3 seconds.) On the answer Sheet, find the number 26, and darken the letter under which you just drew a line. (Pause 5 seconds.)

Look at Sample 15. (Pause slightly.) There are four boxes with a different time in each. Find the latest time, and write the last two numbers of that time on the line in its box. (Pause 4 seconds.) Now, on the Answer Sheet, find the number you wrote on the line in the box, and darken the letter E as in egg. (Pause 5 seconds.)

Look at Sample 16. (Pause slightly.) The number in each box represents a number of parcels. Find the box with the largest number of parcels. (Pause 3 seconds.) Write the letter C as in cat on the line in that box. (Pause 3 seconds.) On the Answer Sheet, darken the number-letter combination for that box. (Pause 5 seconds.)

Look at the four boxes in Sample 16 again. (Pause slightly.) If the second box has more parcels than the first box, write an E as in egg in the first box. (Pause 4 seconds.) Otherwise, write a D as in dog in the next-to-last box. (Pause 4 seconds.) Now, on the Answer Sheet, darken the number-letter combination for the box in which you just wrote. (Pause 5 seconds.)

Look at sample 17. (Pause slightly.) If the largest circle has the smallest number, write an A as in apple in that circle. (Pause 3 seconds.) Otherwise, write a B as in boy in the second circle. (Pause 3 seconds.) On the Answer Sheet, darken the number-letter combination in the circle in which you just wrote.

End of Following Oral Instructions Questions – Practice Test 1

PRACTICE TEST 2

Look at Sample 1. (Pause slightly.) Draw a line under the second number. (Pause 3 seconds.) On the Answer Sheet, find that number, and darken the letter A as in apple. (Pause 5 seconds.)

Look at Sample 2. (Pause slightly.) Draw a circle around the last letter. (Pause 3 seconds.) On the Answer Sheet, find the number 78 and darken the letter you circled. (Pause 5 seconds.)

Look at Sample 3. (Pause slightly.) There are three letters and three numbers. (Pause slightly.) Underline the first letter and the last number. (Pause 4 seconds.) On the Answer Sheet, darken the number-letter combination you just underlined. (Pause 5 seconds.)

Look at Sample 4. (Pause slightly.) Circle the largest number. (Pause 3 seconds.) Now, find that number on the Answer Sheet, and darken the letter B as in boy. (Pause 5 seconds.)

Look at Sample 5. (Pause slightly.) Find the letter A as in apple, and write the number 8 beside it. (Pause 3 seconds.) On the Answer Sheet, darken the number-letter combination you have made. (Pause 5 seconds.)

Look at Sample 6. (Pause slightly.) There are four different size boxes with a number in each. (Pause slightly.) In the next-to-last box, write the letter B as in boy next to the number. (Pause 3 seconds.) On the Answer Sheet, darken the number-letter combination you have made. (Pause 5 seconds.)

Look at Sample 7. (Pause slightly.) There are four numbers in Sample 7. (Pause slightly.) If 68 is less than 86 and the letter C as in cat comes before the letter D as in dog in the alphabet, underline the first number. (Pause 3 seconds.) Otherwise, underline the last number. (Pause 3 seconds.) On the Answer Sheet, find the number you underlined, and darken the letter A as in apple. (Pause 5 seconds.)

Look at Sample 8. (Pause slightly.) There are two boxes and two circles. (Pause slightly.) If 5 is greater than 2 and 9 is less than 12, write the letter C as in cat in the smaller circle. (Pause 3 seconds.) If not, write the letter A as in apple in the larger square. (Pause 3 seconds.) On the Answer Sheet, darken the number-letter combination you have made. (Pause 5 seconds.)

Look at Sample 9. (Pause slightly.) Write the letter D as in dog in the smallest box. (Pause 3 seconds.) On the Answer Sheet, darken the number-letter combination you have made. (Pause 4 seconds.)

Look at Sample 10. (Pause slightly.) There are five letters with a line before each. (Pause slightly.) If the second letter comes before the third letter in the alphabet, write the number 36 on the line before the first letter. (Pause 4 seconds.) Otherwise, write the number 47 on the last line. (Pause 3 seconds.) On the Answer Sheet, darken the number-letter combination you have made. (Pause 5 seconds.)

Look at the boxes and circles in Sample 11. (Pause slightly.) Write the letter B as in boy in the second box. (Pause 4 seconds.) On the Answer Sheet, darken B as in boy for the number in that box. (Pause 5 seconds.)

Look at Sample 11 again. (Pause slightly.) Write the letter C as in cat in the largest box. (Pause 3 seconds.) On the Answer Sheet, find the number 33 and darken the letter E. (Pause 5 seconds.)

continued on next page

PRACTICE TEST 2
continued

Look at Sample 12. (Pause slightly.) There are five numbers in Sample 12. (Pause slightly.) If the second number is larger than the last number, write the letter D as in dog by the last number. (Pause 2 seconds.) Otherwise, write the letter D as in dog by the first number. (Pause 4 seconds.) On the Answer Sheet, darken the number-letter combination you have made. (Pause 5 seconds.)

Sample 13 has a word with four lines under it. (Pause slightly.) On the first line, write the last letter of the word. (Pause 2 seconds.) On the last line, write the second letter of the word. (Pause 3 seconds.) Write the first letter on the second line, and write the third letter on the third line. (Pause 5 seconds.) Find number 54 on the Answer Sheet, darken the letter on the last line. (Pause 5 seconds.)

Look at Sample 14. (Pause slightly.) Listed in the five boxes are various mail delivery times. (Pause slightly.) Write the letter A as in apple in the box with the latest delivery time. (Pause 3 seconds.) On the Answer Sheet, find the number that would be created by using the last two digits of the time in the box in which you wrote the letter A as in apple, and darken the letter E as in egg. (Pause 5 seconds.)

In Sample 15, there is a line. (Pause slightly.) If 33 is greater than 22 and 44 is less than 11, write the number 11 on the line. (Pause 4 seconds.) Otherwise, write the number 44 on the line. (Pause 3 seconds.) On the Answer Sheet, find the number you wrote, and darken the letter C as in cat. (Pause 5 seconds.)

Look at Sample 16. (Pause slightly.) Each box has a number of letters to be postmarked. Find the box with the greatest number of letters to be postmarked. (Pause 3 seconds.) Write the letter B as in boy in that box. (Pause 2 seconds.) On the Answer Sheet, darken the number-letter combination you have made. (Pause 5 seconds.)

Look at Sample 17. (Pause slightly.) You will see the names of four cities with a number of parcels going to each city under each city's name. (Pause slightly.) Find the city with the largest number of parcels going to it, and circle the first letter in that city's name. (Pause 4 seconds.) On the Answer Sheet, find the number 17, and darken the letter you just circled. (Pause 5 seconds.)

Look at Sample 17 again. (Pause slightly.) If 56 is greater than 23 but less than 95, underline the second letter in the name of the city with the least number of parcels. (Pause 3 seconds.) Then find the number 39 on the Answer Sheet, and darken the letter you just underlined. (Pause 4 seconds.) Otherwise, darken the letter A as in apple at number 39 on the Answer Sheet. (Pause 5 seconds.)

In Sample 18, there are three boxes with a time of the day in each. (Pause slightly.) Find the box with the latest time in it. (Pause 3 seconds.) On the Answer Sheet, find the number that would be created by using the first two digits of that time, and darken the letter B as in boy.

End of Following Oral Instructions Questions – Practice Test 2

PRACTICE TEST 3

Look at Sample 1. (Pause slightly.) Draw a line under the fourth number. (Pause 2 seconds.) Now, on the Answer Sheet, darken the letter C as in cat for the number you underlined. (Pause 5 seconds.)

Look at Sample 2. (Pause slightly.) Write the letter D as in dog in the second box. (Pause 3 seconds.) Now, on the Answer Sheet, darken the number-letter combination you have made. (Pause 5 seconds.)

In Sample 3 there are four letters. (Pause slightly.) Draw a circle around the second letter. (Pause 2 seconds.) Find number 35 on the Answer Sheet, and darken the letter you circled. (Pause 5 seconds.)

In Sample 4 there are four boxes. (Pause slightly.) In each box is a number of parcels to be delivered. (Pause slightly.) In the box with the most parcels to be delivered, write the letter E as in egg. (Pause 3 seconds.) On the Answer Sheet, darken the number-letter combination you have made. (Pause 5 seconds.)

Look at Sample 4 again. (Pause slightly.) If 44 is greater than 48, write the letter A as in apple in the box with the lowest number. (Pause 3 seconds.) Otherwise, write the letter D as in dog in that box. (Pause 3 seconds.) On the Answer Sheet, darken the number-letter combination you have made. (Pause 5 seconds.)

Look at Sample 5. (Pause slightly.) There are four boxes of different sizes with a letter in each. (Pause slightly.) Write the number 68 in the smallest box. (Pause 3 seconds.) On the Answer Sheet, darken the number-letter combination you just made. (Pause 5 seconds.)

Looking at Sample 5 again, find the next-to-smallest box. (Pause slightly.) If 22 is less than 67, write the number 8 in that box. (Pause 4 seconds.) Otherwise, write the number 8 in the last box. (Pause 3 seconds.) Now, on the Answer Sheet, find the number 85, and darken the letter A as in apple. (Pause 5 seconds.)

In Sample 6, there are four circles with a time of day in each. (Pause slightly.) In the circle with the earliest time, write a D as in dog. (Pause 3 seconds.) On the Answer Sheet, find the number that would be created by using the last two digits of earliest time, and darken the letter D as in dog. (Pause 5 seconds.)

In Sample 7, five days of the week listed. If 44 is greater than 39, underline the second letter of the first day listed. (Pause 3 seconds.) If not, underline the seventh letter of the second day listed. (Pause 3 seconds.) On the Answer Sheet, find the number 36, and darken the letter you underlined. (Pause 5 seconds.)

Look at Sample 7 again. (Pause slightly.) If the name of the last day of the week listed begins with the letter R as in rat, draw a line under the last letter of the first day listed. (Pause 5 seconds.) Otherwise, darken the letter A as in apple at number 83 on the Answer Sheet. (Pause 5 seconds.)

Look at Sample 8. (Pause slightly.) There are four boxes with a number in each. (Pause slightly.) Write the letter C as in cat in the box that has the number closest to 77. (Pause 4 seconds.) On the Answer Sheet, darken the number-letter combination you have made. (Pause 5 seconds.)

continued on next page

PRACTICE TEST 3
continued

Look at Sample 9. (Pause slightly.) Each box contains a mail delivery time. (Pause slightly.) If any of the mail delivery times is after 5:55 PM, darken the letter E as in egg at number 38 on the Answer Sheet. (Pause 4 seconds.) Otherwise, darken the letter B as in boy at that number. (Pause 5 seconds.)

Look at Sample 10. (Pause slightly.) There are three boxes and two circles of different sizes. (Pause slightly.) If B as in boy comes before D as in dog in the alphabet, and if 23 is less than 34, darken the letter A as in apple on the Answer Sheet at the number found in the smallest box. (Pause 4 seconds.) Otherwise, darken the letter E as in egg at the number found in the smaller circle. (Pause 5 seconds.)

Look at Sample 10 again. (Pause slightly.) If the number in the largest box is smaller than the number in the largest circle, darken the letter B as in boy on the Answer Sheet at the number found in the largest circle. (Pause 5 seconds.) Otherwise, darken the letter A as in apple on the Answer Sheet at the number found in the smaller circle. (Pause 5 second.)

Look at Sample 11. (Pause slightly.) If the second number is an odd number and the first number is an even number, underline the first number. (Pause 4 seconds.) Then, on the Answer Sheet, find the number you underlined, and darken the letter A as in apple. (Pause 4 seconds.) Otherwise, find the second number on the Answer Sheet, and darken the letter B as in boy. (Pause 5 seconds.)

Look at the letters in Sample 12. (Pause slightly.) There are five lines, one for each letter. Circle the E as in egg, and write the number 58 under the fourth letter. (Pause 3 seconds.) If the number you just wrote is under the letter you circled, darken that number-letter combination on the Answer Sheet. (Pause 5 seconds.) Otherwise, at number 58 on the Answer Sheet, darken the letter above the number 58. (Pause 5 seconds.)

Look at Sample 13. (Pause slightly.) Draw a circle around the second number. (Pause 2 seconds.) Draw a circle around the last number. (Pause 2 seconds.) Draw a circle around the first number. (Pause 2 seconds.) On the Answer Sheet, find the second number you circled, and darken the letter D as in dog. (Pause 5 seconds.)

Look at Sample 13 again. (Pause slightly.) If the number you did not circle is larger than 78, darken the letter A as in apple on the Answer Sheet at the number you did not circle. (Pause 3 seconds.) Otherwise, darken the letter E as in egg on the Answer Sheet at the number you did not circle. (Pause 5 seconds.)

Look at Sample 14. (Pause slightly.) There are two squares and two lines. (Pause slightly.) Write the letter E as in egg in the smaller square. (Pause 3 seconds.) Write the number 72 on the first line. (Pause 2 seconds.) Darken this number-letter combination on the Answer Sheet. (Pause 5 seconds.)

Look at Sample 14 again. (Pause slightly.) If 12 is less than 15, write the letter D as in dog in the largest square, and write the number 22 on the last line. (Pause 3 seconds.) Then, on the Answer Sheet, darken this number-letter combination. (Pause 4 seconds.) Otherwise, darken 64-C.

End of Following Oral Instructions Questions – Practice Test 3

PRACTICE TEST 4

Look at Sample 1. (Pause slightly.) Underline the fifth letter in the sequence. (Pause 3 seconds.) On the Answer Sheet, find the number 44, and darken the letter that you underlined. (Pause 5 seconds.)

Look at Sample 2. (Pause slightly.) There are four different size circles with a letter in each. (Pause slightly.) In the smallest circle, do nothing. (Pause slightly.) In the largest circle, write the number 23. (Pause 3 seconds.) On the Answer Sheet, darken the number-letter combination you have made. (Pause 5 seconds.)

Look at the numbers in Sample 3. (Pause slightly.) Draw a line under the numbers greater than 27 but less than 43. (Pause 4 seconds.) On the Answer Sheet, darken the letter B as in boy for the numbers you underlined. (Pause 5 seconds.)

Look at Sample 4. (Pause slightly.) If 21 is greater than 27, draw a line under the last letter. (Pause 2 seconds.) Otherwise, draw a line under the third letter. (Pause 2 seconds.) On the Answer Sheet, find the number 62, and darken the letter you underlined. (Pause 5 seconds.)

Look at Sample 5. (Pause slightly.) There are two circles and two boxes of different sizes with a number in each. (Pause 2 seconds.) If 6 is greater than 5 and 8 is less than 7, write the letter C as in cat in the larger box. (Pause 3 seconds.) Otherwise, write the letter A as in apple in the larger circle. (Pause 3 seconds.) On the Answer Sheet, darken the number-letter combination you have made. (Pause 5 seconds.)

Look at the five circles in Sample 6. (Pause slightly.) The circles contain different mail delivery times. (Pause slightly.) Write the letter D as in dog in the circle that has the latest delivery time. (Pause 3 seconds.) On the Answer Sheet, find the number that would be created by using the first two numbers of the time in that circle, and darken the letter D as in dog. (Pause 5 seconds.)

Look at the circles and words in Sample 7. (Pause slightly.) Write the first letter of the last word in the first circle. (Pause 3 seconds.) Write the middle letter of the first word in the second circle. (Pause 3 seconds.) Write the last letter of the second word in the last circle. (Pause 3 seconds.) On the Answer Sheet, darken the number-letter combinations you have made. (Pause 5 seconds.)

Look at Sample 8. (Pause slightly.) If March comes before April in the calendar year, write the letter B as in boy in the first box. (Pause 4 seconds.) Otherwise, write the letter C as in cat in the second box. (Pause 4 seconds.) Now, on the Answer Sheet, darken the number-letter combination you have made. (Pause 5 seconds.)

Look at the X's and O's in Sample 9. (Pause slightly.) Draw a line under all of the X's. (Pause 3 seconds.) Count the number of X's you underlined, and write that number at the end of the series of X's and O's. (Pause 3 seconds.) Now, add 52 to that number. (Pause 3 seconds.) Find the resulting number on the Answer Sheet, and darken the letter A as in apple. (Pause 5 seconds.)

Look at Sample 10. (Pause slightly.) Write the letter D as in dog next to the numbers that are greater than 12 but less than 32. (Pause 4 seconds.) Now, on the Answer Sheet, darken the number-letter combinations you have made. (Pause 5 seconds.)

continued on next page

PRACTICE TEST 4
continued

Look at Sample 11. (Pause slightly.) Draw a line under the sixth number. (Pause 3 seconds.) Draw two lines under the third number. (Pause 3 seconds.) Now, on the Answer Sheet, find the number you underlined twice and darken the letter C as in cat. (Pause 5 seconds.)

Look at Sample 12. (Pause slightly.) There are three boxes with a number in each. (Pause slightly.) The first box has mail for Portland and Seattle. (Pause slightly.) The second box has mail for Fargo and Butte. (Pause slightly.) On the line in the third box, write the letter A. (Pause 3 seconds.) On the Answer Sheet, darken the number-letter combination you have made. (Pause 5 seconds.)

Look at Sample 12 again. (Pause slightly.) Write the letter E as in egg in the box that has mail for Fargo and Butte. (Pause 3 seconds.) Write the letter B as in boy in the box that has mail for Portland and Seattle. (Pause 3 seconds.) Now, on the Answer Sheet, darken the number-letter combinations you have just made.

End of Following Oral Instructions Questions – Practice Test 4

PRACTICE TEST 5

Look at the circles and words in Sample 1. (Pause slightly.) Write the last letter of the first word in the second circle. (Pause 3 seconds.) Write the first letter of the last word in the first circle. (Pause 3 seconds.) Write the third letter of the second word in the last circle. (Pause 3 seconds.) On the Answer Sheet, darken the number-letter combinations you have made. (Pause 5 seconds.)

Look at the three boxes in Sample 2. (Pause slightly.) If the smallest box has the largest number, write the letter B as in boy in that box. (Pause 3 seconds.) Otherwise, write the letter E as in egg in the largest box. (Pause 3 seconds.) On the Answer Sheet, darken the number-letter combination you have made. (Pause 5 seconds.)

Look at Sample 3. (Pause slightly.) Each of the four boxes contains the name of a city and the number of parcels to be delivered to that city. (Pause slightly.) If the last box has the largest number of parcels to be delivered, write the letter A as in apple next to the number in that box. (Pause 3 seconds.) Otherwise, write the letter C as in cat on the line next to the number in the first box. (Pause 3 seconds.) On the Answer Sheet, darken the number-letter combination you have made. (Pause 5 seconds.)

Look at Sample 4. (Pause slightly.) Draw a line under the numbers that are greater than 12 but less than 42. (Pause 4 seconds.) On the Answer Sheet, darken the letter B as in boy for the numbers you underlined. (Pause 5 seconds.)

Look at Sample 5. (Pause slightly.) Draw a line under each letter A as in apple that you see in the sequence. (Pause 3 seconds.) Count the number of A's you underlined, and write that number at the front of the sequence. (Pause 3 seconds.) Subtract 3 from that number. (Pause 3 seconds.) Find the resulting number on the Answer Sheet, and darken the letter A as in apple. (Pause 5 seconds.)

Look at Sample 6. (Pause slightly.) There are two boxes and two circles of different sizes. (Pause slightly.) Write the number 22 next to the letter in the smaller box. (Pause 3 seconds.) Write the number 53 next to the letter in the larger circle. (Pause 3 seconds.) On the Answer Sheet, darken the number-letter combinations you have made. (Pause 5 seconds.)

Look at Sample 7. (Pause slightly.) Write the letter C as in cat in the last box. (Pause 3 seconds.) In the first box, do nothing. (Pause slightly.) In the third box, write the letter E as in egg. (Pause 3 seconds.) On the Answer Sheet, darken the number-letter combinations you have made.

Look at Sample 8. (Pause slightly.) Each of the three boxes contains the name of a city and the number of express parcels to be delivered to that city. (Pause slightly.) Find the city with the second highest number of express parcels, and write the first letter of that city's name on the line in its box. (Pause 3 seconds.) On the Answer Sheet, darken the number-letter combination you have made. (Pause 5 seconds.)

Look at Sample 9. (Pause slightly.) If 8 is greater than 6 and 15 is less than 23, write the number 71 in front of the third letter. (Pause 3 seconds.) Otherwise, write the number 34 in front of the fourth letter. (Pause 3 seconds.) On the Answer Sheet, darken the number-letter combination you have made. (Pause 5 seconds.)

Look at Sample 10. (Pause slightly.) Draw a line under the numbers greater than 3 but less than 17. (Pause 4 seconds.) On the Answer Sheet, find the numbers you underlined, and darken the letter B as in boy for each. (Pause 5 seconds.)

Look at Sample 10 again. (Pause slightly.) Draw two lines under the numbers greater than 31 but less than 58. (Pause 3 seconds.) On the Answer Sheet, find the numbers under which you drew two lines, and darken the letter A as in apple for each.

End of Following Oral Instructions Questions – Practice Test 5

PRACTICE TEST 6

Look at Sample 1. (Pause slightly.) Draw a line under the fifth letter from the left. (Pause 3 seconds.) On the Answer Sheet, find the number 47, and darken the letter you underlined. (Pause 5 seconds.)

Look at Sample 2. (Pause slightly.) There are five circles, each containing a letter with a line beside it. (Pause slightly.) On the line in the last circle, write the smallest of the following numbers: 82, 78, 59, 64, 69. (Pause 3 seconds.) On the line in the third circle, write the number 21. (Pause 3 seconds.) On the line in the first circle, do nothing. (Pause slightly.) On the line in the second circle, write the largest of the following numbers: 80, 78, 56, 82, 79. (Pause 3 seconds.) On the Answer Sheet, darken the number-letter combinations you have made. (Pause 5 seconds.)

Look at Sample 3. (Pause slightly.) If there are 365 days in the calendar year and if Ronald Reagan is the current president of the United States, write a D as in dog on the line in the fourth box. (Pause 3 seconds.) Otherwise, write a C as in cat on the lines in the second and third boxes. (Pause 3 seconds.) On the Answer Sheet, darken the number-letter combination or combinations you have made. (Pause 5 seconds.)

Look at the X's and Y's in Sample 4. (Pause slightly.) Count the number of X's, and write the number of X's at the end of the line X's and Y's. (Pause 4 seconds.) Count the number of Y's, and write the number of Y's under the number of X's at the end of the line. (Pause 4 seconds.) Then subtract the number of Y's from the number of X's. (Pause 3 seconds.) Find the resulting number on the Answer Sheet, and darken the letter D as in dog. (Pause 5 seconds.)

Look at the numbers in Sample 5. (Pause slightly.) Draw a line under all the even numbers that are less than 27. (Pause 3 seconds.) On the Answer Sheet, find the numbers you underlined, and darken the letter A as in apple for each. (Pause 5 seconds.)

Look at Sample 5 again. (Pause slightly.) Circle the even numbers that are greater than 56. (Pause 3 seconds.) On the Answer Sheet, find the numbers you circled, and darken the letter E as in egg for each. (Pause 5 seconds.)

Look at the circles in Sample 6. (Pause slightly.) Each circle contains a mail collection time. (Pause slightly.) Write the letter B as in boy on the line in the circle with the earliest collection time. (Pause 3 seconds.) On the same line in the same circle, write the number that would be created by using the last two digits of the time in that circle. (Pause 3 seconds.) On your Answer Sheet, darken the number-letter combination you have made. (Pause 5 seconds.)

Look at Sample 6 again. (Pause slightly.) If 5 is greater than 3 and 13 is less than 15, write the letter E as in egg in the last circle. (Pause 3 seconds.) If not, write the letter B as in boy in the third circle. (Pause 3 seconds.) On the line beside the letter in the circle in which you just wrote, write the number that would be created by using the first two digits of the time in that circle. (Pause 3 seconds.) On the Answer Sheet, darken the number-letter combination you have made. (Pause 5 seconds.)

Look at Sample 7. (Pause slightly.) Write the number 65 by the letter on the right. (Pause 3 seconds.) Now, on the Answer Sheet, darken the number-letter combination you have made. (Pause 5 seconds.)

continued on next page

PRACTICE TEST 6
continued

Look at Sample 8. (Pause slightly.) There are three circles and three words. (Pause slightly.) Write the first letter of the second word in the second circle. (Pause 3 seconds.) Write the last letter of the first word in the last circle. (Pause 3 seconds.) Write the first letter of the third word in the first circle. (Pause 3 seconds.) On the Answer Sheet, darken the number-letter combinations you have made. (Pause 5 seconds.)

Look at the two boxes in Sample 9. (Pause slightly.) In the first box is the number of Priority Mail packages in route to the Jacksonville Post Offices. (Pause slightly.) In the second box is the number of Priority Mail packages in route to the Boston Post Office. (Pause slightly.) Write the letter D as in dog in the box that has the number of Priority Mail packages in route to the Jacksonville Post Office. (Pause 3 seconds.) Now, on the Answer Sheet, darken the number-letter combination you have made. (Pause 5 seconds.)

Look at Sample 9 again. (Pause slightly.) Write the letter B as in boy in the box with the smaller number of Priority Mail packages. (Pause 3 seconds.) On the Answer Sheet, darken the number-letter combination you have made. (Pause 5 seconds.)

Look at Sample 10. (Pause slightly.) There are three circles, each containing the name of a city. (Pause slightly.) The city of Gulfport has the latest mail delivery time. (Pause slightly.) The city of Waveland has the earliest delivery time. (Pause slightly.) The city of Biloxi has the middle delivery time. (Pause slightly.) Write the letter C as in cat in the circle with the city that has the earliest delivery time. (Pause 3 seconds.) On your Answer Sheet, darken the number-letter combination you have made.

End of Following Oral Instructions Questions – Practice Test 6

Practice Test 1

1. 22-E
2. 3-C
3. 5-E
4. 8-A
5. 67-D
6. 21-E
7. 45-A
8. 15-D
9. 7-D
10. 72-E
11. 77-A
12. 59-A
13. 30-C
14. 78-C, 88-D, 26-C
15. 25-E
16. 62-C, 39-D
17. 11-B

Practice Test 2

1. 11-A
2. 78-B
3. 3-A
4. 82-B
5. 8-A
6. 5-B
7. 27-A
8. 4-C
9. 9-D
10. 36-E
11. 2-B, 33-E
12. 62-D
13. 54-A
14. 10-E
15. 44-C
16. 64-B
17. 17-C, 39-E
18. 30-B

Practice Test 3

1. 42-C
2. 11-D
3. 35-E
4. 73-E, 37-D
5. 68-D, 85-A
6. 30-D
7. 36-E, 83-A
8. 79-C
9. 38-B
10. 7-A, 2-A
11. 34-A
12. 58-E
13. 71-D, 61-E
14. 72-E, 22-D

Practice Test 4

1. 44-D
2. 23-A
3. 28-B, 3 0-B, 41-B
4. 62-E
5. 19-A
6. 71-D
7. 14-C, 37-B, 21-E
8. 85-B
9. 60-A
10. 18-D, 31-D, 26-D
11. 73-C
12. 64-A, 67-B, 43-E

Practice Test 5

1. 37-A, 76-B, 18-D
2. 12-E
3. 48-C
4. 29-B, 41-B, 36-B
5. 6-A
6. 53-D, 22-E
7. 78-C, 27-E
8. 51-C
9. 71-C
10. 8-B, 14-B, 15-B, 32-A, 57-A

Practice Test 6

1. 47-E
2. 59-B, 21-A, 82-D
3. 26-C, 33-C
4. 2-D
5. 14-A, 24-A, 58-E, 80-E
6. 50-B, 70-E
7. 65-C
8. 79-A, 61-E, 63-C
9. 85-D, 49-B
10. 88-C

About the Confusing
Duplicate Application Systems

Until recently, there was only one Postal application system. This system, I call it the Original System, is one of the most secretive, frustrating, and confusing creations ever conceived by man. Many people believe that its real purpose is to prevent you from actually applying and to drive you nuts while doing so. And I don't necessarily disagree. Unfortunately, as of the publish date of this book, the Original System was still in use for some jobs and tests.

Recently they launched the new eCareer application system. This new system is supposed to simplify the process in a number of ways. The best thing about it is that there's no more waiting for test dates. You can now apply for jobs and exams literally anytime you want. Another improvement is that everything is handled electronically. But, even though it offers some improvements, the application process itself is a monster. And due to an unbelievable number of programming and human errors, the eCareer job search function is a joke. Bottom line ... Since the Postal Service is federal agency, the new "improved" application system is naturally a mistake-laden bureaucratic nightmare. It still seems like their goal is to push us to the edge of insanity.

All jobs/exams were supposed to be moved over to eCareer, and this should happen eventually, but it certainly had not happened yet as of the publish date of this book. As I write these words, **eCareer is being used for many jobs and exams ... but some are still on the old system ... and even worse, some seem to randomly float back and forth between the two systems.** Beginning on the next page are details on what jobs/exams go with which system as of the publish date of this book. To find if anything has changed when you plan to apply, check Pathfinder Perks (page 19) for any updates.

The net result is mass confusion. Both application systems are equally frustrating, just in different ways. Most people have no idea what to do or which way to go. And the Postal Service doesn't offer any real help or guidance. As of the publish date of this book, both systems were active on the Postal website, and there were links to the two different systems randomly scattered around the site. However, there were no clear instructions for either system or specific info about what jobs or exams go with which system. And there's no such thing as contacting them to ask questions. No organization does a better job of hiding from the public than the good old U.S. Postal Service.

That's where I come in. I'm not sure if I should be proud of this or not, but for some reason I'm able to navigate through bureaucratic mazes and find short cuts to make the process more manageable. My brain just doesn't work exactly like everybody else's. Ask my kids. They will happily talk at length about how their Dad seems to be a little more strange than other Dads.

To help you successfully manage the application process, first I will explain what jobs and exams go with which system ... and what jobs and exams float between the two systems. The chart on the next page includes all the jobs along with the respective exams where applicable.

Then – for both systems – I will give you instructions, warn you about obstacles, and share tips for overcoming them. We will look at the new eCareer system first since this is where many jobs are now posted and where all jobs should eventually be posted.

What Jobs & Exams Go with Which System?

Let me start with a note to explain why some of the some of this info is ambiguous. The main reason is that we're talking about the U.S. Postal Service, and almost nothing about the U.S. Postal Service is straightforward and absolute. But more to the point in this particular case, things basically went haywire when they first brought the new eCareer application system online. Several jobs/exams simply disappeared temporarily. When they began to randomly resurface, the postings did not necessarily appear where expected, and some proceeded to undertake unusual migrations. The below chart is an accurate portrait of the situation as of the publish date of this book, but as I have preached over and over, stay tuned to Pathfinder Perks (page 19) for any updates.

Exam	Job	System
230/238/240	Motor Vehicle Operator	eCareer
230/238/240	Tractor Trailer Operator	eCareer
473/473E	City Carrier	eCareer
473/473E	Mail Handler	eCareer
473/473E	Mail Processing Clerk	eCareer
473/473E	Rural Carrier Associate	eCareer
473/473E	Sales, Service, and Distribution Associate	eCareer
916	Custodial Maintenance	eCareer
943/943E	Automotive Mechanic	eCareer
944/944E	Automotive Technician	eCareer
955/955E	Building Equipment Mechanic	eCareer
955/955E	Electronic Technician	eCareer
955/955E	Mail Processing Equipment Mechanic	eCareer
955/955E	Maintenance Mechanic	eCareer
NA	Postmaster Relief / Replacement	eCareer
NA	Professional Corporate Jobs	eCareer
NA	Temporary Relief / Rural Carrier	eCareer
NA	Transitional City Carrier	eCareer
Note: Some of the above jobs/exams have definitely moved to eCareer and no longer appear on the original system. Others have appeared at least once on eCareer and "supposedly" will no longer be posted on the original system. However, as you should have already learned by now, when it comes to the Postal Service, you cannot always trust the word "supposedly". To be safe, I recommend checking both systems just in case.		
710	Data Conversion Operator	Both
N/A	Casual Jobs	Both
Note: These jobs/exams have randomly appeared on both systems since the changeover, so you absolutely need to check both systems when searching for such postings.		

Late Breaking News

I updated this chart literally as the book was going to press. Two exams that had been missing in action finally reappeared, which enabled me to provide confirmed facts on them rather than relying on comments from my Postal contacts. I was particularly delighted to obtain this final info, but as mentioned above, you still need to check both systems to be safe.

New eCareer Application System

About eCareer

Now it's time to try to make some sense out of the eCareer system. Be forewarned that this will take a good bit of time and a bunch of pages. But don't blame me. All I'm doing is trying to make the process as simple, painless, and successful for you as possible. You will find that the Postal Service shares virtually nothing with you on the topics we will discuss over the next several pages.

In eCareer, everything revolves around job postings. (The original system is just the opposite with everything revolving around exam announcements.) Every time a single job opens up, it will be posted on eCareer. Every time they need to hire one single person, it will be posted on eCareer.

As mentioned previously, the new system is far more convenient but a nightmare to use. Many functions simply don't work because of glitches and errors. After a lot of experimenting, the good news is that I've found ways to get around these obstacles and to trick eCareer into working for you.

I won't ask if you feel sorry for people who attempt to apply without guidance because I already know the answer. You don't feel sorry for them at all because they are your competition. You want every single one of them to fail so that they don't get between you and your job. Come on now. Let's play nice. Once you have your job, it's okay if they learn about our little secret. Besides, if you are the only person who ever buys a copy of this book, I won't be able to feed my family!

eCareer Sequence & Timing

The eCareer system consists of six basics steps as recapped below:

1. <u>Create an eCareer Profile/Account</u>
True to form, they made a bureaucratic mountain out of what should be a little molehill. In the time it takes me to show you how to get through this maze, you could have delivered a ton of mail.

2. <u>Search for jobs</u>
This step sounds simple enough, but as mentioned a number of times, the job search function is so problematic that there's no way you will find all the postings without big time help.

3. <u>Apply</u>
Once you find a job that interests you, applying and completing the testing process may cause your hair to turn prematurely gray and/or fall out.

4. <u>Take an exam (if required)</u>
You must complete the testing process within only several days of applying. The problem is that all Postal exams carry 80-95% failure rates, and this leaves you very little time for test preparation.

5. <u>Interview</u>
If you have one of the top few scores, you will be invited to an employment interview unlike anything you've ever experienced before.

6. <u>If you don't get the job, continue applying and consider retaking the exam (if required)</u>
If you don't get the first job, continue applying for other jobs. If you didn't get invited to an interview because your exam score wasn't good enough, consider retaking the exam to improve your score.

Once you learn how to navigate around eCareer's problems, these steps can be accomplished rapidly … which is both good and bad. Let's say that you've already chosen your preferred job. Beginning from that point, here's a sequence of events with timing:

- You create an eCareer online profile/account. If you use my instructions as a checklist to gather all the needed information before starting, this can probably be completed in a half hour or so. Of course it will take time to gather the information, but I cannot begin to guess how long this will take. For some it will easy and painless, and for others it will be a monumental task. If you are obsessive-compulsive like me, it will take no time at all because you have meticulous records at your fingertips. If you are like a certain person who shall remain nameless and who is a little less organized, it may take you quite a while. (Okay, if you insist, I will give you a hint about who this person is – she wears a wedding ring that looks just like mine, only smaller.)

- Next you will search for job openings. The eCareer job search function is a joke, but once you learn how to trick it into working for you, a job search takes no time at all. You could literally find a job to apply for in minutes. Of course, if there is not a posting for your preferred job(s) or locations(s) at that particular time, you will need to continue searching until one is posted. But, again, there's no way to guess how long it will take if you must wait for a posting to appear.

- Once you find a job to apply for, if you follow my directions, the application itself should take a half hour or so – probably less.

- If the job requires an exam, you must complete the testing process in a matter of days.

Taking the exam is the last step that is under your control. It is all up to them from this point. This means that things won't necessarily move as rapidly after the exam. For the most part, everything depends upon your exam score. If you do not have one of the top few scores, you won't even be invited to an interview. If you do have a top score, you will be invited to an interview. But again, from this point it's all in their hands, so it's difficult to make realistic predictions.

If the job does not require an exam, they will review the applications and invite a few of the best qualified applicants to an interview. If an exam is not required, it's all in their hands once you apply, so from that point it's difficult to make realistic predictions.

So, how much control do you have over the eCareer process?

- ➢ Do you have control over creating an account? Yes.
- ➢ Do you have control over the job search? Yes.
- ➢ Do you have control over the application? Yes.
- ➢ Do you do have control over the exam? Yes and no. See the below explanation.

You must complete the testing process within several days of applying. You have no control over this deadline. But within this range of several days, you do have control over the particular date and time you take the test. The most important item you have control over, however, is your exam score. You have complete control over the choice of whether or not to prepare for the exam.

Allow me to preach yet again … if you are required to take an exam … if a study guide is available for your exam … and if you really want to succeed … you must order your guide immediately upon identifying the exam and before applying for a job. Once you apply, you will have only several days to complete the testing process. If you wait until after applying, it may be too late to even order a guide, much less to do the necessary study and practice work. If you really want a job, you must do everything possible to achieve the highest possible score, which means _you must order a guide immediately upon identifying the exam and before applying for a job … and you must use it!_

Create an eCareer Profile/Account

Instructions & Tips

There are nine steps (listed below) involved in creating an online eCareer profile or account. We will discuss each step individually over the next several pages.

- Registration

- Personal Data

- Work Experience

- Education / Training

- General Eligibility

- Veterans Preference

- Attachments

- Assessments

- Review & Release

The very first thing I need to do is share some very important tips with you that could make the difference between success and failure.

Tip #1 – You must have an active email account!
Under the new eCareer system, everything is done electronically. All contacts are made via email. So if you don't already have a valid email account, get one right now!

Tip #2 – No, you cannot just attach your resume and submit the application!
You are required to go through every step providing the specific info requested. Some items are mandatory, and others are optional. You must provide details for every mandatory item. If you skip a mandatory item, you cannot progress any farther or submit the application. You should reply to the optional items as well if at all possible.

Tip #3 – Save frequently!
You will be given an opportunity to save your information at least once on every page. Use every opportunity to save. If your computer shuts down for any reason, if you are timed out for inactivity, or if anything at all happens, all the information that you entered since the last save will be lost.

Tip #4 – Don't get timed out!
After a certain period of inactivity you will be timed out. The problem is that the period of inactivity is defined different ways. Depending upon which statement you believe, it may be as short as 10 minutes or as long as 30 minutes. The moral of this story is to be prepared so that you are not forced to leave the application inactive while searching for info. Per the instructions given over the next several pages, gather all the necessary information before you start.

Tip #5 – You must use the keyboard to copy and paste.
There will be various points where you enter text about your education, training, experience, etc. It is often easier to use a word processor function like Microsoft Word to create this text and then copy and paste the text into your application. You can spell check (very important!), do a word and/or character count, etc. when using Word. Some fields allow a limited number of words or characters. But when working in eCareer, you cannot right click the mouse or use the tool bar to copy and paste. These functions simply do not work on eCareer. To copy in eCareer, highlight the text and then hit the Ctrl key and the "C" (♦Copy) key. To paste in eCareer, place the cursor in the proper spot and then hit the Ctrl key and the "V" (♦Paste) key. After you paste text into your application or profile, proofread it paying particular attention to punctuation marks. Incompatible formats often seem to cause punctuation marks to undergo weird mutations.

Tip #6 – KSA's
Remember the nifty subject of KSA's that we discussed at the beginning of the book? "KSA" is an acronym for Knowledge, Skills, and Abilities. What other employers refer to as a skill-set, the Postal Service calls a KSA. Different jobs call for different KSA's. A job posting may or may not include the KSA's required that that particular position. But, whether they tell you about the KSA's or not, you are expected demonstrate the necessary KSA's in your application. (And at the interview as well, but we will talk about that later.) To the Postal Service, KSA's are important for any job, but they are far more important for technical maintenance jobs than for more normal processing and delivery jobs. How important this topic is to you depends upon the specific job you are seeking. The KSA's for different jobs are discussed beginning on page 336. So, where are you supposed to describe your mastery of the KSA's? As appropriate, include KSA information in the following sections of your profile/account and your application. We will discuss this KSA topic more as we cover the various sections of the profile/account and the application over the next several pages.

Profile/Account
- Work Experience
- Education & Training

Application
- Cover Letter
- Summary of Accomplishments

Beginning on the next page we will discuss the registration step.

Registration

To begin the process, go to *www.usps.com/employment* and click the "Create your eCareer profile" link. This will take you to the Registration page where you choose a username and password. (Note: This web address was valid as of the publish date of this book. However, future website changes may result in this URL being revised. If so, go to *www.usps.com* and look for a jobs or careers link that will take you to the desired page.)

Let's talk about usernames and passwords a bit. We just discussed the username and password for eCareer. What you don't know yet but will soon learn is that you must select another username and password later to login to your assessment (testing) account if an exam is required for your desired job. Having two sets of usernames and passwords for what seems to be a single Postal function causes confusion for most applicants. They have a difficult time remembering two sets of login info and trying to figure out which to use where.

Is there any way to get around this need for two sets of login info? If we could use the same login info for both purposes, wouldn't that be a lot easier? The answer to both questions is YES. Here's the deal ... There is criteria that the username and password must meet for both eCareer and the assessment account, but the assessment criteria is more demanding. So, if you make sure that the username and password you pick for eCareer also meets the assessment criteria, you can use the very same username and password for both. No more trying to remember two sets of login info and which to use where. So let's go over the assessment criteria to assure that the username and password you pick will indeed work for both. We will not discuss the eCareer criteria because, if our login info meets the assessment criteria, it will automatically work for eCareer.

Username / Login ID
- Must include at least six characters.
- That's it. That's the only criteria. As long as it has at least six characters, it's okay.

Password
- Must include at least eight characters.
  - At least one of these characters must be an upper case letter. (A, B, C, etc.)
  - At least one of these characters must be a lower case letter. (a, b, c, etc.)
  - At least one of these characters must be a number. (1, 2, 3, etc.)
  - At least one of these characters must be a symbol. (' ~ ! @ # $ % ^ & * = _ + | ; : , . < > ?)
- May not contain blank spaces.
- May not contain two or more consecutive identical characters. (For instance, you cannot use the word "pretty" because the letter "t" appears twice consecutively.)
- May not contain any of your personal data such as name, social security number, zip code, phone number, email address, or username/login ID. (Pay particular attention to the fact that the password cannot contain your username/login ID. For instance, if your username/login ID is "Cowboy", then your password cannot be "Cowboy&1". Even though this password meets the criteria for number of characters, uppercase letters, lowercase letters, numbers, and symbols, it is not acceptable because it contains your username/login ID "Cowboy". Lots of people don't catch this point and try to include their username/login ID as part of the password so it will be easier to remember. But, doing this is simply not acceptable.)

Before we leave this subject, let me remind you to record your username and password in a safe place so you can find it later. But if you do forget your login info, as with other online utilities, both eCareer and the assessment account have functions available to assist you.

After selecting your login info, the rest of the registration page is simple. Just enter your name, enter your email address, agree to their privacy policy, and click "Save and Continue". The next step is Personal Data.

Personal Data

This section is quick and easy. All you do is enter your name, mailing address, email address, and phone numbers. Then click "Work Experience" to continue.

Work Experience

Entering information about your current and/or prior employers is not terribly demanding, but there are a few important points you should bear in mind …

- You must include your work history for the last seven years or back to your 16th birthday if you are under the age of 23.

- Date gaps are not acceptable. If you were out of work for a period of time, make an entry with "Unemployed" as the company name and include a beginning and ending date for this period along with any appropriate comments. If you were unemployed because you were in school for a period of time, make a similar entry with "Student / Unemployed" as the company name.

- Try to enter accurate information. If you don't have exact dates, estimate as closely as possible. If it is not possible to obtain requested information, enter "unknown" as a response. If a former employer is no longer in business, enter "out of business".

- To assure that you have all needed records on hand before starting, be aware that your salary and your supervisor's name and phone number are required for current and prior employers in addition to basic contact information.

- You can include an unlimited number of former employers. Every time you click the "Add" button, it opens a new form for entering info on another employer.

- The "Grade Level" field is only applicable to government jobs and can be left blank for non-government jobs you've held.

- Use the "Description" box to describe job responsibilities, etc. As mentioned earlier, this is one of the spots where you can demonstrate mastery of KSA's (page 336). Don't be concerned if you cannot cover all the KSA's here because there will be other spots available later.

- To revise or correct information already entered, choose a job by selecting the dark box to the left of it and hit the "Edit" button. If you come back to apply for a different Postal job, you may want to edit an entry by revising the description to highlight aspects that are more relevant to the second job you are applying for.

- When you finish entering/editing info for a job or period of unemployment, click "Save". This will save your info and condense it into the Work Experience table with only key details displayed.

After completing this section, click "Education / Training" to continue.

Education / Training

This section is managed very similarly to how we handled Work Experience. Click "Add" to open a form for a new entry, click "Save" when finished with that entry, and click "Edit" to revise or correct information already entered. Again, you can include an unlimited number of entries. Again, this is an area where you can demonstrate KSA's (page 336). As you enter details on education and training, focus on how it contributed to mastery of particular KSA's. And again, if you apply for a different Postal job, you can edit an entry later by revising the description to highlight aspects that are more relevant to the second job. Every time you finish an entry, click "Save". After completing this section, click "General Eligibility" to continue.

General Eligibility

This is a simple section where you just reply to six questions to assure that you are indeed eligible for Postal employment. There's only one potential issue for males born after December 31, 1959. If you fit this description, you must provide your Selective Service Number to confirm that you have registered with the Selective Service System. I'm willing to bet that nobody has this number on the tip of their tongue. If you don't have this number handy, call the Selective Service System at phone number 847-688-6888 to get it. They will provide your Selective Service Number after asking for your date of birth and social security number to confirm your identity. According to the Selective Service System website, you cannot request the number online or by email; it is only available via phone. When you are finished with this section, click "Veterans Preference" to continue.

Veterans Preference

If you're not a military veteran, answer "No" to all four questions. If you are military veteran, answer the questions, enter your service information, and upload the requested supporting documents. If you do not have the documents in digital form, you will need to scan them into electronic files first. The files must be less than 2 MB in size and may be formatted as any of the following type files: .doc, .txt, .pdf, .html, .htm, .tif, .gif, .jpeg, .jpg, .xls

Attachments

This one will be easy to discuss because there's probably nothing you need to do. A statement in this section says:

"If the vacancy announcement requests supporting documents, please attach them here. If an attachment is not specifically requested, it may not be considered."

I have not seen any normal entry-level jobs that request attachments. Some professional corporate jobs (perhaps engineering, healthcare, etc. positions) may request that certifications, diplomas, etc. be attached, but I have not even seen attachments requested in any of these type postings either. The bottom line is that, unless specific attachments are requested, you should ignore this section.

Assessments

When the Postal Service implemented all their recent changes, for some reason they started to often use the term "assessment" in place of "exam" or "test". You will still see the words "exam" and "test" used occasionally, but "assessment" seems to be the current catchword.

There are three important points on this page you need to know about:

- Your candidate ID number is displayed on this page. This will be discussed more later, but the candidate ID number is extremely important. You need to make a note of this number. Do not lose it! You will need to use this number for taking exams and other functions.

- This page is where records will be kept for your test scores. Every time you take an exam, the results will be recorded and displayed on this page.

- There is only one question for you to answer: "Have you received an Exam History Code from the United States Postal Service?" They do not explain this at all, but here's the story ...

  o If you took any Postal exams (1) in the last few years before eCareer, (2) in pencil & paper format, and (3) that are still actively being used, they would have sent you an Applicant Eligibility Notice when all the recent changes were implemented.

  o Included on this form would be a record of the related exams you had taken, your exam scores, and an Exam History Code number that identifies you and your exam records.

  o If you answer yes to the above question, you will be prompted to enter your Exam History Code number. Once you enter this number, the exams and scores from your Applicant Eligibility Notice will be recorded and displayed on this page.

  o Most exams can be retaken after 120 days. If the tests included on the Applicant Eligibility Notice were taken over 120 days ago, you have a choice. You can use those scores when applying, or you can choose to retake the exam if you want to try for a better score. But if you retake the exam, you cannot select which score to keep. The most recent score is always retained, and the older score is deleted.

  o Even if you received an Applicant Eligibility Notice and an Exam History Code, you can answer "No" if you choose. If you do, you are automatically scheduled to retake the exam.

  o All of this Applicant Eligibility Notice and Exam History Code stuff is completely irrelevant for most applicants because very few people will have already taken any exams.

The next step is Review & Release, which is self-explanatory. You will review your profile and, if everything is accurate, complete and finalize your account.

Review & Release

When reaching this section, the screen is cut in half. The bottom half is a PDF page view of your Candidate Overview, which is simply a recap of all the information you just entered. You are to review this information for accuracy. If there is an error, you should go back to the proper page to make corrections. You can save a copy of and print the Candidate Overview if desired. If everything is correct, complete the registration process as described below.

At the top of the screen, there are two actions to be taken. First you must choose whether to "Release" or "Lock" your profile. If you Release it, the Postal Service can attempt to match you with other suitable job opportunities at any time and contact you if such a match is found. If you Lock it, the Postal Service will only consider you for jobs that you specifically applied for. For most people, releasing your profile is obviously the better choice.

The second action to be taken at the top of the screen, and the final step of the registration process, is to click the "Complete" button if everything on your Candidate Overview is accurate. Your registration is now complete. You now have an online eCareer profile/account. You will receive a confirming email message almost immediately bearing the subject "Acknowledge Candidate" and simply saying "Thank you for registering with USPS". You are now ready to start searching and applying for jobs.

What now?

First of all, when you want to return to your eCareer account in the future for any reason, (1) just go to *www.usps.com/employment* and click "Login now" and (2) use your username and password to sign in on the login page. (Note: This web address was valid as of the publish date of this book. However, future website changes may result in this URL being revised. If so, go to *www.usps.com* and look for a jobs or careers link that will take you to the desired page.)

While in your account, there are a number of tools available to you as described below:

- Under the Candidate Profile tab, you can …
  - View your profile.
  - Edit your profile.
  - Click the "View Roadmap" button for easier navigation.
  - Change your username.
  - Delete your registration.

- Under the Candidate Profile tab, you can …
  - Search for jobs.
  - Save search queries.
  - Save "favorite" job postings.
  - Review and check status of your applications.
  - Complete unfinished applications.
  - Delete/withdraw applications.

Beginning on the next page, we will discuss the nightmarish eCareer job search function.

Search for Jobs on eCareer

Why the eCareer Job Search Doesn't Really Work

You can begin a job search from two different starting points:

1. As described on the previous page, login to your eCareer account, click the Job Opportunities tab, and then select Job Search.

2. Go to *www.usps.com/employment*, and click "Search jobs online". If you choose this route, you will be given opportunities to and you will need to login to your eCareer account before you can apply for a job. (Note: The above URL was valid as of the publish date of this book. However, future website changes may result in this URL being revised. If so, go to *www.usps.com* and look for a jobs or careers link that will take you to the search page.)

This brings me to the point of having to discuss the actual job search function. But, it's difficult to decide where to begin because the eCareer job search has so very many problems. Let's start by looking at an illustration of the job search page:

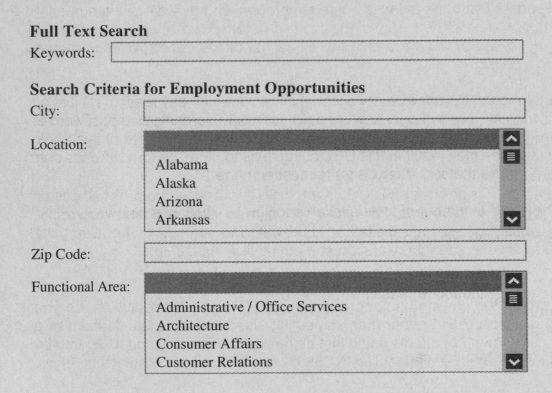

Per this illustration, you are *supposed* to be able to search by text (job title), by city, by location (state), by zip code, and by functional area (job type). But there's a big difference between what you're *supposed* to be able to do and what you can actually do. I've got a little secret to share with you ... none of these search functions really work as intended, and some of them simply do not work at all. Beginning on the next page, we will discuss the search functions individually, all their problems, and how to get around these problems. Every problem discussed indeed existed as of the publish date of this book. Some of these problems may be fixed in the future, but I would not make any bets about when or if that might happen.

Full Text Search

Keywords: [   ]

Many search problems are caused by human error and inconsistent postings. In the case of text searches, job postings seem to be entered by the over 30,000 local Postmasters and supervisors nationwide. There are obviously no specifics for how a job is posted because the same job might be posted a zillion different ways. And there are obviously no preformatted selections. The bottom line is that, with no specific posting criteria and over 30,000 individuals posting a zillion different ways, there's no single text search that can cover all these possibilities. For example, let's look at a few ways that a Rural Carrier Associate job might be posted. A proper posting would look like this:

RURAL CARRIER ASSOCIATE - HOUSTON TX NC58632107 EXTERNAL

This sample has a proper job title (spelled correctly), the city/state, a posting number, and the term EXTERNAL which indicates that this is a public posting rather than an internal posting intended only for current Postal employees. Sometimes a posting will include additional information relevant to the particular job described, but an accurate posting should have at least the items of information displayed above. If you did a text search for the specific terms "RURAL CARRIER ASSOCIATE", this posting would be reported. But if the job was posted improperly in any way ... if the posting did not exactly match your search terms ... it would not be reported. How many ways can this posting be convoluted? Following are just a few of the actual variations (along with comments) that I've observed for this type job:

RCA - HOUSTON TX NC58632107 EXTERNAL
The job title is abbreviated, so this posting would not be reported if you searched for "Rural Carrier Associate".

URAL CARRIER ASSOCIATE - HOUSTON TX NC58632107 EXTERNAL
The word "Rural" is misspelled. This particular mistake where the "R" is dropped from "Rural" seems to happen often. It could be any of the words, however, that are misspelled or posted incorrectly. For instance, the word "Carrier" is often misspelled or abbreviated to something like "Carr", the word "Associate" is often misspelled or abbreviated to something like "Assoc", etc.

POSTING NC58632107
Everything was left out except the posting number, and the word "Posting" was included so you would be aware that this is a job posting rather than something else like maybe an elephant or a submarine or a birthday cake. Any other items could just as easily be left out or added in. And by the way, it is not unusual to see simply a number like "NC58632107" without any other information.

And these are only a few possible variations. There's no way to guess or search for all the different improper posting variations. So, if you do a text search for the job title "Rural Carrier Associate", you will have some postings reported, but you will absolutely not get 100% of the postings for this type job. How many did you miss? There's no way to know. And, the very job and/or location you prefer could well be one of the postings that did not report because it was entered improperly.

So if you cannot trust the text search, what do you do? You never use the text search function as it was intended because you simply cannot trust it. Instead, search per my suggestions given at the end of this job search section.

City Search

City: [   ]

You would logically assume that, in order to search for jobs posted for a particular city, you should enter the name of that city – or perhaps the city and the state – in the "City" search box. But you would be wrong if you made this assumption. As a matter of fact, it is simply wrong to use any form of the word "logical" when discussing the U.S. Postal Service.

The city search issue is a programming problem. This explanation is going to be confusing no matter how I try to approach it. The best way is probably point by point …

• The U.S is broken down into 74 Postal districts, each of which is under a district office in a centrally located large city.

• Geographically, a district may cover only a single densely populated metropolitan area, part of a state, a whole state, or even two or more states if they are smaller and/or less populated.

• The city search function only recognizes cities where district offices are located. It simply does not recognize any cities other than the 74 where there are district offices.

• Let's use the Denver district as an example. The Denver district office covers two full states – Colorado and Wyoming. What happens if we search for jobs at various cities in these states?
   o If we search for jobs in Cheyenne, Wyoming, absolutely no jobs will be reported.
   o If we search for jobs in Colorado Springs, Colorado, absolutely no jobs will be reported.
   o If we search in any Colorado or Wyoming cities except Denver, no jobs will be reported.
   o But if we search for jobs in Denver, it will attempt to report all jobs in the Denver District … which really means all jobs in both states.

The problem is obvious. There's no reason for people in Grand Junction, Colorado to ever dream of searching under Denver if they wanted a job in Grand Junction. And how in the world would people in Casper, Wyoming ever know to search under Denver – in a completely different state – if they wanted a job in Casper.

It's the same all across the U.S. If you want a job in Montgomery, Alabama, would you search under Birmingham? If you're in Amarillo, Texas, would you ever dream of searching under Fort Worth?

So what do you do? Simply *never* use the city search function because you cannot trust it. Instead, search per my suggestions given at the end of this job search section.

Next we will discuss the location (state) search.

Location (State) Search

Location:

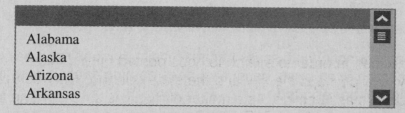

Alabama
Alaska
Arizona
Arkansas

To use this search function, you choose a location by highlighting it. Only five choices are displayed at a time, so you must scroll up or down to see all of them. The fifty states are listed alphabetically followed by Washington DC, Puerto Rico, Guam, and Virgin Islands. The very first selection, a blank field, is the default choice that indicates you want to see job postings for all the locations because you did not select one specific location.

This function tries to work properly, but failure is assured by a limit on the number of postings that can be reported. When eCareer was first launched, the limit was 30 postings. Before long they realized that this limit was too restrictive, so they doubled it to 60. Wow! Like that's going to help.

What happens if you search for all postings in any particular state? What happens is that it reports the first 60 postings in that state, and that's it. At any given time, there may be hundreds of jobs posted for any state you happen to choose, but you will only see 60 of them.

This function is obviously very limited. If you can only see 60 postings per state, odds are that your preferred job and/or location will simply not be reported. And if you did not know about the limit of 60 reports, you would believe that all jobs in your state had truly been reported, so you would never know about the other postings ... including the one that you really wanted but did not see.

So if you cannot trust the location search, what do you do? You do not use this function as it was intended because you cannot trust it. Instead, search per my suggestions given at the end of this job search section.

Next we will discuss the zip code search.

Zip Code Search

Zip Code: [   ]

This will be the easiest search function to discuss because it simply does not work – period! I have no idea why the zip code search even exists because it does nothing at all. It does not matter what zip code you enter, nothing will be reported.

The city search was almost as bad, but it at least recognized the district office cities. The zip code search does not even do that. It does not recognize any zip codes whether they are associated with a district office or not.

So, don't waste your time trying to search by zip code. Instead, search per my suggestions given at the end of this job search section.

(Is it just me, or do you also find it hard to believe that the U.S. Postal Service ... the very people who invented zip codes ... has a job search function that does not recognize them? I have all kinds of wise cracks that I'd love to share on this subject, but maybe I better leave well enough alone before I get everybody in the Postal organization mad at me!)

Next we will discuss the functional area search.

Functional Area Search

Functional Area: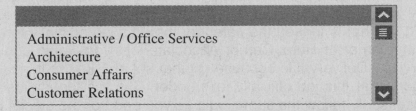

Here you search for postings by functional area ... which simply means by job type. Similar to the location search, you choose a functional area by highlighting it. Only five choices are displayed at a time, so you must scroll up or down to see all of them. The first selection, a blank field, is the default choice that indicates you want to see job postings for all functional areas because you did not select a specific one. Listed below are the 39 functional area choices available for your search. Some of these areas are self-explanatory, some relate only to professional corporate jobs (page 36), and some sound like random titles chosen by a practical joker.

Administrative / Office Services	Information Technology
Architecture	Intelligent Mail / Address Quality
Consumer Affairs	Labor Relations
Customer Relations	Legal
Customer Service / Delivery	Maintenance
Diversity	Marketing / Advertising
Economics	Operations
Education	Other
Emergency Preparedness	Postal Inspection / Law Enforcement
Employee Development / Training	Processing and Distribution
Engineering	Public Affairs / Communication
Environmental Services / Sustainability	Real Estate
Expedited Mail Services	Retail
Facilities	Sales
Finance / Accounting	Shipping / Mailing Services
Global Business	Statistics
Government Relations	Strategic Planning
Healthcare	Supply Management / Purchasing
Human Resources	Transportation / Network Operations
Industrial Engineering	

So far, everything about the functional area search sounds rather logical, but you're forgetting one of the most important lessons I've shared with you. Never ever use any form of the word "logical" when referring the U.S. Postal Service.

The functional area search suffers from the same problems as the text search – human error and inconsistent postings. There are obviously no guidelines or preformatted selections for posting jobs. As discussed earlier, postings seem to be entered by local Postmasters and supervisors ... which means that there's over 30,000 individuals posting jobs ... and none of them seem to post the same job in the same way or under the same functional area. As a matter of fact, it almost seems like they go out of their way to post jobs in the most illogical fashion possible. To help you see exactly how big this problem is, let's look at a real example.

I've experimented with the eCareer job search function almost daily since it went online and found shocking errors every time. For instance, if you were personally going to post a retail (front counter) clerk job, you would likely post it under the Customer Service / Delivery title because (1) that seems like the logical place and (2) that is indeed the category that this job officially falls under. If you were going to post a City Carrier or Rural Carrier Associate job, you would again likely post it under the Customer Service / Delivery title because (1) that seems like the logical place and (2) that is indeed the category that this job officially falls under. But, the thousands of Postal reps who post jobs do not necessarily follow the same logic as you and I or the official job categories. I have literally found such customer service and delivery jobs posted under all the below titles:

Administrative / Office Services	Operations
Consumer Affairs	Other
Customer Relations	Processing and Distribution
Customer Service / Delivery	Retail
Diversity	Sales
Expedited Mail Services	Shipping / Mailing Services

Plus, even worse, I've seen all kinds of jobs posted under no category … under the blank category that is the very first and default functional area choice. When jobs are posted in this fashion, they will simply never be reported when you search under any logical or illogical choice.

So, where will the different jobs most likely be found? I will answer this question job by job below. But, be aware that you cannot trust these answers when searching because – regardless of where jobs are supposed to be posted – there's no telling where they will really and truly be found.

Job	Functional Area
Automotive Mechanic / Technician	Transportation / Network Operations
Building Equipment Mechanic	Maintenance
Casual Jobs	Various (depends on the particular job)
City Carrier	Customer Service / Delivery
Custodial Maintenance	Maintenance
Data Conversion Operator	Processing and Distribution
Electronic Technician	Maintenance
Mail Handler	Processing and Distribution
Mail Processing Clerk	Processing and Distribution
Mail Processing Equipment Mechanic	Maintenance
Maintenance Mechanic	Maintenance
Motor Vehicle Operator / Tractor Trailer Operator	Transportation / Network Operations
Postmaster Relief / Replacement	Customer Service / Delivery
Professional Corporate Jobs	Various (depends on the particular job)
Rural Carrier Associate	Customer Service / Delivery
Sales, Service, and Distribution Associate	Customer Service / Delivery
Temporary Relief Carrier	Customer Service / Delivery
Transitional City Carrier	Customer Service / Delivery

If you cannot fully trust the functional area search, what do you do? You use this search per my suggestions on the next page to assure that you don't miss job postings.

How to Trick the eCareer Job Search into Working for You

As we discuss how to really search, refer to the below illustration.

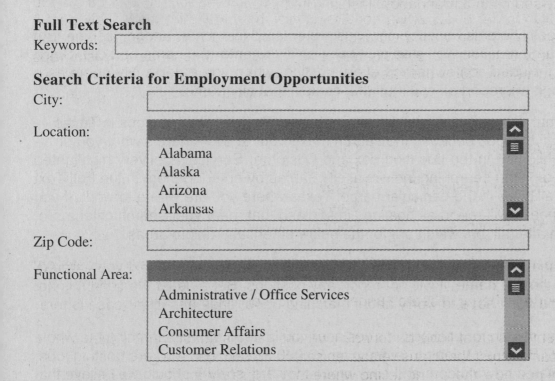

Full Text Search

Keywords: [   ]

Search Criteria for Employment Opportunities

City: [   ]

Location:
- Alabama
- Alaska
- Arizona
- Arkansas

Zip Code: [   ]

Functional Area:
- Administrative / Office Services
- Architecture
- Consumer Affairs
- Customer Relations

Forget the City and Zip Code searches because they simply don't work. What we will plan for is a multi-filtered approach using the Location and Functional Area searches primarily … and perhaps using the the Full Text Search on an as-needed basis … but only per my instructions.

First choose your state in the Location box and select the first default blank option in the Functional Area box. What you just asked for is all postings in your state regardless of which functional areas they fall under. When you click start, it will attempt to report all job postings in your state limited only by the quantity restriction of 60 postings. If less than 60 postings are reported, you are literally looking at every current job opening in your state. If exactly 60 postings are reported, this means that you are not seeing all the postings. It maxed out at 60 and could not report any more due to the quantity restriction. And this is almost certainly what will happen because there will almost always be more than 60 postings in any state. If this does indeed happen, try the below search plan.

This plan calls for a series of multi-filtered searches. For each of these searches, choose your state in the Location box. Then choose one Functional Area for each search. Start with "Administrative / Office Services", then "Architecture", then "Consumer Affairs", and so on down the list until you've searched every single functional area. This is the only way that you can be sure that you truly saw each and every current posting in your state. If you want to look for postings in another state, simply repeat the process for that particular state and any others you choose.

This leaves us with one possible problem area. What if you do one of our multi-filtered searches for all postings in your state in a particular job category, say "Customer Service / Delivery", and 60 postings are reported? Per our discussion on the quantity limit of 60 postings, this obviously means that you are not seeing all of the available jobs. It tried to report all postings that fit your criteria, but the quantity limit stopped it cold at number 60. How do you get to see the rest of the postings?

To see the rest of the postings, you need to do a search for areas smaller than the whole state. But how? You can't search by individual cities, can you? We already found that the city search function simply does not work. But, after playing around with eCareer, I found a way to short circuit the system and do a city search in a roundabout fashion like this …

The text search didn't really help us because postings are entered in such a random fashion. But guess what, the text search function works as a city search if you enter the name of a city. Since the name of the city is included somewhere in every posting, when you enter a city name as a keyword or search term, it will report all postings that contain that city name.

For example, let's say that you are searching for all Customer Service / Delivery jobs in Texas --- but you are not seeing all the jobs because the search maxed out at 60 --- here's what you do --- while leaving Texas highlighted in the Location box and Customer Service / Delivery highlighted in the Functional Area box, start searching individual city names by entering them in the Full Text Search box. Search for all cities in the particular part of Texas where you are willing to work. If you enter Midland, for instance, it will report all postings in Midland that meet your search criteria. So, you can do a city search after all, but watch out for the below potential problem areas:

- You must spell the name of the city exactly right. It searches for exactly the text you entered, so if you misspelled the city name, it will not report any postings. But at least the search is not case sensitive, so you don't have to worry about matching upper case and lower case letters.

- So, why don't you just search for postings in cities near you instead of first searching the whole state as I suggested? Because I don't trust the over 30,000 Postal reps who are posting jobs. We've already discovered how random and error prone they are, so why should we believe that they will always spell city names correctly? Just as mentioned above, the posting will not be reported if the text fails to match due to misspellings. Hopefully such mistakes will be rare, but I would rather err on the side of caution to assure that you don't miss any postings.

- If it is possible for a city name to be abbreviated, you must search all possible abbreviations and/or spellings for that city. For instance, there may be several Texas postings under the city name Fort Worth, and there may be several others under the abbreviated name Ft Worth. If you want to see all the postings, you must search all possible variations.

- Remember the Postal district office problem that interfered with the City Search function? Well a similar problem can surface when using the Full Text Search function to search for cities. If you enter the name of a city where a Postal district office happens to be located, it will report postings for all cities that fall under that district office. For instance, Midland TX is not a district office location. So if you search for Midland, you will only see jobs in Midland. But Dallas is a district office. So if you search for Dallas, in addition to seeing jobs in Dallas, you will see postings for a number of cities across northeast Texas that fall under the Dallas district office.

- There are 13 cities named Midland in different states across the U.S. If you search for the city name Midland while Texas is highlighted in the Location box, it will only report postings for Midland TX. But if you don't have a state name highlighted in the Location box, it will report postings for all of the 13 different cities named Midland.

- And finally, enter one city name only. If you enter two names, like maybe Midland and Dallas, no postings will be reported because it is not possible for two different city names to be included in a single posting (except in the rare occasion that one of the cities is a district office and the other city happens to fall under the jurisdiction of that district office).

Search Tips

1. When you do a search and click "Start", the search results are reported on a new page. If there are no postings to report, the new page will say "This table does not contain any data". If there are postings to report, they will be listed in a table with a maximum of 15 postings per page. Since there will likely be more than 15 postings and there is a reporting limit of 60 postings, there may be up to four pages with 15 postings per page. Below are illustrations of the navigation buttons on the report pages. For this example, we will assume that 49 job postings were reported under your search criteria.

⏮ ⏪ ◀ **Row 1 of 49** ▼ ⏬ ⏭

This illustration is telling you that you are now looking at a page/table that begins with posting number 1 out of 49 postings reported. Since each page/table can only display 15 postings, what you're really looking at are postings 1 through 15. Postings 16 through 30 will be on page two, postings 31 through 45 will be on page three, and postings 46 through 49 will be on page four.

Here's how you navigate between postings and/or pages:

▼ This button advances you one posting forward. If you are looking at report page one, you are seeing postings 1 through 15. Clicking this button will advance you one posting forward, so you will still be on page one, but you will be looking at postings 2 through 16. Click it again, and you will still be on page one, but you will be looking at postings 3 through 17, etc.

⏬ This button advances you one page. Clicking this button while on page one will advance you to page two where postings 16 through 30 are displayed.

⏭ This button advances you to the very last page. Referring back to our illustration, clicking this button while on pages one, two, or three will advance you to page four – the very last page – where postings 46 through 49 are displayed.

▲
⏫ These buttons serve exactly the opposite functions. From top to bottom, they will take you
⏮ back one posting, back one page, and back to the very first page.

Here's a dangerous item they don't tell you about. Let's say you did one search and now you're going back to do another. Let's also say that your first search reported three pages of postings and that you are going directly back to the main search page from posting page 3. If you go directly back to the main search page from posting page 3 of the first search, when you do the second search you will be taken straight to posting page 3 for the second search. It will skip right by pages 1 and 2, and you may never realize that you completely missed two pages of postings. Every time you do an additional search, you will be taken directly to the same posting page (1, 2, 3, or 4) that you were on in the prior search immediately before returning to the main search page. The moral of this story is to always click the ⏮ button to return to posting page 1 before going back for the next search. This way you are assured that you will start the next search on posting page 1 and not miss any job opportunities.

2. By the way, to return from a reports page to the main search page, use the eCareer navigation buttons ... either the [◀ Back] or the [◀ Return to Search] button. If you use your web browser's back button ⇦, you will get an error message saying that this button will not work and you must use the eCareer navigation buttons.

3. When returning to the main search page to begin a new search using all different criteria, always click the reset button [Reset] to clear the previous search criteria so that your second search will not be restricted by the first search's criteria. Note that I said to click the reset button if you want to do a new search using all new criteria. If your second search is just a refinement of the first search ... for instance, you are still searching the same state but looking in a different city or functional area ... leave the state selection and just change your selection for the one new item.

4. Search often and consistently. New postings can appear randomly at any time as job openings occur. Jobs are posted for a limited period of time. Some postings are up for a few weeks, but others are only there for a few days. And you can only find jobs and apply for them during the brief period of time they are posted. This means that you need to search at least twice a week to assure that you don't miss any opportunities. Look at it this way ... If you did a search today and did not search again for two or three weeks, several postings may have come and gone during that period of time, and you never even saw them. The ideal job that you really wanted may have gone up and come down in between your searches, and you missed out entirely because you were too lazy to go back to search more often. As I've preached time and again, please do not let laziness cost you such a wonderful job opportunity.

5. It is not unusual to see several postings for the same city that look almost identical. For instance, you may see twelve City Carrier postings for Houston, TX. But, if you look closely, you will see that the posting number for each is different. What this means is that they have twelve openings in Houston for City Carriers jobs. They intend to hire a total of twelve people in Houston to fill these jobs. If you are interested in a City Carrier job in Houston, apply for all twelve postings – you just multiplied your chances by twelve. If you don't get job #1, you're still in the running for job #2 ... if you don't get job #2, you're still in the running for job #3 ... and so on. There's no limit on the number of applications you can submit or the number of jobs you can apply for.

6. Some postings will be for one particular type job that is available at multiple locations. This is most often true for Casual job postings. Such a posting will typically say something like this ...

> "Openings are for Post Offices within the 123 zip code areas which include but are not limited to the following Postal facilities:"

Following this statement will be a list of cities – perhaps only several cities or as many as a few dozen cities. After the list of cities will be a statement similar to this ...

> "Positions will be filled as vacancies occur."

This obviously means that they have some job openings now, and they expect more to open up in the near future. So, they are collecting applications for use in filling the immediate jobs and to keep on file for filling the future jobs. If you don't get contacted about a job right away, bear in mind that there's always a possibility that they will call you for another job that opens up later.

Beginning on the next page we will discuss the actual application process.

Apply

Instructions & Tips

The application process is basically a duplicate of the registration process with some extra steps thrown in to make sure that it measures up to the bureaucratic standards expected of a federal agency. Included are the below steps that will be discussed over the next several pages:

- Order a Study Guide before Applying (if required)
- Personal Data
- Work Experience
- Education / Training
- General Eligibility
- Veterans Preference
- Cover Letter
- Attachments
- Summary of Accomplishments & References
- Driving History
- Authorization & Release
- EEO & Disability
- Send Application
- Application Acknowledgement
- Exam Notification (if required)

So, if you want to apply for a job, where do you start? With a job posting ... which means that you really started by doing a search (as instructed on the previous several pages) so you could find a job posting in the first place. Below is a sample of what job postings look like on a reports page:

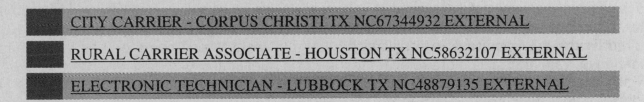

If you want to apply for one of these jobs, you can select it by clicking the dark box to the left of the posting. Then click the Apply button [Apply] at the bottom of the page.

Or you can click on one of the postings. Postings are hyperlinks that take you to a detail page for the selected job. (Without reviewing the detail page, you may not want to start an application as described above because you wouldn't know exactly what you were applying for.) If you decide to proceed with the application, you would click the Apply button [Apply] on the detail page.

Beginning on the next page we will discuss the application process step-by-step.

Order a Study Guide before Applying (if required)

I've preached this important message throughout the book and will continue to do so until the very last page. If the job you're applying for requires an exam, and if there is a study guide available for that exam, *it is imperative that you order a study guide immediately upon identifying the exam and before you apply for the job!* Once you apply, you will have only several days before the deadline for taking the exam. If you wait until after applying, it may be too late to even order a study guide, much less to do all the necessary study and practice work. If you really want a job, you must do everything feasible to achieve the highest possible score, and the only way to improve your score is to study and practice with an up-to-date and effective study guide. If you've chosen your preferred job ... if that job requires an exam ... and if there is a study guide available for that exam ... order you study guide now before it is too late.

Personal Data

You already took care of this task. When creating an eCareer account, you provided all the Personal Data requested, and it was retained in your online profile. So this section *should* automatically be filled in for you. However, "should" is a dangerous word. Check closely to assure that all your info is indeed there and accurate. Also, in some pre-populated sections, they intentionally leave certain items blank and require you to respond all over again. And, they may throw in a few new questions that were not included when creating your profile/account. Bottom line ... You need to review the pre-populated information closely and respond to any blank or new questions.

Work Experience

This is another pre-populated section. You already gave your work history when creating a profile. But, again, you must review the pre-populated information closely and respond to any blank or new questions. And as discussed earlier, if your current information does not adequately demonstrate the KSA's required by the job you are now applying for, you may want to edit some entries to emphasize skills and experience that are more relevant to the job in question.

Education / Training

This is again a pre-populated section that you must review for accuracy and respond to any blank or new questions. And again, if your current information does not adequately demonstrate the KSA's required by the job you are now applying for, you may want to edit some entries to emphasize education or training that is more relevant to the job in question.

General Eligibility

Same story ... review the pre-populated information and respond to any blank or new questions. But this time there is neither the need nor opportunity to address KSA's by editing entries.

Veterans Preference

Yet again you need to review the pre-populated info and respond to any blank or new questions. In this section, there is neither the need nor opportunity to address KSA's by editing entries.

Cover Letter

You do not have to include a cover letter with your application. It is optional. You can just leave this section blank. But if you don't include a cover letter, you're a real dummy. This is your chance to shine ... and another chance to demonstrate mastery of KSA's (page 336), by the way.

The cover letter is a sales tool. The product being sold is you. You need to sell them on the idea that your qualifications enable you to meet or exceed their needs. Employers, including Postmasters and Postal supervisors, are completely self-centered. All they care about is having their needs met, and the only thing they care about you is whether or not you can meet those needs better than other applicants. But it's okay for them to be selfish because this is the way they are supposed to be and this is the way they are paid to perform.

To paraphrase President John F. Kennedy ... "Ask not what the Postal Service can do for you; ask what you can do for the Postal Service." This entire situation – everything about this application – is about what you have to offer the Postal Service. What they have to offer you is irrelevant.

Sales pros talk about features and benefits, and as of now you're a sales pro. You have features to offer, but what's important is how those features will benefit the Postal Service. So that's what you need to sell – the benefits you will provide as an employee.

To do all this, first look back at the posting and the KSA's for the job you're applying for. This is where they tell you exactly what they need, what they want, and what they are looking for. And the specific words and terms they use are very important. Using their own words (within reason), you want to highlight your mastery of the job responsibilities, KSA's etc.

Be brief and concise. With cover letters, *less is more* ...meaning that you should make your points in a professional but brief fashion. A long boring letter with unrelated content is a big turnoff. A single high impact paragraph will often do the job. Never use more than two or three paragraphs.

Start out by saying how excited you are about the job and the chance to work for the U.S. Postal Service. You might mention how this has long been your goal and how thrilled you are that it may now be coming to pass. The tone should always be upbeat displaying excitement, motivation, etc.

Always conclude by thanking them for the opportunity to apply and mentioning how much you are looking forward to an interview to explore ways that you can contribute to their operations. Remember, it's all about them and what you can do for the Postal Service. It's not about you.

There are many books available about cover letters. I encourage you to find and review one at a library or bookstore. My comments deal specifically with creating a cover letter on the eCareer application system, but it would not hurt you to learn more about cover letters in general.

When you enter a cover letter, it is not permanently retained in your online profile. Once you submit the application, the cover letter is gone. And this is good because, if you apply for another job, you need to write another cover letter that deals specifically with the demands of that job. A generic cover letter that you think will cover any job is the worst cover letter in the world. Each cover letter should be specific to the job in question. However, so that you can use the old cover letter as a starting point next time, you can save it by copying and pasting it (page 278) into Microsoft Word or a similar program.

Attachments

As explained when we were creating your profile, unless specific attachments are requested in a job posting, you should ignore this section.

Summary of Accomplishments & References

This is a rather mysterious section. It talks about describing qualifications and accomplishments that demonstrate your grasp of the job requirements (KSA's). And it talks about references. But mostly it leaves a great deal unsaid.

If you are applying for a position that demands particular skills, training, or education, it's easy to understand the importance of your qualifications and accomplishments. But most people apply for normal mail processing and delivery jobs. Are you supposed to complete this section if you are applying for a regular non-technical job?

What about the references? Are you only supposed to give references for people who can confirm the qualifications and accomplishments you claimed? If you don't include any information about qualifications and accomplishments, are you supposed to leave the references blank too?

It would be nice if you could contact them to ask questions like this, but you cannot. As discussed earlier, they don't want to hear from you – period! Nobody in the word does a better job of hiding from the public than the good old U.S. Postal Service.

If you cannot ask them questions, it sure would be nice to have a friend who has inside information to offer. Guess what? You do have a friend like that … Me.

Let me start by giving a little history of the eCareer application system. It started out as an internal system used only by Postal employees applying for transfer/promotion to a higher position. Over time it was decided that this system would be an efficient way to handle public applicants as well, so an external version of eCareer was developed. The external version is similar, but it does not come with the abundance of instructions provided to internal applicants. I happen to have the internal instructions. Some of extra details I provide come from these internal instructions … including the below information on this Summary of Accomplishments & References section.

Basically, you only need to enter a Summary of Accomplishments if the posting includes specialized KSA's. In such a case, describe your qualifications and accomplishments in a "narrative format", which means in a resume type format. The objective is to demonstrate that you are prepared by your past performance to meet each of the requirements stated in the job posting.

It is not really necessary to complete a Summary of Accomplishments if you are applying for one of the more normal type jobs we discussed like City Carrier, Mail Handler, Clerk, Sales and Service Associate, Rural Carrier Associate, Data Conversion Operator, etc.

However, it is recommended that you provide references whether or not you include a Summary of Accomplishments. You can include up to three "personal or professional references who can support the information in your application". Notice that they are to be references who can support you and your application as a whole, not just support a Summary of Accomplishments.

Driving History

This is a straightforward section where you answer four questions that ask ...

1. If you have a valid state driver's license.

2. If you have held a valid state license for at least the past two years.

3. If you have been found guilty of a moving violation (not parking violations) with the last 5 years.

4. If you have been in an accident in the last 5 years.

If you answer yes to question 3, you must provide the below information for each violation:
- Charge (speeding, reckless driving, etc.)
- Date
- Place (city, town, state)
- Law Enforcing Authority (city police, state police, etc.)
- Action Taken (fined, forfeited, collateral)
- Was permit or license revoked or suspended?

If you answer yes to question 4, you must provide the below information for each accident:
- Place (city, town, state)
- Date
- How did the accident happen?
- Damage to your vehicle? (%)
- Damage to other vehicle? (%)
- Who made the damage payment?
- Was anyone killed?
- Were you judged at fault?
- Court or legal body that made judgment

It is imperative that you answer honestly because they will check your driving record. If you did not answer honestly with full details, you will not be considered for employment.

Authorization & Release

Three subjects are covered in this section:

1. If you have ever used other names, you are to provide those names along with dates used.

2. You are to list all previous addresses for the last five years.

3. If you have ever been convicted of a crime, if you are now under charges for any offense against the law, or if you were ever convicted by special/general court martial while in the military, you are to provide full details for any such incident.

EEO & Disability

In this section you are asked to voluntarily answer questions about your ethnicity, race, sex, and physical or mental disabilities. You are not required to answer the questions, and your responses will not be considered part of your application and will have no impact on your potential employment. The purpose is to "evaluate the effectiveness of the Postal Service's effort in promoting its equal employment opportunity policy and in identifying and eliminating barriers which impede that policy."

Send Application

In this final section you (1) review a PDF recap of your application and edit if necessary, (2) agree to the Postal Data Privacy Statement, (3) release your profile so the Postal Service can consider you for other jobs in addition to the ones you've applied for, and (4) click "Send Application". You are now finished with this stage of the process. You application has been submitted.

Acknowledgement of Application

Almost immediately after applying, you will receive an email message entitled Acknowledgement of Application. This message will thank you for applying and explain that "you will be considered under the competitive procedures for this vacancy".

Exam Notification (if required)

If the job requires an exam, you will receive a second email message with instructions for creating an online assessment account and advising the deadline for completing the assessment process (for taking the exam). In some cases this message is received almost immediately, and in other cases it is not received for a few days.

What now?

If the job does require an exam, follow the emailed instructions to create an assessment account and take the exam. Allow me to again emphasize an important point that has been mentioned before and will soon be mentioned again. If you there is a study guide available for your exam, at this point you should already have it and be preparing. As will be discussed shortly, you now only have a few days before the deadline for taking your exam. At this point it may be too late to even get a study guide, much less to do all the necessary study and practice work. Hopefully you are now reviewing this book as you make plans to apply. If so, you still have time to order and make full use of a study guide. Hopefully you have not already applied. If you have already applied, *order you study guide right now this very minute* so you can make the best possible use of what little time remains.

If the job does not require an exam, there is nothing more you can do except wait and hope to receive an interview invitation.

And finally, if you released your profile so the Postal Service can consider you for other positions, don't be surprised if you receive correspondence about a job that you don't recognize. If you are interested in this job, they will tell you what actions are necessary to be considered for that job.

Can you apply for a job without creating an eCareer profile/account?

Yes and no. (Don't you just hate a stupid answer like "yes and no". But since the Postal Service is such an ambiguous operation, ambiguous replies are often necessary.)

It is indeed possible to search for jobs without creating an account. And it is possible to apply without creating an account. But when doing so, you are actually creating an account without even knowing it. As explained below, this is not a good route to follow. It leads to great confusion. I will explain how this works for one reason only ... so you will not accidently get caught in this trap.

You can search jobs without creating an account by going to *www.usps.com/employment*, and click "Search jobs online". This will take you to a search page that works exactly as discussed in the job search section of the book several pages back. (Note: The above URL was valid as of the publish date of this book. However, future website changes may result in this URL being revised. If so, go to *www.usps.com* and look for a jobs or careers link that will take you to the search page.)

If you find a job that you like, you can apply for it without already having an account. To do so, follow the same application instructions I gave you several pages back with one exception ... None of the application sections will be pre-populated because you have not yet provided any info. So, you will need to provide all new information from scratch.

Here's where things get strange. The first step in applying without an account is a page where you (1) provide your name and email address, (2) agree to their Privacy Policy, and (3) click "Save and Continue". What you just did was create an account without realizing it unless you read all the fine print carefully. As you continue with the application, information is retained very much as it was when you were creating an account per our discussion several pages back.

What happens next? You receive a mind-blowing email message. One statement in the fine print that you probably did not see said this:

> You will receive a system generated email containing your temporary username and password. You will have an opportunity to change the username and password the next time you log in. Please retain your username and password information for future access to your career profile and job application.

Here's the actual content of the message you will receive. (I made up the username and password, but this is exactly how they are formatted.)

From: XXXXXXXXXXXXX
To: XXXXXXXXXXXXXX
Sent: XXXXXXXXXXXXXX
Subject: Access Authorization

We have regenerated your password.

Your new password is: fSOhKi9a

Your user name is: RG58124763

Kind Regards,

Human Resources

What in the world is this message trying to tell you? Do you have any idea what this password and user name is supposed to be for? It says that they "regenerated" your password. Wouldn't that lead you to believe that this is a replacement for a prior password or perhaps that this is something you requested? But you didn't create a password yet or request a replacement, did you? Are you beginning to believe my wisecracks about a conspiracy to drive us all nuts?

Even though they don't explain this, when you apply without already having an eCareer account, they are using the information provided to set up an account for you. Once you finish the appying, the only thing missing from your account is login info. Since you were not given the opportunity to pick your own username and password, they emailed you temporary ones.

You are to use these temporary items to login and then choose your own permanent username and password. But the message certainly did not tell you that the temporary username and password are for the eCareer system. And, it didn't even give you a web address where you should go to use these items to login and choose you own permanent username and password. In short, this email message simply causes confusion and does more harm than good.

To login using these temporary items, just as described before, go to *www.usps.com/employment* and click "Login now". This will take you to a page where you can use your temporary username and password to login. You will then be prompted to choose a permanent username and password. (Note: This web address was valid as of the publish date of this book. However, future website changes may result in this URL being revised. If so, go to *www.usps.com* and look for a jobs or careers link that will take you to the login page.)

Let's go over this one more time …
- Why did I explain how to do this without an account? So you won't get caught in this trap.
- Are you going to try it anyway? No!
- Are you going to follow my directions and do it the right way? Yes!
- Are you tired of my lecture yet? Yes!

You know, you're no different than my kids. Just about the time I get started on a good long lecture, they tune me out. The only difference is that they can't slam the book closed to shut me up. So, I will shut up voluntarily to assure you keep the book open and keep learning what you need to succeed.

Next we will discuss the exam step of the eCareer process. If the job you've chosen requires and exam, this section is extremely important to you. If your job does not require an exam, you can skip this exam information and go directly to the "Continue Applying if Not Successful" section.

Take an Exam (if required)

About eCareer Exams

As mentioned previously, toward the end of the application process you are advised if an exam is required. Following are the various possible scenarios depending upon your circumstances. (Note: The reference to taking exams every 120 days is true for most tests. When applying for and/or taking an exam, you will be advised of the specific number of days for your particular test.)

- If you have taken the same exam within the last 120 days, you are advised that you do not need to take an exam at this time and that your existing score will be used for this application.

- If you took the same exam over 120 days ago, you will be asked if you would like to retake the exam or to use your existing score.

- If you are already scheduled to take the same test due to an earlier application, you're advised that, once you take the scheduled exam, that score will be used for the new application.

- If you have never taken the exam and are not presently scheduled to take it, after finishing your application and clicking "Send", a screen will come up that confirms your application was sent and contains the below message:

> The job you have applied for has an assessment requirement. Below is your candidate identification number. Write down this number and keep it in a secure location. You will need this number to register for an assessment. You will receive an email message with instructions for how to sign up and take the exam. You will have a limited time frame with which to complete all required assessment steps; please read the email message carefully and follow all instructions regarding the assessment process. Failure to follow instructions related to assessment processes may cause your application to be rejected. You may also view your candidate identification number by clicking on the Assessments tab in your Candidate Profile.

Candidate ID: | 99999999 |

As indicated, you will indeed receive an email message that instructs you to go to a particular web address where you will create an assessment account so that you can complete the process. Next we will discuss creating your assessment account.

Create an Assessment Account

Following the instructions in the email message described above takes you to a verification page where you enter your candidate ID and your name. Then you are taken to a registration page where you choose a Login ID/username and password for your assessment account. You, however, have already chosen login info that works for both your eCareer and assessment accounts (page 279). So, enter the same login info you chose before and continue.

When logging in to your assessment account, you are taken to a Console page that is broken into the following three sections:

- Current Status – Recap of current actions and steps to be taken.

- Appointments – Recap of appointments for exams, etc.

- Messages – Brief reminders about scheduled tests, exam history, score reports, etc.

With most exams, when first logging in, there is a Current Status reminder to complete the About You step, which is simply a questionnaire similar to the EEO section (page 300) of the application.

Electronic Exam 230/238/240

After logging in to your assessment account, you will be told that the assessment (self-administered questionnaire) must be completed by a certain date, and you will be given a link in the Current Status section to begin. After completing this questionnaire, you will be sent an email message advising your eligibility and/or telling you to login to your assessment account to view your score.

Electronic Exams 473/473E & 955/955E

After applying for a job filled from one of these exams and logging in to your assessment account, you will be advised that the testing process must be completed by a specified date that basically allows you about two weeks. Both these exams consist of two sessions as detailed below:

- Session 1 is a Personal Characteristics & Experience Inventory test. You will be provided with link in the Current Status section to access this part of the exam, and you will take it on your own without supervision. You do not receive a score for this session. It is simply a pass/fail test. If you pass, you are almost immediately emailed instructions for taking the session 2. If you do not pass, you are advised via email that you are not eligible to take session 2.

- If you pass Session 1, you are given a link in the Current Status section of your assessment account to schedule Session 2 at a supervised testing site. After completing this session, you are sent an email advising your eligibility and/or telling you to login to your assessment account to view your score. You will be invited to take this session at a site (or a number of sites) as close to you home as possible, and you will be offered a variety of dates and times as well.

  o The Postal Service has contracted an outside company to administer their exams, and this company has access to hundreds of testing sites nationwide. If you live in a large city, you may be offered the choice of dozens of testing sites. If you live in a less populated area, there may be only a few choices. If you live in a very rural location, you may need to drive some distance to a city where sites are available. If preferred, you can choose other geographical areas to take the test. You can enter the zip code for any location in the U.S., and they will offer you testing sites at or near that location.

  o You have absolute control over when (within the time frame specified) and where you take the exam. This is an extremely important point. Allow me to explain … You can apply for a job filled from one of these exams anywhere in the U.S. and take the test close to home. This tremendously expands your geographical limitations without any inconvenience. You see, under the original application system, if you wanted to apply for jobs at other locations, you had to travel to those locations to take the test. Every time you took an exam, the score was only applicable to local jobs. An exam or score from New York could not help you get a job in California in any way at all. But under eCareer, you can conveniently apply for jobs anywhere nationwide but take the test at home!

  o You must adhere to the time frame given to complete the testing process. Once you apply for a job, you are given about two weeks to wrap everything up. But be aware that after you complete session 1, they expect you to complete session 2 in only one week. They give you a variety of locations, dates, and times for session 2, but those choices all fall within about one week of when you took session 1. So if you take session 1 right after applying, your time frame in effect was reduced from two weeks to about one week. Just the opposite, if you wait until the two weeks are almost up …if you wait until the last couple of days … before taking session 1, there will not be enough time left to schedule you for session 2. The moral of this story is that you don't necessarily need to take session 1 immediately after applying, but don't wait too long or you will lose out altogether.

Electronic Exam 943/944

After logging in to your assessment account, you are given a link in the Current Status section to schedule this exam and advised that the testing process must be completed by a certain date. After completing the test, you are sent an email message advising your eligibility and/or telling you to login to your assessment account to view your score. Using your home zip code as a key, you will be invited to take the exam at a site (or sites) as close to you home as possible. You will be offered a variety of dates and times as well.

- An outside company has been contracted to administer Postal exams, and this company has hundreds of testing sites nationwide. If you live in a large city, you may be offered the choice of dozens of testing sites. If you live in a less populated area, there may be only a few choices. If you live in a very rural location, you may need to drive to a city where sites are available. You can also choose other geographical areas to take the test. You can enter the zip code for any location in the U.S., and they will offer you testing sites at or near that location.

- You have absolute control over when (within the time frame specified) and where you take the exam. This is extremely important. Allow me to explain ... You can apply for a job filled from these exams anywhere in the U.S. and take the test close to home. This tremendously and conveniently expands your geographical limitations. Under the original application system, if you wanted to apply for jobs at other locations, you had to travel to those locations to take the test. Every time you took an exam, the score was only applicable to local jobs. An exam or score from New York could not help you get a job in California in any way at all. But under eCareer, you can conveniently apply for jobs anywhere nationwide but take the test at home!

Hybrid Exams 710 & 916

As of the publish date of this book, these exams were hybrids. Their application and administration processes were being handled partially on an electronic basis and partially on paper. You apply for jobs online, and you schedule the exams online with your assessment account. But the exams are pencil and paper tests taken the old fashioned way. Details follow:

- After applying, you get a message in the Messages section of your assessment account like the below example. This is an actual message received in response to an application submitted 2/12/09. I included all the dates to give you an idea of the time frame involved.

> The next step is to schedule your assessment. You must log back into this site between 3/7/09 12:00:00 AM and 3/10/09 11:59:59 PM to schedule an appointment to take the assessment. If you do not schedule yourself by 3/10/09 11:59:59 PM, you will be considered ineligible for the position. The exact dates, times, and locations of the assessment are not yet determined but will be around 3/11/09 12:00:00 AM and 3/14/09 11:59:59 PM.

- When you log back into your assessment account during the specified dates, you are given a link in the Current Status section to schedule the exam and you are offered various test dates, times, and sites as close to you home as possible.

  o An outside company has been contracted to administer Postal exams, and this company has hundreds of testing sites nationwide. If you live in a large city, you may be offered the choice of dozens of testing sites. If you live in a less populated area, there may be only a few choices. If you live in a very rural location, you may need to drive to a city where sites are available. You can choose other locations to take the test. You can enter the zip code for any location in the U.S., and they will offer you testing sites at or near that location.

- ○ You have absolute control over when (within the time frame specified) and where you take the exam. This is extremely important. Allow me to explain … You can apply for a job filled from these exams anywhere in the U.S. and take the test close to home. This conveniently expands your geographical limitations. Under the original application system, if you wanted to apply for jobs at other locations, you had to travel to those locations to take the test. Every time you took an exam, the score was only applicable to local jobs. An exam or score from New York could not help you get a job in California in any way at all. But under eCareer, you can conveniently apply for jobs anywhere but take the test at home!

- A final important point before we leave these hybrids and move on … As you will see when we discuss the original application system shortly, exam 710 is one of the tests that was migrating back and forth between eCareer and the original system as of the publish date of this book. How it is scheduled and administered varies radically depending upon the application system involved. Again, as you will see shortly, the process is completely different when applying under the old original application system.

What's next?

After collecting the applications and exam scores submitted during the period of time that the job posting was up, applicants with the highest scores are invited to interviews. If there is one job to be filled (which is usually the case), one of the interviewed applicants is hired. All other applicants are notified electronically that their applications were not successful, and they are encouraged to apply for other positions if so desired. This process can take anywhere from several weeks to a few months, so do not be concerned if you don't hear anything from them right away.

If you make it through the interview, depending upon the particular job, there may be various other steps in the hiring process. All info on these steps will be communicated electronically – typically via your online eCareer account.

Continue Applying if Not Successful

If you were not successful … if you did not get the job … *do not give up!* This is where the diligence and motivation I've been preaching come in. Continue searching and applying. Do not let discouragement and laziness cost you such a valuable opportunity.

You now have an exam score recorded in your online account, and this score is valid for six years (or until you retake the exam as discussed on the next page). Continue to diligently search for other jobs filled from that exam and apply for them using your existing score.

If you find a job posting you like that calls for a different test, apply for the job and take that test as well. There is no limit to the number of jobs you can apply for or the number of exams you can take. If you want to, you can apply for every job they post and take every exam they offer.

And don't foget about jobs that do not require exams. This mostly includes temporary and part-time jobs. But as discussed before, some of these jobs offer fulltime hours, fulltime wages, and partial benefits … and some of them can be stepping stones to career positions.

Use Your Score to Apply for Jobs Nationwide!

Don't forget one of the big benefits of eCareer ... You can use your exam score to apply for jobs anywhere in the U.S. You now have an exam score that is valid for six years (or until you retake the exam as discussed below), and you can use this score to apply for jobs anywhere in the U.S. that are filled from that test. Depending upon how flexible (or maybe how desperate) you are, you may have better luck trying to get a job somewhere other than your hometown. And if you've ever considered relocating to another city or state, this may be your golden opportunity.

Consider Retaking the Exam (if required)

If you have applied several times without success, there may be various reasons. But if the job requires an exam, and if you have never even been invited to an interview, the reason is almost certainly your exam score.

Per our earlier discussions, virtually everything revolves around exam scores. When they choose who to invite to interviews, the decision is based almost exclusively upon exam scores. And one of the few items you have control over is exam scores.

If your exam score is the likely problem, there are two options available:

1. Retake the exam to improve your score. Specific details are provided when you take an exam, but you can retake most tests after 120 days. So if your current score isn't working for you, retake the exam as soon as you can. If you apply and it has been over 120 days since you took the exam, you will be given the choice of using your current exam score or retaking the test. If you want to try to improve your score, choose to retake the test. But remember that they always keep the most recent score and delete the oldest score. You cannot choose which score to keep. So do everything possible to assure that your new score is indeed higher.

2. What can you do to assure that your new score is indeed higher? There is only one thing you can do ... prepare for the test with an up-to-date and effective study guide (if a study guide is available for the exam you are taking). At various points in this book we have discussed how to prepare for exams and the benefits of a performance proven study guide. If you did not prepare for your test the first time, you have discovered the consequences first hand. If you did attempt to prepare the first time, maybe this time you need to take your test preparation more seriously and apply yourself more diligently. Your exam score is the only item you have control over. Use that control wisely.

Contact Info for eCareer Help

After applying, you will receive an email message providing the below contact info:

Jobs and Employment Help
If you have jobs or employment questions, you are told to go to *www.usps.com/employment* and click the "Contact Us" link at the bottom of the page. However, as of the publish date of this book, there was no "Contact Us" link on that page. That's okay, though, because I have the actual email address you should use for jobs and employment support: *ExamAdmin@usps.gov*

Assessment Help
If you have any problems with your assessment account or with online assessments, for support contact *USPS_Support@panpowered.com* via email.

Apply for jobs & take exams anytime you want!
No more waiting for test dates!

Because you haven't learned about the old original application system yet, you have no idea what a fantastic benefit this is. We will cover the original system in detail shortly because it is still in use for some jobs and exams. For now, the below recap will make my point:

How the original system works ...

You have absolutely no control under the original system. It is an unbelievable process. You will likely get discouraged simply reading the below steps involved.

1. Let's say that they have decided to give an exam in your hometown. The first thing that happens is that they open an application period and post an exam announcement online. The application period may be as short as a few days or as long as a few months; it varies radically from district to district and from test to test. The decision to offer a test is always a last minute affair. There is no such thing as advance notice.

2. Finding when and where to look for exam announcements under the original system is one of the most challenging tasks known to mankind. For every one person who manages to actually apply for an exam, hundreds desperately want to but cannot find the way. (You won't have to worry about this because I will give you specific directions.) Despite these obstacles, Postal jobs are so popular that thousands of people apply every time an exam is announced under the original system. For instance, over 160,000 people applied on one occasion when a test was offered in Chicago. Imagine what the number of applicants would be if the opportunity was easily accessible and truly made known to the public.

3. So, let's say that I apply for the exam. What happens next? They mail me a scheduling notice that tells me when and where to report for the exam. When will I get this notice? I'm supposed to receive it approximately two weeks before the scheduled test date. But, as I've said before, there's often a big difference between what is *supposed to* happen and what really happens. Sometimes it is delivered only a day or two before. And, of course, there are occasions where it is not delivered until after the test date.

4. Okay, so I'm supposed to get a scheduling notice a couple of weeks before the test date, but how soon after applying will I be sent the notice? Once I apply, how long until I actually take the test? It is not possible to answer this question. I may end up taking the test only a few weeks after applying. However, I know of many cases where the test was not given until months – even over a year – after applying. And every now and then they simply cancel the exam without telling anybody. So, unaware that my test had been cancelled, I could be still waiting to hear from them two or three years from now.

5. Assuming that I do get to take the test at some point and that I get a passing score, what's next? This is the part you will not believe. My name is placed on a hiring register – which is simply a list of people who passed the exam ranked in order by score. When a job opens up, they call in the highest name/score on the register, then the next one down, and so on until either the list is depleted or it becomes so old that it is no longer functional. It typically takes at least two years for the hiring register to be used up or declared non-functional, and it can take five or six years. Putting it all together, my name is on a list with thousands of other applicants, and I will not be called in until they work their way down the list to my name.

6. How soon will I be called in? If I aced the exam … if I diligently prepared for the exam with an effective study guide … if my name is literally at or near the very top of the list … I may get called within a reasonable period of time. If I'm not at the top of the list, it may be years before they reach my name, and there's a good chance that they will never reach my name. Eventually they will deplete the hiring register or decide to retire it, and the process will start all over again with a new exam announcement, etc.

7. So, if I failed the exam or if I did not get called because my name was not at the top of the list, what are my options? There are no options. The only thing I can do is wait a few years until the list is used up and they offer the exam again. Then I take it again and hope for the best.

8. That's my story; what about you? Let's say that you wake up one morning and decide "I want to get a Post Office job". What do you do? Well, let's assume that you are stubborn enough to keep plugging away at the Postal Service website until you eventually find where they post exam announcements. The bad news is that you almost certainly will not find a test posted for your hometown. So, let's say that you find a way to talk to somebody at the Postal district office over your area … which makes you a miracle worker because district offices are supposed to be completely inaccessible to the public. What do they tell you? They tell you that (1) they just gave the test several months ago, (2) they will not offer the exam again until the current register is exhausted, (3) the exam will therefore not be offered again for a few years, and finally (4) there is nothing you can do but wait a few years until the next test is given.

9. By the way, what I've been talking about is trying to take an exam and get a job only in your hometown. Under the original application system, when you take a test, you are only applying for local jobs, and you are only eligible for local jobs. If you want to try for a job in another location, you must wait for the test to be offered at that other location and go take the exam there. Under the original application system, everything is handled on a local basis. If you want to be considered for jobs in several different areas, you must go through the same maddening process for each of those areas … you must wait for exams to be offered in those areas and go take the tests in those areas one by one.

You can apply for jobs anytime under eCareer …

Just the opposite, under eCareer you have total control all the way through the test taking step. You are not dependent upon Postal Service action (or inaction) until after you take the exam. When you see a posting you like, you can immediately apply and take the test (if required). Within a matter of days, you have completed the process. The eCareer system definitely has problems, but compared to the original system where you could only apply once every few years … where you could only apply if you managed to find your way to the hidden announcements … and where you could only apply if you happened to check at the exact right time every few years … eCareer is fabulous!

You can take exams anytime under eCareer …

The above facts describe how you can apply for jobs anytime under eCareer. Since applying for a job and applying for an exam are accomplished simultaneously with eCareer, this basically means that you can take exams anytime as well. And, of course, this makes eCareer a far better system. But per the following explanation, there is another – and maybe even better – test taking benefit available under eCareer.

Let's say that I want a job as a City Carrier in Houston TX. This means that I must take exam 473E. Let's also say that I've been checking the job postings for a few weeks, but I haven't seen a City Carrier job posted for Houston yet. I will keep looking and find a posting sooner or later, but is there anything I can do now to speed up the process? Yes. I can go ahead and take the test now.

"Wait a minute" you say. "You can't take the test yet because you didn't find a posting in Houston yet. And you can't take the test until you find a posting and apply for the job." Guess what? You're wrong. I *can* take the test now. And if I take the test now, I will already have my score when I apply for the job in Houston. So I can speed up the process by skipping the exam step once I do apply.

You know what your problem is? You're not as sneaky and devious as me. If you want to find ways around a frustrating bureaucratic system, you've got to play the game, and here's how it works.

Since I can't apply in Houston and take the test for Houston yet, I will apply for any job anywhere in the U.S. that is filled from the 473E exam. And this will be easy because, even if my particular job in Houston is not posted right now, there are always hundreds of jobs posted somewhere in the U.S. that call for exam 473E.

So, let's say that I find a posting for a City Carrier job in Florida … or a Rural Carrier Associate job in California … or a Sales, Service, and Distribution Associate job in Montana. It doesn't matter where or what the job is as long as it is is filled from exam 473E. So, I apply for the job, conveniently take the 473E exam right here in Houston, and receive my score. How did this help?

Remember our discussion about how your exam score is good for six years and you can use it to apply for any jobs anywhere that are filled from that test? Well, that's what I'm going to do. As soon as a job posting appears for Houston, I immediately apply using the score I already have. That's it. I'm done. Quick and easy. It took me all of maybe fifteen minutes. If I prepared diligently for the test and scored well, I should be called in for an interview within a few weeks. And doing anything with the federal government that quickly – especially going through the hiring process for a federal job that quickly – is nothing short of a miracle.

But what about the job in Florida (or wherever)? What if they contact me about that job? If I scored well enough to be invited for an interview in Houston, won't they probably invite me to an interview in Florida as well? Yes, they will likely contact me about the job in Florida. But that's no problem.

When they email me about an interview in Florida, they will give me contact information for a reply. I must respond (1) to confirm that I am still interested in the job and to schedule my interview, or (2) to decline the invitation. So, my response will say that I am no longer interested/available or that I have decided against a move to Florida or whatever. I can decline the invitation with no concerns or negative ramifications. The fact that I applied for a job in Florida will have absolutely no effect on other applications I submit. Whether or not I accepted or declined the Florida interview invitation will have absolutely no effect on other applications I submit.

Bottom line … Even if there's not a posting right now for the particular job or location I prefer … I can use this strategy to take exams immediately without any negative effects whatsoever … which will expedite my future applications for jobs filled from that exam.

Now you see why being able to apply and take exams anytime is such a big deal. Again, eCareer certainly has its problems, but compared to the original application system, eCareer is a dream!

There's less competition for jobs under eCareer!

As soon as eCareer came out, I immediately realized that there would be a great advantage for truly motivated applicants. Since then, my observation has been confirmed by many contacts within the Postal Service. This advantage has to do with less competition for jobs.

To explain, we will first look at how the original application system worked as detailed a few pages back. Let's say that I took a test in Philadelphia PA under the original system. After taking the test, my name was included on a hiring register with thousands of other applicants. This register is simply a list of all the people who passed the test ranked in order by score. So, what happens next?

Let's say that a job opens up at the Post Office on 63rd Street in Philadelphia. How do they fill this job? By calling in the top few people on the list for an interview. What does this mean to me? It means that I am competing with literally thousands of people for one job. What are the chances of me getting this job? Slim to none. The only people that have a real chance for a job are the ones with the highest scores … the ones at the top of the list.

Under the original system, if I did not ace the exam, the sad truth is that I will probably never be called in for a job. And even if I aced the exam, I am competing with thousands of other people, and surely some of them aced it as well. So I am still competing with a bunch of people for only a few jobs. One of the biggest problems with the original application system was the incredible level of competition you faced.

So, how is eCareer better? Under the original system, the Postal Service was responsible for keeping up with everything. The only thing an applicant had to do was take a test. From that point on, it was up to the Postal Service to maintain records and contact the appropriate applicants when jobs opened up. But under eCareer, everything is under the applicant's control.

Under eCareer, the only thing the Postal Service does is give you a test. That's it. From that point on, it's all up to you. It's up to you to routinely and consistently search for job postings. And it's up to you to apply when you find a job that you like.

The problem for most applicants …and the advantage for you … is that most people are lazy. Most people are not motivated enough and will not invest the time and energy required to consistently search for job openings. Oh sure, they may start out searching every now and then … but sooner or later they will get tired and frustrated … so sooner or later they will either stop searching or search so erratically that they miss most of the jobs. You, on the other hand, will search consistently and diligently … you will find the job openings … and you will apply.

How does this affect the level of competition? Think back to the job on 63rd Street in Philadelphia. Under eCareer, the only applicants considered will be those who searched consistently, found the posting, and applied. And, how many people in the Philadelphia metro area want a job at this one specific Post Office anyway? How many people are you really competing with? Well, it won't be thousands for sure. According to my Postal contacts, due to inherent laziness, it's not unusual if only a handful of people apply for a particular job. How many people are you competing with now? Not many at all. Your chances are far better even if you didn't ace the exam. The competition is far lower, so you simply don't need to worry as much about how many people scored higher than you.

Under eCareer, motivated and diligent applicants have a great advantage. Lazy applicants – which means most of the applicants – will simply never follow through or get the jobs.

Original Application System

For the most part, the original application system revolves around exam announcements and erratic testing dates. The only exceptions are a few temporary jobs that do not require exams. (The new eCareer system is just the opposite; it revolves around job postings.) You may have a hard time believing all that I tell you about the original system, but it is all true. Just ask anyone who ever tried to apply under the old system. But don't stand too close when asking. They may end up unintentionally taking their frustrations out on you.

Original System Sequence

The original application system consists of six basics steps as recapped below:

1. Search for Open Announcements
This sounds simple enough, but without a road map, you're almost guaranteed to get lost. You will understand better when we discuss this step in detail shortly.

2. Apply
Once you find an open announcement, the actual application process is actually quick and easy. Unfortunately, this is absolutely the only part of the original system that is quick and easy.

3. Exam Scheduling Notice (if required)
If the job requires an exam, after applying you will eventually be sent an exam scheduling notice. And you take the exam exactly when and where they tell you, or you don't take it – period. There's no flexibility, and there's no such thing as rescheduling.

4. Take an Exam (if required)
Regardless of the application system, all exams still carry 80-95% failure rates, so test preparation is still important. But timing is a real issue. The test may not actually be given until several months after you apply, and you will only get several days notice once the test date is scheduled.

5. Employment Process & Hiring Register (if required)
Assuming you're not one of the 80-95% who fail, you and everyone else who passed the exam are included on a hiring register ranked in order by score. You are now competing with thousands of other applicants, and you have virtually no chance unless you are at or near the top of the list.

6. If Not Successful, Continue Applying and/or Retake the Exam (if required)
If your interview does not go well, or if you did not even get invited to an interview because your score wasn't good enough, you can try again by retaking the exam the next time it if offered. If that doesn't discourage you, the really bad news is that the test may not be offered again for a few years.

Did the above recap give you a warm and fuzzy feeling about the good old U.S. Postal Service? Sorry if it sounds discouraging, but you are far better off knowing the real facts than operating under false assumptions. And now you're beginning to better understand why the new eCareer system – even with all its problems – is such an improvement. Starting on the next page we will look at each original application system step in detail. I will give you instructions for each step, warn you about the obstacles, and share tips for overcoming these obstacles.

Search for Open Announcements

The first thing I must do, before telling you where and how to search for announcements online, is share with you several important points that will significantly affect your search.

1. There are two types of announcements ... exam announcements and job announcements.

   • If there is an exam required for a particular job, they announce the exam, not the job. What they are really announcing is an application period that may be as short as a few days or as long as a few months; it varies radically from location to location and from test to test. You can only apply for an exam during this limited application window. It is not possible to apply before or after. If you miss the opportunity, you must wait for the next announcement.

   • If the job does not require an exam, they announce the job itself. Under the original system, only temporary and casual jobs are handled in this manner. Again, what they are really announcing is an application period that may be anywhere from a few days to a few months long, and you can only apply during the limited application window – not before or after. If you miss the opportunity, you must wait for another job to be announced.

2. Both exam and job announcements are posted by individual districts or facilities on a horribly erratic as-needed basis. The decision to offer a test or post a job always seems to be made at the last minute. There is no such thing as advance notice or regularly scheduled exams. So if you don't continuously search for announcements ... meaning at least twice a week ... if you happen skip several days or a few weeks ... you will almost certainly miss announcements.

   What do I mean by "a horribly erratic as-needed basis"? I mean that it may be anywhere from a few weeks to a few months to a few years before the same exam or job is announced again.

   • With a job announcement, nobody knows when a particular job will open up, so there's no way to predict when a job announcement will be posted.

   • Exams are even goofier. As will be explained in detail shortly, everyone who passes a test is placed on a hiring register – which is simply a list of names ranked in order by score. As jobs filled from that exam open up, they call in the highest scores/names for interviews. Eventually, when the list is depleted or is no longer functional, they give the test again and build a new register. There could very well be thousands of names on the register, so it could take years to deplete it, and they will not offer the test again until that happens.

3. What does an announcement look like? There are two realistic samples at the top of the next page followed by explanations. The top sample is an exam announcement, and the bottom one is obviously a job announcement. Note that they are identical except for number/title columns.

City/State	Announcement No.	Exam No.	Exam Title	Opening Date	Closing Date
Wichita, KS	289235	710	Clerical Abilities	07/13/2009	07/26/2009

City/State	Announcement No.	Job Title	Opening Date	Closing Date
Van Nuys, CA	293402	Casual or Temporary Position	08/01/2009	08/30/2009

- The City/State is the key location for this event. Usually, this location is responsible for a larger area surrounding it. When you apply for an exam or job, you may be applying for employment anywhere in the surrounding area or in another facility that falls under the jurisdiction of this key location, not just in that one city or at one facility in that city.

- The Announcement Number identifies the specific job or exam opportunity announced.

- For exam announcements, the Exam Number and Exam Title identify the test being offered.

- For job announcements, the Job Title identifies the position to be filled. Under the original system, however, the only job announcements are for casual jobs. And since casual jobs can be for literally any type function, the Job Title really doesn't tell you anything at all.

- The Opening Date is when the application period begins for that particular exam or job … the first date that you can apply. It is not possible to apply before this date. As a matter of fact, the announcement will not be posted online until this date.

- The Closing Date is when the application period ends … the last date that you can apply. The announcement disappears at midnight on this date.

- Note that, for exam announcements, a test date is not given because it is not yet known. We will discuss this more in the Exam Scheduling Notice section.

So, where and how do you find online announcements? Go to the below web address:

https://uspsapps.hr-services.org/UspsLocate.asp?strExam=&strOpenID=

(Note: This web address was valid as of the publish date of this book. However, future website changes may result in this URL being revised. If so, go to *www.usps.com* and look for a jobs or careers link that will take you to the desired page.)

With the eCareer system, I gave you links to follow rather than a web address because the eCareer URL is a million miles long. But with the original system, the link chain is so convoluted that you may never get where you need to be if I only gave you the links. With the original system, it's easier and safer to just enter the URL into your web browser's address bar.

So, what do you find when arriving at this URL? A realistic illustration of the search page is given at the top of the next page followed by a discussion on each element of the search page.

Here's what the job search page actually looks like ...

Position Selected:

Select a State: | Select a State/Possession   ▼ |

< Back | Continue >

Let's discuss the job search point by point:

➢ The first item is the "Position Selected" function. What should you do with this? Nothing. Why? Because this function does not really exit. I have no idea why it is there because it has never worked. So you simply ignore it.

➢ Next is the "Select a State" drop down window. When you click the drop down arrow, all fifty states and the District of Columbia (Washington D.C.) appear as choices. Click one of these choices to select it.

➢ Clicking the "Continue >" button will take you to a screen where all open announcements posted under the original application system for the selected state will be displayed. (Remember, most postings now are on the eCareer system. You're only looking on the original system for the few jobs/exams that may still appear here as previously discussed.) This screen is split in half with "Examination Openings" at the top and "Casual/Temporary Openings" at the bottom.

➢ If you want to return to the main search page to begin another search in another state, click the search system's "< Back" button or the "Back" button in your web browser's tool bar.

Until eCareer, searching the original system for all open announcements in a state would yield a very lengthy list of postings. Since most postings are now on eCareer, such a search now yields only a few ... if any ... announcements. Searching the original system only takes a few minutes, and you really need to do so, because – as previously discussed – some jobs/exams continue to appear on the original system, and some float back and forth between the two systems.

Apply

Once you find an announcement, applying could not be easier. As we discuss the application process, refer again to these two sample announcements:

City/State	Announcement No.	Exam No.	Exam Title	Opening Date	Closing Date
Wichita, KS	289235	710	Clerical Abilities	07/13/2009	07/26/2009

City/State	Announcement No.	Job Title	Opening Date	Closing Date
Van Nuys, CA	293402	Casual or Temporary Position	08/01/2009	08/30/2009

For both exam and job announcements, the announcement number is a hyperlink. Clicking on the announcement number will take you to an online application for that particular job or exam. And the application could not be simpler. All they ask for is your name, social security number, mailing address, phone number, email address, and some demographic information. That's it. That's all they want for now. But what does "for now" mean? Read on to see …

Exam Scheduling Notice (if required)

After applying for an exam on the original system, they mail you a scheduling notice advising when and where to report for the exam. Included with this notice are a few basic instructions and a few sample questions just so you will have an idea what the exam looks like.

You are supposed to receive this scheduling notice about two weeks before the scheduled test date. But as I've said before, there's often a big difference between what is *supposed to* happen and what really does happen. Sometimes the notice is delivered only a day or two before the test date. And, of course, there are occasions where it is not delivered until after the test date.

How soon after applying will you be sent this notice? How long after you apply will you actually get to take the test? It is not possible to answer this question. You may end up taking the test only a few weeks after applying. However, I know of many cases where the test was not given until many months – even over a year – after applying. And every now and then they simply cancel the exam without telling anybody. And, of course, there's no such thing as contacting them to inquire. After applying, the only thing you can do is wait ... and hope ... to receive a scheduling notice.

What does all this mean to you? Other than frustrating you, what it mostly impacts is your plan for test preparation. Since you have no idea how soon the test will actually be given after you apply, how can you make a plan for effective test preparation? In this situation, only one plan will work:

1. If a study guide is available for your test, hopefully (as I have preached over and over again) you ordered one immediately upon identifying your preferred job/exam and before applying. If not, order your study guide immediately after applying.

2. Following the guide's instructions, begin a diligent test prep program immediately after applying (or immediately upon receiving the guide if you did not order one until after applying). Since you have no idea when the test will be given, and since it literally could be given within a matter of days or weeks, you cannot afford to delay. You must start your test preparation right away.

3. If you complete your test preparation and still have not received a scheduling notice ...

   • Review the study guide and retake at least one practice exam periodically. Do this at least once every two weeks. Once a week would be even better.

   • If your scheduling notice is received a week or two before the test date, use that time for intense review and to retake all the practice exams possible.

   • What's the logic behind this plan?

      ➤ You cannot delay your test preparation until receiving a scheduling notice because you could very well end up without enough time to fully prepare. But, if you do all your test prep work immediately after applying, it could be months before you really take the exam. And while you're waiting to take the test, you will naturally forget or lose much the skills and speed that you worked so hard to master.

      ➤ However, this plan enables you to retain the needed skills and speed via occasional brief reviews while waiting to take the test and a final intense review just before the test.

Take an Exam (if required)

Eventually the scheduling notice and your test date finally arrive. What happens now?

What happens is that you either take the test exactly as scheduled, or you do not take it at all. The official Postal policy is that there is no such thing as rescheduling. The test location, date, and time are completely inflexible. And if you do not take it now as scheduled, it could be months or years before the next opportunity is presented. (Again we see how the new eCareer system – even with all its problems – is so much better than the original system.)

Is it really true that you cannot reschedule even in the event of something major like an emergency? For the most part this is indeed really true, but some Postal districts and/or facilities may be a little bit more flexible than others. The scheduling notice is a booklet, and you will find a return address on the first page of the booklet at the top left corner. Generally the only way to contact them about this testing event is by sending a letter to the return address. Occasionally a phone number is included with the return address, and if so you can contact them much more conveniently by phone. In some cases a phone number is provided on the very back of the booklet in the section labeled Directions / Other Information. But, sadly, it is rare that they provide a phone number at all.

What about the exam score? When do you get it? That's a very good question, but unfortunately there is no good answer for this question. When you take a pencil & paper exam under the original application system, they always tell you that you should receive your score via mail within a few weeks. And while I'm sure that it really is their intention to send out scores within a few weeks, in truth it rarely happens that fast. Some people do indeed receive their scores in a few weeks, but many others are still waiting months later. Two people who took the same test sitting right next to each other may receive their scores months apart. And, officially, there's no way to inquire about your score. However, there is one way to attempt an inquiry. Referring again to the return address on your scheduling notice, you can inquire by mail, and they may respond. But if there's a phone number on the scheduling notice, and if you inquire by phone, the answer will almost always be: "I have no idea. You have to wait until you get your score in the mail. There's nothing I can do."

Employment Process & Hiring Register (if required)

There are basically two different employment processes under the original application system. As detailed below, there is one process for jobs that do not require an exam (which really means casual jobs under the original system) and another process for jobs that do require exams.

Jobs that Do <u>Not</u> Require Exams (Casual Jobs)

When you applied for one of these jobs under the original system, you provided only basic contact information. Under this system, all applicants are generally mailed a typical extensive employment application. You are instructed to fully complete this application and return it by mail to a particular address. They review these applications and call in a select number of applicants for interviews.

Jobs that <u>Do</u> Require Exams

The process for jobs that do require exams is far more complicated. The names of all applicants who passed the exam are placed on a hiring register ... which is simply a list of names ranked in order by score. When a local job filled from that exam opens up, they send interview invitations by mail to a few of the highest names on the register. (Remember, under the original system, taking an exam only makes you eligible for jobs in the local area where you took the test.) Included with the interview invitation is a typical extensive employment application and other forms that you are to complete and return by a particular date. As you will recall, you only provided basic contact info when you originally applied to take the exam.

How soon will you be invited to an interview? If you diligently prepared with an effective study guide and aced the exam – if you managed to score high enough to be at or near the top of the hiring register – you may get invited within a reasonable period of time. Here's the problem ... there will probably be thousands of names on the hiring register. So, if you're not at the top of the list, it may be years before they reach your name, and there's a good chance that they will never reach your name. Eventually they will deplete the hiring register or decide to retire it, and the process will start all over again with a new exam. If they still have not contacted you when this happens, your exam score and all records of you application are voided. So you must take the exam again if you want to considered for a job.

If Not Successful, Continue Applying and/or
Retake the Exam (if required)

If your application for a job that does <u>not</u> require an exam was unsuccessful, continue searching and applying for similar jobs in hopes that they will find you to be a better candidate next time. But as mentioned before, there's no way to predict when the next similar announcement will appear. You must simply continue to search consistently and diligently.

If you applied for a job that <u>does</u> require an exam but you were never invited to an interview, there can only be one reason – because your score was not high enough. In this case, there's two things you need to do if you still wish to pursue a Postal job:

1. Continue searching consistently and diligently other exam announcements you can apply for. But under the original system, as discussed before, it will likely be months … and maybe even a few years … before the exam is offered again.

2. When you have a chance to take the test again (and if there is a study guide available for that exam), let's get serious this time about test preparation. If you did not get a guide and/or prepare last time, you learned the consequences the hard way. So this time make sure to get a guide and use it. If you got a guide last time but were not really diligent about your study and practice, let's get with the program this time. Failure is no fun.

Under the original application system, the one and only thing you have control over is your score … or at least whether or not you effectively prepare in order to achieve your highest possible score. You have absolutely no control over any other steps under the original system. Again I plead with you, do not let plain old fashioned laziness cost you such a valuable career opportunity!

Ace Your Employment Interview

As you well know, the interview is a critical element in the employment process that can make you or break you. The most important element is your exam score (if the job requires an exam). You will simply never be invited to an interview if your score is not good enough. But assuming that you prepared diligently for your exam and scored high enough to be invited to an interview, the interview then becomes the final deciding factor.

About the Interview

A Postal job Interview is unlike any other employment interview you can imagine. A Postal interview shares some common items with other interviews, but for the most part it simply a whole different world. There are many books available about employment interviews in general. I encourage you to find one of these books at a library or bookstore and review it in order to prepare yourself for the interview as fully as possible.

How are interviews conducted? There are a number of variables that affect this issue. For instance, different Postal districts and facilities have their own ideas about how to approach interviews. So, interviews for the same job but at different locations may be approached in different ways. Plus, interviews are conducted by local postmasters and other Postal representatives ... which means that there are more than 30,000 people nationwide who conduct Postal interviews. Each of these people is an individual with their own ideas about interviews, so each one will conduct interviews a little differently. And on top of that, the very same person may approach interviews differently from one day to the next based upon how they feel on a particular day, if they had an argument with their spouse that morning, if the traffic was bad on the way to work, etc.

Possible Interview Scenarios

Depending upon the situation, there are a few basic scenarios you might expect:

1. If you applied under either eCareer or the original system for a casual, temporary, transitional, etc. job that does <u>not</u> require exam ...

   • Many applicants may be invited to a bulk prescreening interview. The objective in such a case is to simultaneously (1) weed out applicants who do not fit the necessary criteria and/or who decide not to pursue the job after learning more about it and (2) identify qualified applicants who should be given full consideration for the job. These qualified applicants may be invited back later for individual interviews.

   • Or, based upon the applications, they may invite only a few of the promising applicants to individual interviews.

   • Or, they could do almost anything in between these two extremes.

2. If you applied under the original application system for a job that <u>does</u> require an exam ...

   • Again they may invite many applicants to a bulk prescreening interview.

   • Or, they may invite only a few of the top scorers to individual interviews.

   • Or, they could do almost anything in between these two extremes.

3. If you applied under eCareer for a job that <u>does</u> require an exam, there is typically only one scenario ... They invite only a few of the top scorers to individual interviews.

Basic Interview Tips

As we begin to discuss your approach to the interview, I first want you to look back over our discussion on the eCareer application cover letter on page 297. All the points I made about the cover letter are just as applicable to the interview. Your goal in the interview is to demonstrate that you can meet their needs better than any other applicant. What they have to offer you is irrelevant. The interview is all about them and what you can do for them. It is not about you. In order to achieve this goal, also as discussed in the cover letter section, you must demonstrate mastery of the KSA's required for the job. (We will cover the KSA's for different jobs beginning on page 336.)

We will first discuss items applicable to any interview; then we will focus on factors only applicable to Postal interviews. We will start with the below self-explanatory basic common sense rules:

- Arrive early. <u>Do not be late!</u>

- Remember – first impressions are lasting.

- Your personal appearance, grooming, attitude, and behavior are being examined.

- Do not chew gum or use any type of tobacco product during the interview.

- Establish eye contact with the interviewer. Failure to do so leaves a poor impression.

- Be attentive and interested. Ask relevant questions.

- Try to relax. Speak clearly and in a normal tone of voice.

- Don't respond too quickly. Pause to think before answering.

- Be prepared to answer honestly about past work experiences and work relationships.

- Do not make excuses for past mistakes. Show that you have learned from them.

- Be prepared to discuss why you want a Postal career and what you can contribute.

- Thank the interviewer for his/her time. Make his/her last impression of you favorable.

Common Interview Questions

Next we will cover a few questions typically posed in individual interviews that can be difficult for many applicants. These questions may not be heard in bulk pre-screening interviews as described a few pages back.

1. Many interviewers start out with one simple request that strikes terror into an applicant's heart: **"Tell me about yourself"**. When faced with this request, most people freeze up and cannot think of an appropriate response to save their life. And the first few seconds of an interview are critical. Right or wrong, hiring decisions are often based upon first impressions. So, we're going to compose your response right now. We're going to create your "Snap Pitch".

   What is a "Snap Pitch" you ask? Snap Pitch is a term I dreamed up years ago, not long after I graduated from college, when I was sales manager for an industrial equipment company. A Snap Pitch is a hard-hitting brief sales pitch used when trying to make a favorable impact in a matter of seconds. Use your imagination. Picture a sales rep who bumps into a prospective customer on the sidewalk, in an elevator, etc. The rep has only seconds to make his pitch, so he must make every second count. Now picture yourself hearing "Tell me about yourself" and needing a similar brief hard-hitting reply. That reply is your personal Snap Pitch.

   In case you didn't realize it, during the course of the last paragraph you became my sales rep, and I became your sales manager. Now that we have the proper relationship established, I must teach you the proper sales philosophy.

   You are not one of those greedy sales reps who are willing to lie or cheat to make a sale; you are a professional with the greatest of ethics. You practice "need-satisfaction selling" … the highest form of sales. Rather than simply getting a customer's money, your goal is to assure that the customer receives exactly what is necessary to fulfill a need – no more and no less. I will immediately fire you if I catch you using any approach other than the professional and ethical practice of need-satisfaction selling. It is important that you learn this philosophy because you will use it throughout your interview and when drafting your Snap Pitch.

   Remember, this interview is not about you … It's about them and their needs … It's about how you as a product can fulfill their needs better than other applicant products … In short, it's all about need-satisfaction selling. So your Snap Pitch should be quick recap of how "you" are exactly the product that will fulfill their needs. In essence, it is a short recap of your relevant education/training, work experience, and future goals. It is a brief illustration of your professional qualifications. The Snap Pitch should say nothing of your personal life except for pointing out personal attributes like diligence, motivation, work ethics, etc. Your Snap Pitch must be positive and upbeat, and goals are important. Your goals should include becoming a productive and valued member of the Postal organization (or your own words to that effect). You might mention how this has long been one of your goals and how personally rewarding it would be to finally achieve this goal (or your own words to that effect).

   When it comes to your Snap Pitch, the number one rule is "Less is more". Brief means brief. We're talking about a 30 to 60 second response, not a long and boring recitation of your education, your work experience, and all the other details that make up the story of your life. The interviewer already has your application with all this information, and you will provide additional details on these topics if asked during the interview. Your Snap Pitch is supposed to simply be a brief overview that hits the highlights, not all the sordid little details.

Obviously I cannot really write your Snap Pitch for you. I don't even know you. You must write it yourself based upon your own qualities. But do indeed write it down. Then review it a number of times over several days. If you are like me, every time you look at it you will think of ways to improve it. Eventually it will be finished. Then you need to memorize it and practice saying it aloud comfortably and naturally. Ask a friend or family member to listen and offer suggestions for a better presentation. After several days of preparation, you will have a ready Snap Pitch response for "Tell me about yourself".

If you don't get the first job, hopefully you will diligently search for other postings and apply for other jobs in the future. And hopefully this will lead to future interview invitations. If you go to another interview for the same job, the same Snap Pitch will probably do. (But do review it for possible improvements.) However, if you are invited to additional interviews for different jobs, you may want to tweak your Snap Pitch a bit to more specifically target the new position.

2. Another common frustrating question is "**Where do you see yourself in _____?**" The time period might be a number of months or a number of years. Regardless of the period of time, your reply should reflect a goal of long term employment with the Postal Service and the prospect for growth within the organization if applicable. Your answer should not include anything about your personal life. This is a professional interview, not a personal interview.

3. Perhaps one of the most difficult interview questions is "**What are your weaknesses?**" How do you answer a question like this? There are two schools of thought …

   • Some advisors suggest that you actually point out a strength and use it as a weakness. For instance, you could say that you're a little too much of a perfectionist or a workaholic and that you're trying to get a better grip on this issue. In effect, you just turned a negative into a positive by putting a spin on your answer.

   • But other advisors discourage this tactic saying that the interviewer will likely recognize what you're doing and take a dim view such an answer. These advisors believe that you should truly point out a lesser weakness and immediately describe actions you are taking to improve on it. But do not confess a major issue under any circumstances! Do not ever confess a significant weakness that will cost you the job!

   • You must decide for yourself which approach to use. The decision will be based upon your personality, your true strengths, and your true weaknesses. And to some degree it will be based upon your impression of the interviewer when you get to the interview. Once you get a feel for the interviewer and what he/she is looking for, you may change your mind at the last minute. Spend several days before the interview preparing for this question. I suggest that you prepare two responses – one for each approach. Then you will be ready to handle this question regardless of how the interview goes. As you refine your responses, role play with a friend or relative and ask him/her to critique your presentation. With preparation, you should be ready use either approach without panic when this question comes up.

4. When interviewing for a delivery job, **applicants are frequently asked how they would react if confronted by a bad dog**. Below is a quote from the official Postal policy on this topic:

   "Postal employees must not risk personal injury during mail delivery because of animals. If unsafe conditions exist, report them to your supervisor at once."

The best response to this question would therefore be to postpone delivery until supervisory advice can be obtained in order to avoid an on-the-job injury or incident.

How to Dress for Your Interview

Over the years I have surveyed many Postmasters and other Postal hiring authorities about how applicants should dress for an interview. The below comments are the results of these surveys.

Literally every hiring authority started by saying applicants should dress "professionally". The word "professionally" was used in every single case. When hearing this word used so unanimously, it quickly became obvious that "professional" attire is a key if you want to ace your interview.

Many of those I surveyed shared stories of applicants who came to interviews in jeans, shorts, tee shirts, halter tops, or ragged old clothes that looked like he/or she had just finished mowing the grass or changing the oil in their car. I can absolutely assure you that an applicant who dresses like this for an interview has already lost the job.

Each time I heard the word "professionally", I asked what exactly does that mean. The answers were again virtually unanimous:

- Men should wear dress shoes, slacks, a dress shirt, and a tie. Your clothes should of course be clean, pressed, and presentable. A tie is not absolutely required, but it is highly recommended. Those I surveyed were again virtually unanimous in saying that … if forced to choose between two similarly qualified applicants … if one wore a tie and the other didn't … the applicant with a tie would be chosen because he appeared to be more motivated, professional, etc.

- Whatever ensemble a woman chooses, it should be an equivalent conservative professional outfit. Note that I said "conservative". A number of those I surveyed told stories of women who came to interviews in inappropriate clothing that was cut too low, had too short of a hemline, had slits too high, was overly formfitting, or was otherwise suggestive. Wearing such attire to an interview raises many red flags and will guarantee that you do not get the job.

Note: Most people using this book are seeking normal entry-level positions. The above comments on interview attire are directed to such applicants. People applying for professional corporate jobs are typically expected to dress at a somewhat higher level. For instance, the expected dress code for men interviewing for professional corporate jobs would be suit and tie.

KSA's & the Interview

We come again to the mysterious subject of KSA's. As discussed previously, "KSA" is an acronym for Knowledge, Skills, and Abilities. What other employers refer to as a skill-set, the Postal Service calls a KSA. Different jobs call for different KSA's. A job posting may or may not include the KSA's required that that particular position. But, whether they tell you about the KSA's or not, you are expected demonstrate the necessary KSA's in your application and in your interview.

To the Postal Service, KSA's are important for any job, but they are far more important for technical maintenance jobs that for more normal processing and delivery jobs. How important this topic is to you depends upon the specific job you are seeking.

You will probably be asked about your mastery of relevant KSA's during your interview. But if not, you should know the KSA's and bring them up yourself as appropriate. The KSA's for different jobs are discussed beginning on page 336. It is essential that you familiarize yourself with the KSA's for your particular job so that you can demonstrate mastery of these KSA's on your application and in your interview.

Official Postal Interview Checklist

Below is a copy of the official checklist they will use when interviewing you. Notice that, for each topic, the interviewer makes notes from both your application and your interview. We will discuss each section of the checklist individually over the next several pages.

Item	Application Review	Interview Results
Work Setting and Job Content • Similar work content • Similar work environment • Similar level of supervision • Safety requirements • Applicant expectations of job • Applicant expectations of environment		
Conscientiousness • Time and attendance • Task and assignment completion • Admission of errors/mistakes • Responsibility for money/property • Performance of job in safe manner • "Doing what it takes to get the job done"		
Adaptability • Changes in work schedules • Changes in work load or priorities • Changes in supervision or staffing • Changes in working conditions		
Cooperation • Working with others in sequenced tasks (i.e., work proceeds from one person to another) • Working with others on shared tasks • Assisting customers or coworkers • Conflicts with coworkers, superiors, subordinates, or customers		
Communication • Taking direction from supervisors and others as required • Using instructions to perform work effectively • Transmitting information to supervisors, coworkers, and customers as necessary		
Customer Service • Responding to customer request in person or by telephone • Dealing with dissatisfied customers or inappropriate behavior • Directing customers to the appropriate source for their needs • Creating positive impression of organization		
Basic English Competence		

Work Setting and Job Content

Item	Application Review	Interview Results
Work Setting and Job Content • Similar work content • Similar work environment • Similar level of supervision • Safety requirements • Applicant expectations of job • Applicant expectations of environment		

In this section they obviously want to know if your previous work experience (1) will enable you to smoothly transition into your new Postal job and (2) has contributed to your ability to perform the responsibilities of the Postal job. Note the below details:

• Work content refers to actual functions performed in previous jobs. In particular, does your experience indicate mastery of the necessary KSA's?

• Work environment refers to circumstances under which you have worked. Are you experienced and comfortable working outside in the weather? (Think mail carrier.) Are you experienced and comfortable in an industrial environment that may operate 24 hours a day? (Think internal jobs like mail sorter/processor.)

• Level of supervision is self-explanatory. Do you have the self-discipline needed to work without constant supervision? (Think mail carrier.) Are you comfortable with consistent supervision? (Think internal jobs like mail sorter/processor.)

• They preach safety big time and expect employees to follow all safety guidelines on the job. If you went through any safety training on a previous job or received any kind of safety award, make very sure to bring this subject up if they don't. For jobs that involve driving, brag about your clean record and your safe driving practices.

• They want to make sure that you have realistic expectations of the job responsibilities and the working environment. They don't want to hire you only to have you quit in a few months because the job is not what you expected. When you applied, the original job posting should have included a full job description. Plus, I have included the KSA's beginning on page 336. Study the job description and KSA's thoroughly so you can display (1) that you have a full understanding/expectation of the job and the environment and (2) that you are quite happy to accept the job, the responsibilities, the working conditions, etc.

Conscientiousness

Item	Application Review	Interview Results
Conscientiousness • Time and attendance • Task and assignment completion • Admission of errors/mistakes • Responsibility for money/property • Performance of job in safe manner • "Doing what it takes to get the job done"		

Below are several synonyms for the word conscientious:

attentive	diligent	exacting	industrious	persistent	reliable
careful	earnest	faithful	meticulous	punctual	thorough

An ideal employee would meet all these descriptions, and they obviously want to know to what degree you meet these descriptions. As appropriate during the interview, you should be prepared to quote instances from prior employment (1) that prove you do indeed meet these descriptions and (2) that show you have demonstrated the specific features itemized in this section of the checklist. Notice that the subject of safety appears yet again in this section.

Adaptability

Item	Application Review	Interview Results
Adaptability • Changes in work schedules • Changes in work load or priorities • Changes in supervision or staffing • Changes in working conditions		

Some people are quite inflexible and resistant to change. In addition to a smooth transition into your new Postal job, they are looking for assurance that you will be a flexible employee comfortable with on-the-job changes.

The Postal Service is a dynamic organization continually evolving and adapting to its environment. They expect employees to be able to adapt as well to changing conditions. You will undoubtedly be asked how open you are to varying schedules, responsibilities, etc. Obviously you need to assure them that you are one of the most flexible individuals in the world who has no problem with adapting to ever-changing work conditions.

Cooperation

Item	Application Review	Interview Results
Cooperation • Working with others in sequenced tasks (i.e., work proceeds from one person to another) • Working with others on shared tasks • Assisting customers or coworkers • Conflicts with coworkers, superiors, subordinates, or customers		

The U.S. Postal Service is one of the most diverse workplaces in the world. They have employees of every imaginable ethnic background, nationality, race, religion, etc. This is generally viewed as an asset, but there are some who find it difficult to work with such a diverse mixture of individuals. In addition to looking for you to be a true team member who can work and share tasks well with coworkers, they seek assurance that you can relate well to such a diverse mixture of people. They are keenly interested in any on-the-job conflicts you've had. Hopefully you can assure them that you have had no such conflicts and that you find it easy to get along with just about anybody. If the job you seek includes customer contact, it would be good to refer to your excellent history of customer service (if your previous jobs included customer service).

Communication

Item	Application Review	Interview Results
Communication • Taking direction from supervisors and others as required • Using instructions to perform work effectively • Transmitting information to supervisors, coworkers, and customers as necessary		

Communication is another big issue with them. During the interview, they are interested in two aspects of communication:

1. In recent years, an ever-growing percentage of Postal employees claim English as their second language. However, in order to communicate with customers, supervisors, and coworkers, an employee must have a functional grasp of English. One purpose of the interview is to determine if a potential employee does indeed have a sufficient grasp of English. (See the last section of the interview checklist – Basic English Competence – for more information of this topic.)

2. Some people are simply better communicators than others. Another purpose of the interview is to judge if your communication skills will enable you to effectively communicate on the job. This includes both understanding information shared with you and sharing information with others. You may be asked to quote instances of effective communication when working for previous employers. Of course, how you communicate during the interview will be the best measure of your communication skills.

Customer Service

Item	Application Review	Interview Results
Customer Service • Responding to customer request in person or by telephone • Dealing with dissatisfied customers or inappropriate behavior • Directing customers to the appropriate source for their needs • Creating positive impression of organization		

The subject of customer relations was already touched upon in the Cooperation and Communication sections of the checklist. Like most organizations, the U.S. Postal Service exists for one purpose only ... to serve its customers. There are a zillion functions performed behind the scenes that customers never see or even know about, but every function has one eventual main purpose ... to serve customers of the U.S. Postal Service.

If you applied for a job that calls for direct contact with customers, they want to be sure that you have adequate customer service skills, particularly in the situations listed on the checklist. You will likely be asked specifics about how you handled these types of situations when dealing with customers for a previous employer. They may make up scenarios and ask how you would handle them. For instance ... "Let's say that a very unhappy and hostile customer comes in complaining about a delivery that was lost or delayed. How would you handle this customer?" Or maybe ... "What if a customer had a valid question but you did not personally know the answer?" Your replies should demonstrate that you believe customer service and satisfaction is a #1 priority, that you will do everything possible to make the customer happy, that if you don't know the answer you will find it or refer the customer to the proper individual, etc.

In addition, your conduct during the interview will say a lot about you interpersonal skills.

Basic English Competence

Item	Application Review	Interview Results
Basic English Competence		

The title Basic English Competence says it all. As mentioned earlier, an ever-growing percentage of applicants claim English as their second language. This section of the checklist serves one specific purpose. Based upon your communication during the interview, the interviewer will make one simple note ... either "Yes" or "No". Either you have basic English competence, or you don't.

Important Note about the Interview Checklist

I'm sure that you would not do this, but allow me to warn you just in case. When being interviewed, do not let them know that you had access to this interview checklist. Do not mention that you saw something on the checklist, that you came especially prepared for certain subjects thanks to checklist, or anything similar.

Most interviewers would not care that you had the checklist. Some would admire you for having the ingenuity and motivation to find a copy of the checklist and use it to prepare for the interview. Ingenuity and motivation are desirable traits for an employee. But a few may see it as a negative issue and think that you had an unfair advantage.

And you know what, you did have an advantage. The entire purpose of this book is to give you an advantage over other applicants, and I think that by this point you've discovered that the book gave you many distinct advantages. But there was nothing unfair about it.

I worked long and hard to gather all this information (including the interview checklist) and present it to you in an understandable fashion. And unlike most applicants who are simply too lazy, you had the motivation to find and use the best tools available. Both you and I are simply reaping the rewards of our efforts ... and there's absolutely nothing unfair about that!

But, just to be safe, do not say or do anything that would lead them to believe that you had a copy of their interview checklist.

(PS: Don't ask where I got my copy of the checklist. We all have our little secrets.)

Solving the Mystery of the Killer KSA's

About KSA's

As discussed a number of times already, "KSA" is an acronym for Knowledge, Skills, and Abilities. What other employers refer to as a skill-set, the Postal Service calls a KSA. Different jobs call for different KSA's.

A job posting may or may not include the KSA's required that that particular position. But, whether they tell you about the KSA's or not, you are usually expected demonstrate the necessary KSA's in your application and in your interview.

So how in the world are you supposed to demonstrate specific KSA's if they don't tell you what the KSA's are? This is where most applicants get lost. Most applicants don't know a thing about the KSA's and don't do anything about KSA's in their application or interview because most applicants don't have the advantage you do. The advantage is right here in your hand – *this book!*

Over the next several pages we will discuss KSA's (where available) for all entry-level jobs.

KSA's for Technical Maintenance Jobs & How They Impact the Interview

This category of jobs includes the below fulltime positions:

Electronic Technician (page 31)
General Maintenance Group (page 30)
Mail Processing Equipment Maintenance Mechanic (page 32)

As discussed previously, you are supposed to demonstrate mastery of KSA's when applying and interviewing for these jobs. So it would seem logical that postings for these jobs would include info on the required KSA's. But if you keep thinking that the Postal Service uses logic, you'll never get anywhere. Remember ... Never use the word "logical" when describing the U.S. Postal Service.

However, there is some good news about these jobs and their KSA's. Unlike other jobs, postings for these positions do sometimes include the KSA's. This is certainly not always true, but sometimes is definitely better than never.

A general set of KSA's for all technical maintenance jobs follows on the next few pages. Again, if a posting lists specific KSA's, go with what the posting says. But the problem is that postings for the very same job do not always include the same KSA's. So it is still entirely possible for them to expect you to be familiar with KSA's that they never even told you about. Try this approach ...

1. Start out by closely reviewing all information in the job posting and the topics covered on new exam 955E (page 199) and old exams 931, 932, and 933 (page 227). The topics covered on these exams are the technical fields that they feel are important and that they want you to be familiar with. As a matter of fact, you will find that the 20 technical fields covered on old exams 931, 932, and 933 exactly match 20 of the 33 KSA's listed on the next few pages.

2. Until being invited to an interview, you may never be completely sure which KSA's are really required for a particular job. So, when completing your application, demonstrate mastery of as many of the KSA's (listed on the following pages) as possible.

3. The interview for technical maintenance jobs is totally different from interviews for other jobs.

    *   If you are invited to one of these interviews, they will send you a "Maintenance Selection System Candidate Supplemental Application", or a KSA Book as it is more commonly known. This is an approximate 30 page booklet. Listed in this booklet are the exact and specific KSA's for the job. This is probably the only truly accurate listing you will ever see of the KSA's for a particular technical maintenance job.

    *   There is a separate page in this booklet for each KSA where you provide the below info.

        ➤ There is a box beside a statement that says "I do not have education, training, or experience for this KSA". If this statement is true, you are supposed to put a check in the box and go on to the next page/KSA.

        ➤ If you did not check this box, there is a section labeled "Postal and non-Postal training courses completed". Here you list any training courses you've been through that are relevant to this KSA. Current Postal employees seeking a transfer into one of these jobs must fill out this booklet as well. That's why it says "Postal and non-Postal". If you have not been through any training for this KSA, leave this section blank.

➢ The next section on this page is "Duty/task accomplished, how it was accomplished, and dates". Here you describe examples of tasks or duties performed that demonstrate your mastery of this KSA.

➢ The final section on this page is "Verifying Information". Here you include information, if applicable and/or available, of how they could confirm the info you provided.

• The actual interview will be conducted by a panel of several individuals from maintenance management positions and from the human resources department. In addition to judging your potential as an employee in a traditional sense, they will be questioning you to confirm your mastery of the relevant KSA's.

• Following are critical points that will make you or break you at one of these interviews … points that I learned from maintenance managers who actually conduct these interviews.

➢ To get a job, you must claim mastery of every KSA included in the booklet. Do not check the "I do not have education, training, or experience for this KSA" box for any KSA's.

➢ However, you should not lie about the KSA's either. What you do is look back throughout your entire life to come up with examples for KSA's. (This is not something I'm making up. This is exactly I was told by Postal maintenance managers.)

For instance, you may not have on-the-job experience for basic mechanics, but have you ever worked on your car, a household appliance, or anything mechanical. Did you ever help your father do something like this when you were young? Write it up and mention specific items from the KSA like gears, pulleys, belts, etc.

When it comes to knowledge of electricity, have you ever replaced a light fixture or an outlet in your home? If so, you have examples of electrical experience to offer. When you replaced the light fixture, did you know to connect the black wires together and the white wires together rather than connecting a black (hot) wire to a white (neutral) wire? If so, you have knowledge of the National Electrical Code (electrical wiring color codes).

If you have a hobby that can be tied into the KSA in any way (like restoring old cars, woodworking, etc.) use it to your advantage. If you dig far enough, you can probably come up with all kinds of KSA examples from your personal life.

You are not lying or doing anything dishonest. You are downplaying the negative and emphasizing the positive to display your skills in the best – maybe the only – possible fashion. And, you're doing exactly what Postal maintenance managers coach applicants to do. Bottom line … Rather than focusing on weaknesses; focus on your strengths!

➢ Before leaving this subject, I have one final bit of advice. And again, this advice came straight from Postal maintenance managers who actually conduct interviews. If they ask you a technical question at the interview, be assured that they already know the answer. If you do not know the answer, say so. Do not try to bluff or bull your way out of it. They will know what's going on, and you probably just lost the job. They made it clear that this is probably the worst thing you could do. It leads to distrust, and distrust is simply unacceptable if you hope to be trusted with the care and maintenance of extremely expensive equipment that is vital to Postal operations. Being honest and admitting you don't know an answer is always better than trying to bluff a pro.

KSA's for Technical Maintenance Jobs

- Ability to apply theoretical knowledge to practical applications refers to the ability to recall specific theoretical knowledge and apply it to mechanical, electrical, electronic, or computerized maintenance applications such as inspection, troubleshooting, equipment repair and modification, preventive maintenance, and installation of electrical equipment; and isolating combinational (hardware/software) or interactive problems.

- Ability to communicate in writing refers to transmitting written information (e.g., equipment status, recommend repairs) to maintenance, operations, and other personnel.

- Ability to communicate orally refers to receiving/transmitting oral information (such as equipment status, recommend repairs or modifications, parts usage, and technical procedures) to/from maintenance, operations, and other personnel.

- Ability to detect patterns refers to the ability to observe and analyze qualitative factors such as number progressions, spatial relationships, and auditory and visual patterns. This includes combining information and determining how a given set of numbers, objects, or sounds are related to each other.

- Ability to follow instructions refers to the ability to comprehend and execute written and oral instructions such as work orders, checklists, route sheets, and verbal directions and instructions.

- Ability to perform basic mathematical computations refers to the ability to perform basic calculations such as addition, subtraction, multiplication and division with whole numbers, fractions and decimals.

- Ability to perform more complex mathematics refers to the ability to perform calculations such as basic algebra, geometry, scientific notation, and number conversions, as applied to mechanical, electrical and electronic applications.

- Ability to solder refers to the knowledge of, and ability to safely and effectively apply, the appropriate soldering techniques.

- Ability to use hand tools refers to the knowledge of, and proficiency with, various hand tools. This ability involves the safe and efficient use and maintenance of such tools as screwdrivers, wrenches, hammers, pliers, chisels, punches, taps, dies, rules, gauges, and alignment tools.

- Ability to use portable power tools refers to the knowledge of, and proficiency with, various power tools. This ability involves the safe and efficient use and maintenance of power tools such as drills, saws, sanders, and grinders.

- Ability to use shop power equipment refers to the knowledge of and proficiency with shop machines such as bench grinders, drill presses, and table/band saws.

- Ability to use technical drawings refers to the ability to read and comprehend technical materials such as diagrams, schematics, flow charts, and blueprints.

continued on next page

- Ability to use test equipment refers to the knowledge of, and proficiency with, various types of mechanical, electrical and electronic test equipment such as VOMS, oscilloscopes, circuit tracers, amprobes, and RPM meters.

- Ability to use written reference materials refers to the ability to locate, read, and comprehend text material such as handbooks, manuals, bulletins, directives, checklists, and route sheets.

- Ability to work from heights refers to the ability to perform safely and efficiently the duties of the position above floor level such as from ladders, catwalks, walkways, scaffolds, vert-a-lifts, and platforms.

- Ability to work under pressure refers to safely and effectively performing the duties of the position under stress or in emergency situations.

- Ability to work with others refers to the ability to work safely and efficiently in cooperation with fellow employees to perform the duties of the position.

- Ability to work without (immediate) supervision refers to the ability to perform safely and efficiently the duties of the position such as planning and executing work activities without direct supervision.

- Knowledge of basic computer concepts refers to the terminology, usage, and characteristics of digital memory storage/processing devices such as core memory, input-output peripherals, and familiarity with programming concepts; and computer operating systems and utilities.

- Knowledge of basic electricity refers to the theory, terminology, usage, and characteristics of basic electrical principles such as Ohm's Law, Kirchoff's Law, and magnetism, as they apply to such things as AC-DC circuitry and hardware, relays, switches, and circuit breakers.

- Knowledge of basic electronics refers to the theory, terminology, usage, and characteristics of basic electronic principles concerning such things as solid state devices, vacuum tubes, coils, capacitors, resistors, and basic logic circuitry.

- Knowledge of basic mechanics refers to the theory of operation, terminology, usage, and characteristics of basic mechanical principles as they apply to such things as gears, pulleys, cams, pawls, power transmissions, linkages, fasteners, chains, sprockets, and belts; and including hoisting, rigging, roping, pneumatics, and hydraulic devices.

- Knowledge of carpentry refers to the terminology, materials, techniques, and procedures used in carpentry applications such as form construction, building framing, and interior and exterior finishing projects.

- Knowledge of cleaning materials and procedures refers to the terminology, characteristics, storage, preparation, disposal, and usage techniques involved in application and removal of cleaning materials such as alcohols, solvents, detergents, and degreasers. Included is an understanding of the use of compressed air and vacum type cleaning procedures.

- Knowledge of digital electronics refers to the terminology, characteristics, symbololgy, and operation of digital components as used in such things as logic gates, registers, adders, counters, memories, encoders and decoders.

continued on next page

- Knowledge of heating, ventilation, and air conditioning (HVAC) equipment operation refers to the knowledge of equipment operation such as safety considerations, start-up, shut-down, and mechanical/electrical operating characteristics of HVAC equipment (e.g., chillers, direct expansion units, window units, heating equipment). This does not include the knowledge of refrigeration.

- Knowledge of lubrication materials and procedures refers to the terminology, characteristics, storage, preparation, disposal, and usage techniques involved with lubrication materials such as oils, greases, and other types of lubricants.

- Knowledge of mail processing equipment operation refers to the knowledge of machine operation such as safety considerations, start up, shut down, and operating characteristics of mail processing equipment such as conveyors, letter sorters, and cancellers.

- Knowledge of painting refers to the terminology, materials, techniques, and procedures used in painting applications such as surface preparations, application procedures, and usage of protective/identifying materials (e.g., enamels, varnishes, plastics, stains, sealants, decals) and painting equipment.

- Knowledge of plumbing refers to the terminology, materials, techniques, and procedures used in plumbing applications such as installing pipe and tubing, making joints, repairing flush and float valves, and cleaning drains.

- Knowledge of refrigeration refers to the theory, terminology, usage, and characteristics of refrigeration principles as they apply to such things as the refrigeration cycle, compressors, condensers, receivers, evaporators, metering devices, and refrigerant oils.

- Knowledge of safety procedures and equipment refers to the knowledge of industrial hazards (e.g., mechanical, chemical, electrical, electronic) and procedures and techniques established to avoid injuries to self and others such as lock-out devices, protective clothing, and waste disposal techniques.

- Knowledge of the National Electrical Code (NEC) refers to basic knowledge and familiarity with the techniques and procedures specified in the NEC as they apply to electrical installations such as circuit protection, wiring, conduit, power, and lighting circuits.

KSA's for Processing, Distribution, Delivery, and Retail Clerk Jobs

This category of jobs includes the below fulltime and part-time positions:

Customer Service	General
City Carrier (page 26)	Data Conversion Operator (page 42)
Rural Carrier Associate (page 39)	Mail Handler (page 29)
Sales, Service & Distribution Associate (page 27)	Mail Processing Clerk (page 28)
Postmaster Relief / Replacement (page 43)	
Temporary Relief / Rural Carrier (page 41)	
Transitional City Carrier (page 38)	

Without help, successfully applying and/or interviewing for the above jobs is very difficult because postings for these jobs virtually never include the KSA's. Unlike most applicants, however, you have the help that is so desperately needed … this book. I'm going to share the KSA's with you.

Notice that the above jobs are broken down into two groups – Customer Service and General. The Customer Service jobs are obviously positions that include interacting with customers, and the General jobs are positions that do not include interacting with customers. Similarly, there are two sets of KSA's on the next page labeled Customer Service and General.

If applying for a job that requires customer interaction, you are expected to be proficient in both the Customer Service and General KSA's. If applying for jobs that do not require customer interaction, you are expected to be proficient in only the General KSA's.

Note these points about the KSA's:

- The Customer Service "business equipment" and "financial records" KSA's may not be relevant to positions that are strictly delivery jobs where employees do not perform such functions.

- The "Ability to work and deal with people sufficient to work cooperatively …" KSA appears for both groups because it is important whether interacting with customers or coworkers.

Here are some tips to remember when considering KSA's, job descriptions, etc.:

1. If a posting does include KSA's for that job, then use the KSA's in the posting rather than those listed on the next page. In all likelihood the KSA's in the posting will be specific to that job rather than general, so a few of the KSA's on the next page may not be included. The posting may even include a few KSA's that don't appear on the next page if the individual who posted the job felt that additional KSA's were important.

2. Whether the posting includes KSA's or not, pay close attention to the job description, functions, responsibilities, etc. It is important that you express a full understanding of and abilities for all topics related to the job regardless of what those topics are called … KSA's, job description, functions, responsibilities, or whatever.

KSA's for Processing, Distribution, Delivery, and Retail Clerk Jobs

Customer Service KSA's

- Ability to exercise courtesy and self-control in providing appropriate customer service to accomplish established goals of the functional area.

- Ability to interact with a variety of customers to gather information, evaluate service needs, and respond appropriately to unique customer situations.

- Ability to sell products and services includes providing timely and courteous customer service, persuasive selling to customer needs, providing product information, creating/maintaining an aesthetically pleasing retail environment, and completing sales transactions.

- Ability to use technology-based business equipment, such as calculation equipment or computers, sufficient to process customer transactions, input data, and produce numeric and written reports.

- Ability to work and deal with people sufficient to work cooperatively and interact positively with customers and/or coworkers, as well as responding appropriately to changing conditions or unique customer and/or coworker situations.

- Knowledge of financial procedures such as the terminology, materials, techniques, and procedures used in maintaining accurate records of disbursements, receipts, and other financial information and loss prevention.

General KSA's

- Ability to communicate orally refers to expressing spoken ideas or facts clearly and logically when answering questions, giving instructions, and providing information.

- Ability to identify and analyze problems by gathering information form both oral and written sources and developing an appropriate course of action to resolve the situation.

- Ability to perform basic mathematical computations refers to performing basic calculations such as addition, subtraction, multiplication, and division with whole numbers, fractions, and decimals.

- Ability to reference, comprehend, and use information refers to gathering information from both oral and written sources, retaining it for future use, providing it in response to request (e.g., on forms), and using to identify the appropriate course of action to resolve a situation.

- Ability to safely perform the duties common to the position.

- Ability to work and deal with people sufficient to work cooperatively and interact positively with customers and/or coworkers, as well as responding appropriately to changing conditions or unique customer and/or coworker situations.

- Ability to work independently refers to following either spoken or written instructions or directions, multitasking, and organizing time effectively to perform work assignments, either with or without direct supervision.

- Demonstrating conscientiousness and initiative refers to taking care in performing work assignments and working toward task completion.

KSA's for Custodial Maintenance Jobs

I have never seen KSA's published for custodial maintenance jobs (page 35). As a matter of fact, I have never been able to confirm that KSA's even exist for these jobs. A Postal human resources manager once told me that the below items are the only requirements expected of custodial maintenance applicants:

1. Military veteran preference eligibility.

2. An adequate score on exam 916 (page 183).

3. Basic English competency.

4. Ability to work from heights - the ability to perform safely and efficiently the duties of the position above floor level such as from ladders, catwalks, walkways, scaffolds, vert-a-lifts, and platforms.

However, years of experience convince me that applicants for any jobs would be expected to display mastery of the General KSA's listed on the previous page. If applying for a custodial maintenance job, my advice would be to demonstrate that you meet the above items plus as many of the General KSA's as possible.

KSA's for Automotive Mechanic/Technician Jobs

I have never been able to find any KSA's or specific requirements at all for these jobs except for an adequate score on exam 943/944 (page 196) and basic English competency. An automotive mechanic/technician (page 33) applicant must obviously be knowledge about maintenance and repair of automobiles, but that will be proven or disproven by the exam score. However, again, years of experience convince me that applicants for any jobs would be expected to display mastery of the General KSA's on the previous page. I would accordingly advise that you demonstrate mastery of as many of the General KSA's as possible.

KSA's for Professional Corporate Jobs

It is not possible to publish KSA's for the widely diverse category of professional and corporate jobs (page 36). A posting for one of these jobs will include details on the credentials, certifications, etc. required, and in order to be qualified you must indeed meet all of the posted qualifications.

Special Hiring & Testing Benefits for Military Veterans

Eligible veterans may qualify to have 5 or 10 preference points added to a passing test score. (If the veteran fails an exam, no preference points are allowed.) It is therefore possible for an eligible veteran to score over 100 on an exam after adding preference points.

Eligible veterans are given hiring preference. Eligible veterans must be considered for a job before non-veterans. If the job requires an exam, all eligible veterans must be considered in order of score before non-veterans are considered. This is true even if there are non-veterans with higher scores. If none of the eligible veterans are found to be a suitable fit for that job, non-veteran applicants are then considered in order of score. Of course, if no eligible veterans apply for a job that requires an exam, the non-veterans applicants are considered in order of score.

And, as discussed earlier, custodial maintenance jobs (page 35) are restricted to preference eligible military veterans. Only eligible veterans can apply for this job and/or take exam 916 (page 183) used to fill this job.

Eligibility requirements for veterans preference is a confusing topic. Various government agencies have printed probably a bazillion pages on this topic. The problem is that trying to read and digest all this info will likely drive you crazy, and the different agencies often provide conflicting information anyway. And if you ask ten different government agencies or employees the very same question, you may get ten different answers.

To help solve this eligibility puzzle, I have included a list of the basic qualifications on the next page. However, for your own welfare, I must publish the two below disclaimers along with this list.

The qualifications on the following page are a collection of info published by various agencies including the U.S. Postal Service. While I believe that these qualifications are accurate, I cannot guarantee that they are all-encompassing or that they fully address every single question and/or issue related to veterans preference. To assure that you get truly accurate answers to questions about veterans preference, you should inquire directly with the U.S. Postal Service or with the U.S. Department of Veterans Affairs. And, if at all possible, submit your inquiry in writing and request a written response. When dealing with written inquiries and replies, the responding individual will make great effort to assure accuracy because they will be held accountable for the information provided. It is not possible to hold a responder accountable for verbal information because there is no hard evidence of the reply.

As the U.S. becomes involved in additional military actions, preference qualifications will be updated to include veterans of those conflicts. It is not possible for the following list to include conflicts that were occurring as this book was being published or that occurred after the publish date, so veterans of such military actions should make inquiries as described above to confirm their status.

Veterans Preference Qualifications

10 Points – 30% Compensable Disability
Honorably separated veteran who served at any time and has a compensable service-connected disability rating of 30 percent or more

10 Points – Compensable
Honorably separated veteran who served at any time and has a compensable service-connected disability rating of at least 10 percent but less than 30 percent

10 Points – Disability
- Purple Heart recipient
- Honorably separated veteran who qualifies as a disabled veteran because you served on active duty in the Armed Forces at any time, and have a present service-connected disability or are receiving compensation, disability retirement benefits, or pension from the military or the Department of Veterans' Affairs, but do not qualify for the above 10 point entitlements

10 Points – Derived
- Spouse of other than a dishonorably discharged veteran who is disqualified for a federal position along the general lines of his or her usual occupation because of a service-connected disability
- Widow or widower of other than a dishonorably discharged veteran and not divorced from the veteran, has not remarried, or the remarriage was annulled, and the veteran either served between April 8, 1952 and July 10, 1955 or during a war, campaign or expedition for which a campaign badge is authorized and awarded to the veteran
- Widow or widower of a veteran and not divorced from the veteran, or the marriage was annulled, and the veteran died while on active duty that included service as described immediately above under conditions that would not have been the basis for other than an honorable or general discharge
- Mother of a living disabled veteran, and the veteran was separated with an honorable or general discharge from active duty performed at any time and was permanently and totally disabled from a service-connected injury or illness; and the mother (1) is or was married to the father of the veteran, and lives with her totally and permanently disabled husband (either the veteran's father or her husband through remarriage); or (2) is widowed, divorced, or separated from the veteran's father and has not remarried; or (3) remarried but is widowed, divorced, or legally separated from her husband when she claims the preference

5 Points
- Veteran discharged with an honorable or general discharge who served during a war
- Veteran discharged with an honorable or general discharge who served during the period of April 28, 1952 through July 1, 1955; **OR** for more than 180 consecutive days, other than for training, any part of which occurred after January 31, 1955 and before October 15, 1976
- Veteran discharged with an honorable or general discharge who served on active duty (not for training) during the Gulf War from August 2, 1990 through January 2, 1992
- Veteran discharged with an honorable or general discharge who served on active duty (not for training) for more than 180 consecutive days, any part of which occurred during the period beginning September 11, 2001, and ending on the date prescribed by Presidential proclamation or by law as the last day of Operation Iraqi Freedom
- Veteran discharged with an honorable or general discharge that served in a campaign or expedition for which a campaign medal has been authorized and awarded to the veteran

Putting It All Together

Assuming that you've been a good little student, followed my instructions, and did not cheat ... here's an extremely abbreviated overview of the steps I've taught you:

1. Choose your preferred job(s) --- and check Pathfinder Perks online for any relevant updates.

2. Identify your exam (if required) --- and order a test prep guide (if available) immediately upon identifying your exam and before applying.

3. Apply for the job/exam --- and make sure to demonstrate mastery of KSA's in your application.

4. Take the exam (if required) --- and diligently prepare for the exam if you want to achieve your highest possible score and to have any real chance for a job.

5. Ace the employment interview using my insider tips --- and make sure to demonstrate mastery of KSA's in your interview.

6. Get the job --- and live happily ever after!

Of course, accomplishing these steps was not as simple as merely listing them on this page. It took me hundreds of pages to give you all the nitty gritty details, and you invested much effort in learning all that you needed to know and in actually implementing these steps. However, if you follow my plan step-by-step, success is virtually assured.

What does "follow my plan" mean? It means that you really do what I tell you ... that you take the time to learn about the job and exam choices before attempting to apply ... that you take the time to learn how to navigate through the bizarre application systems before attempting to apply ... that you take the time to diligently prepare for your exam before attempting to take it ... and that you take the time to diligently prepare for your interview before going to it.

Success is indeed is waiting for you. You have only to display the necessary motivation and effort. However, success does call for effort. If you want the job, *you* must make the effort; no one else can do it for you. One last time I beg of you ... do not lose this wonderful opportunity due to plain old fashioned laziness. I want you to be one of the winners, not a loser, but the only way that can happen is if you make the necessary effort.

Thousands of Postal employees have used my guides over the years to jump-start their careers. As most of them know, this is the point in my books where I typically get a bit dramatic, and this book is no exception. Hence my concluding comments ...

Do not let this opportunity escape for lack of effort.

Muster the effort. Show the initiative.

Go forth and conquer!

T. W. Parnell

<u>Postal Job & Exam Guides by T. W. Parnell</u>

Complete Postal Exam 473 / 473E
Interactive eGuide

Comprehensive preparation for the new electronic exam featuring ...

* Six complete ultra-realistic online practice exams
* Full info on exam content and effective test-taking tips
* Comprehensive instructions covering every detail of the new test
* Simple memorization techniques for the mind-boggling memory section
* Chart your progress & plan your preparation with automatically scored practice tests

This new electronic study guide offers complete online test preparation with nothing to print and no papers to manage. The information is 100% up-to-date, and the practice tests are virtually identical to the real exam. To quote Mr. Parnell ...

"When it comes to electronic tests, a study guide is either 100% right, or it's 100% wrong. And to master the speed and skills demanded, you must practice extensively with realistic interactive online sample exams formatted precisely like the real thing. Again, the practice exams are either exactly right, or they're completely wrong. There's nothing in between."

All this for only ~~$29.95~~ $19.95 ... *Special Price for Repeat Customer* (details below)

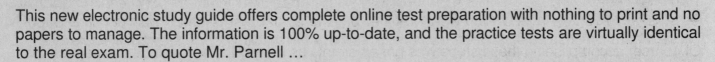

How to Order

Order online at *www.PostalExam.com*. The guide is accessible online immediately upon receipt of your payment. The repeat customer special price is available only to individuals who have a copy of "How to *Really* Get Postal Jobs" and who create an online account as described below.

1. Go to *www.PostalExam.com* and find the blue box near the top right corner of the page that says "Have a book code?"

2. Enter your book code found on the bottom of page 3 in this book, and click "Go".

3. You will be taken to a new page where you enter your email address, choose a password, etc. to create an account.

4. Login to your account where you will be able to check Pathfinder Perks for updated job and exam info, order guides at special repeat customer prices, etc.

Continued on next page.

Postal Job & Exam Guides by T. W. Parnell

Postal Exam 710
Quick Course

Comprehensive preparation for Clerical Abilities Exam 710 featuring ...

- Full info on exam content
- Simple yet effective test-taking tips
- Three complete and realistic practice exams
- All seven sections of the exam – 100% up-to-date
- Quick & easy to use. Just print the PDF, study, and practice.

This guide offers complete test preparation with 100% up-to-date info and ultra-realistic practice tests. Exam 710 is a hybrid. You apply online, but the actual test is taken with pencil & paper. Therefore, to practice realistically, you must practice with realistic pencil & paper sample tests – which is exactly what this guide has to offer.

The guide is provided online as a 90 page PDF file that you must print in order to use it. Be sure you have a functioning printer along with adequate paper and toner. Once you print the guide, study the information and tips, and take the practice tests realistically (meaning follow the directions and time yourself precisely) in order to master the speed and skills demanded. By the time you've completed the practice tests, you should be prepared to ace the exam.

All this for only $29.95 $19.95 ... *Special Price for Repeat Customer* (details below)

●●

How to Order

Order online at *www.PostalExam.com*. The guide is accessible online immediately upon receipt of your payment. The repeat customer special price is available only to individuals who have a copy of "How to *Really* Get Postal Jobs" and who create an online account as described below.

1. Go to *www.PostalExam.com* and find the blue box near the top right corner of the page that says "Have a book code?"

2. Enter your book code found on the bottom of page 3 in this book, and click "Go".

3. You will be taken to a new page where you enter your email address, choose a password, etc. to create an account.

4. Login to your account where you will be able to check Pathfinder Perks for updated job and exam info, order guides at special repeat customer prices, etc.

Continued on next page.

Postal Job & Exam Guides by T. W. Parnell

How to _Really_ Get Postal Jobs

They changed it all ...the application system ... the exams ... it's all new ...

- Apply for Post Office jobs & exams 24/7 --- No more waiting for test dates!
- Step-by-step instructions for the new eCareer application system
- Shortcuts for managing the glitchy new online job search
- Tips from the official Postal interview checklist
- Full details on all jobs & all the new exams

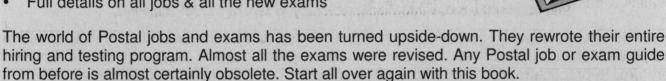

The world of Postal jobs and exams has been turned upside-down. They rewrote their entire hiring and testing program. Almost all the exams were revised. Any Postal job or exam guide from before is almost certainly obsolete. Start all over again with this book.

This essential Postal job search guide offers full info on the new application system, the new online job search, all the jobs, and all the new exams. Plus it comes with insider interview tips from the official checklist they use when interviewing you. Perhaps best of all, it shows you how to get jobs in any economy. The Postal Service processes and delivers mail to 150 million addresses daily. They always need motivated workers whether the economy is up or down.

All this for only $19.95 + S/H (see S/H rates below)

How to Order

Order Online
Visit our website _www.PostalExam.com_ to order online.

Order by Mail
Send the order form on the next page along with your check or money order to the address given.

Shipping & Handling

- **Priority Mail**
  For fast, accurate, and traceable delivery, we ship via Priority Mail for only $6.00 per book to any U.S. address.

- **Express Mail**
  For even faster delivery, Express Mail is available for only $17.50 per book to any U.S. address. Call 1-800-748-1819 for details.

Continued on next page.

Prices, shipping charges, and/or products are subject to change without notice. All sales are final.

352

Order Form

Mail to:

Pathfinder Distributing Inc.
P.O. Box 1368
Pinehurst, TX 77362-1368

Item	Price Each	Quantity	Total
How to *Really* Get Postal Jobs	$19.95	X	=
Priority Mail Shipping & Handling ($6.00 per book)	$ 6.00	X	=
Enclose check/money order made payable to Pathfinder for this amount. **Grand Total** ➡			

Please print the below information carefully to assure correct shipment.

Name	
Mailing Address	
City / State / Zip Code	
Phone Number (with area code)	
E-mail Address (internal use only)	

Prices, shipping charges, and/or products are subject to change without notice. All sales are final.